LIBERALISM

or

HOW TO TURN GOOD MEN INTO

WHINERS

WEENIES

and

WIMPS

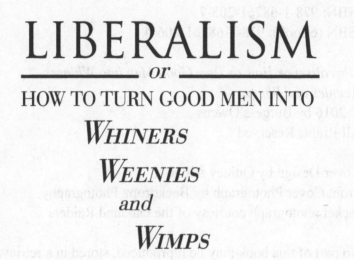

BURGESS OWENS

A POST HILL PRESS BOOK
ISBN: 978-1-68261-205-7
ISBN (eBook): 978-1-68261-206-4

Liberalism or How to Turn Good Men into Whiners,
Weenies and Wimps
© 2016 by Burgess Owens
All Rights Reserved

Cover Design by Quincy Alivio
Front Cover Photograph by Backdropz Photography
Jacket photograph courtesy of the Oakland Raiders

Post Hill Press
posthillpress.com

Second Edition

ACKNOWLEDGEMENTS

It is impossible to express my appreciation for being a very small part of a great legacy, but I'll do my best. The Owens and Kirby families, of which I am a descendent, would make any American proud to be a member of. Not perfect by any means, with all the typical inter-family disputes, these two families though have worked to adhere to heartfelt principles passed down for generations: family, loyalty, commitment, work ethic, and pride in heritage and country. My mom and dad represented the best of that Owens/Kirby legacy. Though they've completed their earthly journey, I continue to seek to live up to their expectations and to make them both proud.

As they encouraged our educational pursuits, it was dad in particular who trained me to reason and ask the big question: Why? Through his many principled stances, he taught me that it's OK not to be liked and NOT to be popular, as long as I was respected. He taught me, during my 10th grade football season, how to deal with a teammate bully. *"Run at him as fast as you can and hit him as hard as you can"*. Conquering fear by running *toward it* instead of *away from it* has been an invaluable life long lesson. My mom's compassion and love for people was my cornerstone during my teenage years of testing. Their example granted me a great love for my race, country, and God. The seeds planted decades ago have now blossomed to an acknowledgment of an omnipotent God who has an absolutely perfect plan for each of us. Living in this country at this time, with the opportunity to defend His nation, is a part of that plan for everyone who is now reading this sentence. Through the eyes of time and perspective, we all have the opportunity to experience life's mountains, deserts, valleys, winding roads, and beautiful scenic way stations. Each, due to its diversity, grants an appreciation for the completeness of His creation. As Americans, we live in a nation that celebrates diversity. I pray that we can come to a place of harmony and consensus in recognizing the unique value of our American culture. It is a culture whose completeness can only be found in Freedom and is one we must together defend.

INTRODUCTION

Our nation now stands at a crossroad. Due to the success of progressive education in our public school system, almost 50% of Americans now welcome the very ideology that their grandfathers and great grandfathers fought and died to defend our country against... Socialism. In previous wars the outcome of battles was determined by the capture and loss of territory. Our nation is at war today but the location of the battle has changed, as has the strategy. Karl Marx, Socialist founder and author of the *Communist Manifesto* was correct when he stated, "The First Battleground is the re-writing of history."

How to Turn Good Men into Whiners, Weenies, and Wimps represents a call to arms for Americans of all stripes who are proud of our nations' culture and values, and who remain committed to ensuring that our history is not rewritten by those who are opposed to our American way. The goal of this book is two-fold. The first is to begin the "resurrection of the once self-sufficient and proud Black community that I grew up in." The second is to highlight the lessons learned from the century-long stealth intrusion of Socialism into the Black community, and then sound the alarm of its destructive nature. The impact of this godless and empathy-free doctrine is no longer hypothetical. It has had its way within the urban Black community for decades with very consistent results… hopeless dependency on Black and White political socialist elitists, the politically correct term: Liberals. With the adoption of Political Free Agency, Americans who love freedom most can together pull our great nation back from the dark and empty abyss of this deceitful ideology.

What happened to the once thriving and nation-leading Black middle class of the 1940s, 50s, and 60s? What was the cause of its decline and the present status of the Black community, now at the top of our nations' misery index? Is it possible that the consequence of Socialism seen there is a foreshadowing of what is to come for our nation? Answers to these and other questions are addressed in this book, along with solutions. For the Black community, the answers to its decades long slide can only come from within .

As we consider the consequences of this battle, it is clear that apathy, ignorance, or life's busy pace is simply no excuse for standing on the sidelines. These are unprecedented times in which our nation, freedoms, and children's futures hang in the balance. As Americans whose culture is defined by its diversity, it is imperative that we are harmonious in prioritizing the welfare of our nation. There is no party, politician, organization, or ideology that should take precedent over it.

How to Turn Good Men into Whiners, Weenies, and Wimps highlights the period during which the Black community stood at the same crossroad as our Nation does today. Due to the path chosen during the early 1900s, the Black American community has paid dearly in loss of lives, souls, hopes, and dreams. Its century-long sacrifice can only be deemed worthwhile, if our nation learns from its journey and chooses not to duplicate its mistake. Allowing the planting of the seeds of Socialism within its once proud, entrepreneurial, and Christian community, in 1910, was indeed a game changer. The consequence of this parasitic ideology can now be seen within every community where it resides. The urban communities of Detroit, Oakland, Philadelphia, New Jersey, Ferguson and others, stand as a warning beacon to our nation.

Coming from within those same communities are Freedom Sentinels, willing to do battle for the hearts and minds of all freedom-loving Americans. These Black American conservatives understand that our nation cannot afford to lose any more ground. They have also proven that above popularity and acceptance... *they love Freedom more.*

CONTENTS

HISTORY/CAREER

Burgess spent his childhood growing up in the Deep South during a time when the barriers of segregation were being torn down. He was the third Black American to be offered a football scholarship at the University of Miami. He earned a Bachelor of Science degree in Biology/Chemistry and simultaneously gained national recognition as a First Team All-American.

During his college career, Burgess was named to *Who's Who among College Students in American Universities and Colleges*. He was inducted to the Hall of Fame of Outstanding College Athletes of America and later to the University of Miami's Hall of Fame and the Orange Bowl Ring of Honor.

Following college, the New York Jets picked Burgess in the NFL 1st round as the draft's first defensive back, and 13th overall pick. Later that year he was selected as the Jets Rookie of the Year and to the NFL's All- Rookie team. He played with the New York Jets for seven years and was selected as the Defensive Team Captain his last three seasons. After being traded to the Oakland Raiders, Burgess led the Raiders defensive squad in tackles during their Championship season and in the 1981 Super Bowl XV game. In his final season, in 1982, he led the Raider's team in interceptions and was selected as a First Alternate to the NFL All Pro-Bowl.

Since retiring from the NFL, Burgess has been involved in the corporate and entrepreneurial arenas. Over the last decade he has traveled throughout the country speaking about the intrinsic principles of freedom that underlie the foundation of our American way of life.

ABOUT THE AUTHOR

Politically I grew up as a Democrat, who supported the ultra-liberal Presidential candidates Eugene McCarthy and later, Jimmy Carter. After retirement from the NFL, I began my journey as an entrepreneur and to an awakening to the plethora of opportunities available within our free enterprise system. I also became aware of a mindset within the Black community that prevented many from seeing those opportunities.

During this period, I came to a realization of the gradual degradation of my once proud and independent Black community. I remembered the introduction of the 1960s Great Society welfare program and the resulting increase of dependent women and young girls—given financial incentives to remain single, pregnant, and jobless. These same programs encouraged black men to abandon their roles as patriarchs, providers, and protectors of their families. In the decades since my youth, I've witnessed the explosion of fatherless families, and an exponential increase in illiteracy and crime.

During the summer of 1990, seven years after retiring from the NFL, I saw firsthand the hopelessness that prevails in the urban inner city. After a business failure and pursuant bankruptcy, I temporarily moved my young family into the basement of a Brooklyn, New York inner city home. For a brief while, I worked as a chimney sweep during the day, built a network marketing business at night, and would finish my day working a midnight shift as a security guard. As I listened to sporadic gunfire one night from the basement apartment, I reflected on the advantages I had over my neighbor. Unlike my neighbor, I understood that my present setback, though painful and extremely humbling, was temporary and would ultimately provide some very important life lessons. I was correct in that assessment.

At the core of my belief, then and now, are the tenets of Faith and Love for my God, Country and Family. There is also the knowledge that in America, starting over is always an option. These tenets, embedded within the Conservative ideology, allow for an eternal optimism that is available to all Americans, regardless of race, creed, gender or color. For as predictable as the physical laws that define gravity and inertia, are the spiritual truths that have defined our country. Those truths have been present from the beginning of the vision called America. They are embedded within each of its founding documents, the Mayflower Compact, the Declaration of Independence, the US Constitution, the Bill of Rights, the Emancipation Proclamation and others. Uniquely ensconced in the Judeo-Christian belief system, is the theme of fairness and meritocracy that has provided the world with its first true societal melting pot. As an ever-evolving nation, for more than 200 years, America has provided an environment in which its citizens can work and strive to find their better selves. This desire to continue to improve, to become better is embedded within the very DNA that defines the American Way.

I Believe ... (SLD)

I believe that my worth is not measured by what I do, by the honors bestowed upon me, or by the material wealth I might obtain. Instead I am measured by the courage I show while standing for my beliefs, by the dedication I exhibit to insure my word is good, and the resolve I undertake to establish that my actions and deeds are honorable.

I believe that the principles upon which our country was built are founded on the bedrock of Eternal truths; that these truths, when applied, build men and women of character and families with purpose and vision.

I believe that men can be inspired by powers from on high as evidenced by the immortal words penned by our country's founding fathers: "We hold these truths to be self-evident that all men are created equal, that they are endowed by their Creator with certain unalienable Rights; that among these are Life, Liberty, and the pursuit of Happiness."

I believe in the concept embodied by the words "We the People." That our country stands as the most unique among all the world's societies because it was not founded on We the Blacks, We the Whites, We the Christians, We the Jews, We the Muslims, We the Buddhists, We the Old, We the Young, We the Rich, or We the Poor, but "WE THE PEOPLE." Though as a nation we are a diverse people we have, through the power of unity and adherence to concrete core beliefs, found the common thread that defines the American Way.

I believe that a country is no better than its people and its people are no better than its dream; that the ability to dream, to hope, and to envision the possibilities is among the greatest and most precious gifts. Living in the freest country in the world we owe it to our creator to "Dream Big." It is a free gift from a Big God.

I believe that success is a matter of choice not chance. As we choose to control our attitude, we begin to control our actions. As we choose to control our actions, we are choosing to form new habits. As we choose to control our habits, we are choosing to define our character. As we choose to define our character, we begin to choose our destiny and our happiness. Success is therefore a matter of choice not chance... your choice.

I believe the impact of our life will be determined by our courage to have a vision, our wisdom to understand and overcome life's obstacles, and our faith to know that we're meant to be.

I believe that we are in life exactly where we see ourselves. If we want to change our station, we'll have to change our vision and expectations.

I believe that to obtain true success we must not look to the past as if it represents the future. The future is a place of opportunity and where our happiness is forged. Live there and learn to enjoy it there.

I believe only through struggle and persistence can we take advantage of the special talents we have hidden within. It is not the Super Bowl ring that I wear but the character and resolve I exhibit during the downtimes, that defines me as a Champion.

I believe failure can be our best friend, if we choose not to quit once we've been formally introduced.

I believe that as "the individual" is empowered with the freedom of choice, self-direction and financial incentives, he will do all within his power to be the very best that he can be. With every effort toward self-improvement will come, as a by-product, an increased value to our communities and country.

I believe that we're all created in the image of God, who loves us and has designed each of us to win. Life's struggles, of which no one is exempt, are opportunities to find our better self. In a land explicitly set aside for Freedom, we're only asked to do our best, do it honorably, do it with confidence, with power, and with high expectations. Remember, we are not alone. "Dream Big."

CHAPTER 1

A TRIBUTE:
THE GREATEST GENERATION

*"For those who grew up in the Deep South, in
the days of the KKK and Jim Crow segregation,
pride in community was not founded on the
embellishment of opportunities lost due to racism.
Instead it was built on the highlighting of the
great accomplishments achieved, in spite of the
obstacles. The "can do" outlook that prevailed in
past generations cleared the pathway to prosperity
and celebrated a creative, courageous, and self-
respecting community determined not to be held
back. They succeeded in their quest."*

- Burgess Owens

My life has been filled with many blessings, the most
important of these being the family, race, country, and era
that I was born into. I was raised in the 1950s- and 60s-Deep
South during the tumultuous era of segregation, Jim Crow
institutional racism, and the KKK. Opportunities outside of
our segregated community, unlike today, were rare. It was
an age when there were no such terms as glass ceilings.

Instead, we had an honest understanding that if you were Black, Jewish, Catholic, Mormon or a woman that you need not apply. In the Deep South none of these groups would consider running for a national, state, or even a city political office. I grew up as a Baptist, worshipping the same faith and God as the white Baptist parishioners. We did so separately. There was no thought, pressure, or desire by either race to integrate our sacred sanctuaries.

I was raised in a family whose ancestral names, Kirby and Owens, I carry to this day with pride. I was privileged to witness the men and women of my parents' generation attack and overcome the institutional racism of their era. They did so with pride, fierce independence, and the greatest of all equalizers, "Success." This they did, as have all other successful American cultures, through the American free market system.

It was a generation determined to show themselves competitive with all other races, determined that it would never be bested. It did so by adopting an attitude of preparation to compete at any time and within any arena to prove their status of equality. The Black community, throughout the early to mid-1900s, had an insatiable thirst for education. This was evident in my 1960s Tallahassee home, where a room was set aside as a library. Entering this room to the right was a shelf from floor to ceiling full of books and magazines... *Ebony* magazine, *The National Geographic* magazine, the *Encyclopedia Britannica*, books on historic Black heroes like Harriett Tubman and Fredrick Douglass, etc. There were also expectations from our parents that we would study and do our homework every night, from Sunday through Thursday, in our library room. Watching TV on school days was forbidden.

This demand for education could also be seen on both sides of my family lineage, the Owens and Kirbys. Each illustrated the commitment of the Black community to aspire, as one generation worked to lift the next to a higher standard. Each of the siblings of my parents' generation, four in the Owens family and thirteen in the Kirby family earned undergraduate or graduate college degrees. They came from homes of hard working farmers and humble independent contractors with very little formal education. Members of my grandparents' generation, including Papa Kirby whose father was a slave, had served our nation with valor as veterans of WWI. My Kirby family's lineage includes a Confederate soldier, the former owner of the 8,000-acre Alta Vista plantation and 137 slaves. The plantation was sold in the mid-1870s to Texas and is now the site of Prairieveiw College, the oldest Black college south of the Mississippi River.[1]

The Owens family, comprised of my dad and his two brothers, exemplified the tenacity and will of the Black community. After serving in WWII, in the Philippines and Germany, they returned home to complete their undergraduate program at Prairieveiw College. Once they graduated they sought postgraduate degrees. These were non-existent for Blacks in the late 1940s, due to Jim Crow segregation laws. The traditional expectation for Black Americans in Deep South Texas, after their 11th grade graduation, was to return to the farm fields to work as manual laborers. My Grandfather, Daddy Wade, was a third grade dropout who owned a scrap metal business and a school bus that transported Black children to school. His school bus enterprise ended when

---

[1]   https://en.wikipedia.org/wiki/Prairie_View_A%26M_University

white members of the school board calculated that he was making more in his two businesses than they were. One of the members was honest and respectful enough of him to let him know the reason for his termination. My grandmother Da, who worked as a domestic and a mortician, finally received her high school equivalency at the age of 50.

My dad was the youngest of three boys. His next older brother, Uncle Emiel, graduated summa cum laude from Prairieveiw College. Along with my dad, he sought postgraduate acceptance from white colleges throughout the Northeast. I recently discovered, among my dad's belonging, a box full of rejection letters that Uncle Emiel had received. As I reviewed letter after letter of rejections, it was easy to conclude that it was his race that was the determining factor. Institutional racism was very prevalent and an accepted practice throughout our country during that era.

Despite numerous rejections, both persisted in their quest until they received acceptance from Ohio State University in Columbus, Ohio. It was from there that my Dad and Uncle received their PhD's—in Agronomy and Economics, respectfully. Both spent the next 60 plus years as college professors, entrepreneurs, researchers, international travelers, authors, mentors, and committed contributors to the youth in their communities.

Soon after graduating, Dad and Uncle Emiel worked on separate projects that miraculously had them both living with their young families at the same time in Liberia, Africa. Thus from 1956 to 1958, at the tender age of five, I had my first international travel experience to the European and African continents.

Uncle Emiel published a book, *Blood on German Snow: An African American Artilleryman in World War II and Beyond,* recounting his WWII experience in Germany with the 777th all-black field artillery unit. In the early 70s he and my dad collaborated on a two-year research project, traveling with migrant's workers from Miami to Maine. Their research was federally funded and later published. Years later, Uncle Emiel authored a second book, *Peacocks in the Field,* recounting his migrant study experience. In the summer of 1990, my dad took six of his pre-teenage grandchildren on a cross-country camping trip, from Florida to New Mexico. He wrote a book of his experience of the many kind acts of Americans, from a wide diversity of backgrounds, and titled his fond experience *Traveling through the Heart of America.* He spent the last seven years of his life working on his life's memoirs, a treasure trove to his progeny.

They both received numerous honors and accolades throughout their careers. In 2008, Uncle Emiel's oldest daughter and accomplished physician, Dr. Sheila Owens Collins, and I accepted on his behalf his last award. It was the "Distinguished Alumni Award" from Ohio State University, a fitting and timely acknowledgement from where his journey had begun.

My dad's oldest brother, Uncle Charles, was yet another example of the "can do" attitude of that great generation. He was the first in the family to volunteer for WWII, and served as an army engineer in Germany. He was a mathematical whiz. In the early 1960s he purchased his own single engine plane, which was a rare occurrence in the White community and totally unheard of in the Black community. He turned his flying passion into a profitable side business by delivering personal mail from the nearby Wichita Falls, Texas army base to bases in Chicago. On one occasion he flew to Tallahassee and allowed me to experience a brief flight. While in mid-flight and without any warning, he tipped up the nose of the plane and purposely sent it into a stall. After getting the panic response he sought from me, he regained control and proceeded to explain airplane lift.

Over the decades of discussions with my Dad and Uncle Emiel, neither mentioned the countless college rejections received prior to their acceptance at Ohio State. Neither bemoaned the institutional racism they faced when they returned from fighting for their country. Whatever obstacles they faced on their road trip from Texas to Ohio in 1950 or inconveniences faced once they arrived in Columbus, I'll never know. It was not important enough to them to discuss them. They instead spoke of their pride in serving their country during WWII. Both emphatically counted it as the most important decision of their lives. They were forever grateful, always competing, progressing forward, and committed to win against the false narratives of "real" institutional racism of their day. For this was not a generation of Whiny, Weenie and Wimpy men, but a small illustration of the tenacious grit of the greatest generation in American history. It was a generation of men and women from a diversity of races, colors and religions who fought, lived and loved—more than anything—being Americans.

The meteoric rise of the 1940s, 50s and 60s black community into the middle class was not a matter of luck or happenstance. It was also taught, earned and expected by the Kirby's. All 13 children went on to experience the American dream buffet, which included higher education, successful marriages, families, business ownerships or long job careers, church and community involvement, college education for their children, vacations, reunions, and lifetimes of added-value to their communities and to their proud Kirby name.

Born to the era of the Great Depression my parents' were raised by poor, hardworking, formally uneducated farmers, business owners and country-loving Christians. They lived in an era centered on such family values as honesty, hard work, loyalty, fidelity and respect. It was a culture in which front doors remained unlocked and where a firm handshake and steady look in the eye was considered of more value than a team of lawyers. After returning from WWI my grandfather's generation transferred their patriotism to their sons, many of who would volunteer for WWII and the Korean War. The common denominator was the pride they shared amongst themselves for their willingness to step up to the plate and serve with valor when our country called for freedom fighters.

My generation was in turn taught, at young ages, about courageous historic freedom fighters like Harriett Tubman and others. These stories were inspiring to me as a pre-teen Black youth, as they were for so many others in our small segregated community of Tallahassee, Florida. Tallahassee is the home of the prominent black college, Florida A & M University (FAMU). FAMU was nationally respected for its high academic standards and consistency in graduating talented bright minds from its ranks. Its athletic department yielded some of the NFL's first Black athletic stars. One of these was Bob Hayes, the worlds fastest human, nicknamed the human bullet. Its electrifying football half-time band, "The Marching 100," was of international acclaim. The band's daily practice sessions could be heard for miles.

Black elementary and junior high youngsters who dreamed of one day earning a place in its ranks emulated its drum roll cadence.

As an impressionable pre-teenage black boy, my exposure to success within my segregated community made it natural to see success as a normal progression of growing up. The vision of graduating from high school and college, starting a business, beginning a career, going into the field of medicine or academia was as much a part of our future as it was for other communities during that era. Black families of my parents' generation, throughout our nation, were actively participating in the post WW2 middle class explosion.[2] It was a time of the housing boom, stimulated by easily affordable mortgages for returning members of the military. Proud patriotic Black men were returning from World War II and the Korean War, using the GI Bill to further their education, start their own businesses, find jobs, start their families and build their new homes. The nation's gross national product rose from about $200 million in 1940 to $300 million in 1950 and to more than $500 million in 1960.[3] Their participation was evident in the self-sustaining, segregated communities growing in the shadow of influential Black colleges like FAMU, Prairieveiw University, Southern University, Jackson State, Morgan State and many more. These colleges represented a pride in academic accomplishment and a gateway to the American dream envisioned by a vast majority of Black citizens. These college campuses were also the settings for learning standards, discipline, respect for

2   https://en.wikipedia.org/wiki/Post%E2%80%93World_War_II_economic_expansion

3   http://economics.about.com/od/useconomichistory/a/post_war.htm

authority and a reflection of Christian-centered families, who espoused the traditional American values.

In and around these campuses was also a setting for an increasingly growing and influential Black middle class. During this era of the 50s and mid-60s, segregated Black communities across the country shared a common vision... "To rise up, to compete, to overcome and to lift others. They were committed to show to the world that they were equal or better to any others." For the entire community, comprised of rich and poor, educated and non-educated, professional and the manual laborer, it was the Black middle class that represented the catalyst for the upward financial trajectory for all. They served as the community's financial stabilizing force as they reinvested their resources of time, talent and income into their community. They served in mentorship roles as volunteer coaches, Boy Scout and Girl Scout leaders. They were actively involved as community project leaders in PTA/children musical programs. They offered both employment and examples for the Black youth as they opened/expanded new businesses and contributed substantially to the community's financial tax base. The children of business owners worked at their family business during the summers. My younger siblings and I would walk on Saturday mornings more than a mile, with brooms in hand, to sweep the driveway of my dad's off campus 12-unit apartment building. When finished sweeping, we'd then walk home. These types of opportunities, along with community cultural activities and experiences allowed their children to continually reset their boundaries.

This new Black middle class, representing the communities best and brightest, took pride in leading their community's meteoric rise upward during this era, while availing themselves to support and encourage others to follow. In our segregated town, it was the Black middle class communities of College Terrace and Jake Gaither Park that represented success within the community and the real life possibilities for the rest of community of the American dream. It was also a place where youngsters, like myself, could live somewhat protected from the harsh realities of institutional racism. Within our community there was simply no personal interaction with White Americans.

My first personal interaction with racism did not come until I was 16 years old, during the integration of Rickards High School. Within my segregated community, confidence was palatable, where *anything* could be accomplished, even with the oppressive policies of white racism. We were taught that our solution—our gateway to success—could be found through hard work, entrepreneurship, education, tenacity, courage, self-respect and loyalty.

The community's expectations of us were high. We grew up projecting that success, even outside of Tallahassee, was not only possible but also inherently predictable. Obstacles were therefore never the focus of discussions, but instead, overcoming and opportunities were.

We were taught patriotism and the etiquette of respecting our flag. We understood that as we reverently folded and unfolded it, that it would be desecrated if allowed to touch the ground. This insight was taught in a community of fathers who had served and returned from WWII before we were born. The pride that they felt collectively for serving had been passed on to each of us. We were taught the benefits of a look in the eye, a firm handshake and a respectful reply of "Yes Sir" or "No Ma'am" to every adult... regardless of race, financial status or profession. With that same firm handshake and promise came a bond more binding than a contract. We were taught to be courageous leaders, not weak and compliant followers. "If it is right, have the courage to do it; if it is wrong, have the courage not to."

The most important lesson taught to us as young boys was that of respect and chivalry for all women. There was no excuse, NONE, for a real man to strike a woman. If women were being disrespected, real men were expected to act and NOT stand idly by. This was the message given and mandated by the 1960s segregated community of Tallahassee, Florida.

Black print publications, such as *Jet* and *Ebony* magazines, were in practically every Black home, school library, physician and dentist office, and barbershop. These publications served as examples of Black success. They shared a consistent theme that was present in all community communications... that our race was capable of ANYTHING when work ethic, preparation and dream power were embraced.

Through private organizations like the Jack and Jill Club and community activities available on the FAMU campus—like Judo training, gymnastics, swimming competition, Boy Scouts and marksmanship/firearm training by the National Rifle Association—the tools of preparation were granted to my generation to break the bonds of institutional indifference.

As children, we were both protected and encouraged within this sheltered segregated environment. From our protective cocoon we would only occasionally get a glimpse of the institutional racism our parents dealt with daily. Entering the seventh grade, I remember our class was distributed old, used textbooks that Leon High the cross-town all-white school was discarding. With the delivery of their brand new textbooks, they no longer needed the older ones. At least once a year our family was reminded of our second-class demarcation as we took our annual road trip to visit our relatives in Texas. All white-owned service stations along the way labeled their rest room facilities, "White Men Only" or "White Women Only." The single, unisex toilet for Blacks, placed in the back of the building and labeled "Colored," was guaranteed to be unkempt and filthy. My parents refused to acquiesce to this very prevalent southern Jim Crow practice and would enter the White Men and Women restrooms anyway. On one of these cross-country trips, two white boys attempted to break in the door while my mother was using the "White Women Only" bathroom. As a ten-year old, from the backseat of our car, I watched as my dad proceeded to get out of the car and to have an altercation with both. Mom was not forced to leave that restroom early and Dad showed his two boys and three girls what was expected of Real Men.

These occasional opportunities to travel outside of our segregated cocoon gave me a chance to observe first hand the courage of my parents' generation. These were men and women who lived their lives determined not to be viewed as victims. Instead through tenacity, grit and by winning they commanded the respect of other Americans. Their confidence came from a lineage of young men who fought and returned home from two World Wars with pride in their family's name and heritage that would not permit submission. This was a generation that understood that overcoming the prejudices of Jim Crow laws and institutionalized racism could only be done by creating value and independence from within. All opportunities to compete head-to-head against the White race were welcomed, embraced and celebrated regardless of the arena. In 1935, the debate team from Wiley College, one of the oldest predominantly black colleges west of the Mississippi River, defeated the reigning national debate champion, the University of Southern California.[4] Proof again that this generation simply refused to be intimated, deterred or victimized by any other race.

It was a generation born during our nations darkest financial times, The Depression, and one that fought and saved the civilized world from the darkest forms of godless totalitarianism... Socialism, Nazism and Communism. (Apparently lost to many through the annals of our progressive education is the acknowledgement that the Soviet Union (Socialist) and the National Socialist German Workers' Party (German Nazis) were allies entering WWII.[5] They shared the same endgame... the *godless centralization of power, totalitarianism.*) This was the generation that changed the heart of America from its tolerant and blind eye to finally see the evils of institutional racism. It was also a generation that understood the divine nature of gratitude. They exhibited their gratitude in words, deeds and loyalty to a nation that, though still imperfect, had granted freedom and opportunities within their segregated communities to make their lives better. They simple refused to fall prey to the today's popular view expressed by English author Aldous Huxley, "Most human beings have an almost infinite capacity for taking things for granted." This was not so with this past "great generation"

---

4   https://en.wikipedia.org/wiki/Wiley_College
5   http://rexcurry.net/socialistwar.html

and the ones that preceded it. For in their hearts had been cultivated an attitude of gratitude.

"The grateful man sees as much in the world to be thankful for, and with him the good outweighs the evil. Love overpowers jealous and light drives darkness out of my life. Pride destroys our gratitude and sets up selfishness in its place. How much happier we are in the presence of a grateful and loving soul, and how careful we should be to cultivate, through the medium of a prayerful life, a thankful attitude toward God and man'[6]

This book is a tribute to the spirit of freedom exhibited by Harriett Tubman, Booker T. Washington, Fredrick Douglass, my parents' generation and the millions who preceded them. It is an acknowledgement of generations past who accepted the challenges of visionaries, leaders, providers and protectors to all for whom they were given responsibility. They accepted their responsibility and contributed to the great human experiment we now call America.

It will be these "past great generations" whom we will one day have to face and answer to. How will we respond to their question, "What did you do with our gifted legacy?" As a community and nation of men will we be able to stand tall, with confidence and with pride and answer, "We stood on your shoulders and became better. We learned to 'Man-Up.'" Or will we, at that day of reckoning, be forced to answer with all timidity, "We were afraid... afraid of what others thought, afraid of what others might say, and afraid of what others might do. We therefore took your proud legacy of Manhood

---

[6]   President Joseph F. Smith, President of the Church of Jesus Chris of the Latter Day Saints

and turned our sons and ourselves into a community and nation of Whiners, Weenies and Wimps."

Black Americans face a critical choice as to their priorities, as does the rest of America. As a Judeo-Christian and capitalist nation, once proudly viewed as the Shining Light on the Hill by the rest of the world, we now stand on the precipice of Socialism, Atheism and decline. Unfortunately, close to 50% of Americans either welcome this new status or are totally unaware of its threat to their own freedoms. To choose our path, it will require that "We the People" understand the true meaning of the ideology of Liberalism/Socialism. Our choice will have immutable consequences, for which no one else can be blamed or credited. Do we choose to remain free, committed to the ideals that have allowed us to be so, or do we choose to subject ourselves to the servitude of the seductive ideology of Liberalism/Socialism? It will be *our choice,* with eternal consequences.

CHAPTER 2
THE SPIRIT OF HARRIETT TUBMAN

1

"I was free, they ought's to be free."

- Harriett Tubman

---

1   http://www.bing.com/images/search?q=harrit+tubman&view=detailv2&&id=828DF
     5C5D0E707CC708DC13B9AE4BFD41A03C99B&selectedIndex=3&ccid=I3ZcwD
     80&simid=608011449918425522&thid=OIP.M23765cc03f3432bb9942be64ff017a9
     eH1&ajaxhist=0

Throughout the early to mid-1800s there were thousands of nameless slaves who found the courage to take the perilous pathway northward that would lead them to freedom. Of the many, there is only one, Harriet Tubman, whose name is synonymous with that great freedom effort. Married to a freed man, it was Harriett Tubman who escaped without his knowledge for fear that he might attempt to thwart her efforts or betray her. It was Harriett Tubman whose love for freedom would have her risk it all, more than 19 times, to bring her family and more than 300 slaves north to the Promised Land. The rewards offered for her capture totaled an astronomical $40,000 (more than $1 million in today's money).[2] On June 2, 1863, abolitionist and former slave James Montgomery led 300 African-American troops of the Union Army's 2nd South Carolina Volunteers on a raid of plantations along the Combahee River. Backed by three gunboats, Harriet Tubman's forces set fire to the plantations and freed 750 slaves.[3] She was credited not only with significant leadership responsibilities for the mission itself, but with singing to calm the slaves and keep the situation in hand. Tubman came under Confederate fire on this mission. General Saxton, who reported the raid to Secretary of War Stanton, said "This is the only military command in American history wherein a woman, black or white, led the raid and under whose inspiration it was originated and conducted." Tubman reported later that most of the freed slaves joined "the colored regiment." She was

---

2   http://mentalfloss.com/article/31251/harriet-tubmans-perfect-record-brains-and-opium-underground-railroad

3   http://www.clarionledger.com/story/journeytojustice/2015/06/02/civil-rights-history-june-8/28353633/

also present for the defeat of the 54th Massachusetts, the black unit led by Robert Gould Shaw.[4]

It was her love for freedom that drove her to work tirelessly as a spy, scout, cook, nurse and recruiter of black soldiers for the Union cause. When not conducting her passengers through the byways and southern homes of the Underground Railroad, she traveled throughout the north soliciting donations to help fund yet another journey. Though illiterate, and at any time could succumb to unpredictable and uncontrollable spells of narcolepsy, she did not allow these obstacles to encumber her mission. When asked why she was so willing to put all at risk so often, her answer was simple yet profound, "I was free, they ought's to be free."

For Harriett Tubman it was her love of freedom that mattered most.

It was this same type of unselfish, courageous, and unheralded spirit that opened doors for the black middle class to unparalleled opportunities and growth, during the early to mid-1900s. This segment of the Black population, the middle class, had learned to negotiate the difficult and exhausting pathway to success that allowed them to enjoy the precious fruits of their labor. These valued lessons were passed on responsibly to the following generations. As with all other American cultures, it was the vision of the Black community to allow each generation to reach higher while standing upon the shoulders of the preceding one. "The American Dream" that our past generations had sacrificed for, is alive and well for today's Black middle class. It is represented by memories Black parents give their children on family trips to Disney

---

[4] http://womenshistory.about.com/od/harriettubman/a/tubman_civilwar.htm

World and cruises throughout the Caribbean. It is seen in the rearing of their children in safe neighborhoods with "state of the art" schools, positive peer group experiences, and acceptance to expensive, prestigious colleges. Millions of middle class Black Americans have experienced international travel and have secured their retirement through healthy IRAs and pension plans. Most importantly, for decades they have created a platform for their children on which the vision of unlimited opportunity was painted. For these members of the black middle class who have thus tasted the fruit of this country's promise of life, liberty and the pursuit of happiness, it is incumbent for the future of our children, race and country that we now embrace the spirit of Harriett Tubman, "I was free, they ought's to be free."

The uniqueness of our society is its perpetuation of opportunity necessary for vertical mobility. It is opportunity that is predicated on the reality of its available to even the less among us. It is the promise that our capitalist system remains both dynamic and economically fluid. For in our country there are no imposed static layers of rich and poor, where at the doorway stands a sentinel granting or denying access. The combination that opens the door to the American dream is available to everyone who has the desire to learn and apply the code. As part of our inherent beauty, we are the one country that allows for as many "do-overs" as the dreamer has the faith and endurance to take. It's the gift that keeps on giving, the eternal mulligan. Our economic system, fluid and growing, allows us to be active participants in its success cycle, regardless of color, creed, gender or economic status. Every American has the opportunity to go from broke to wealthy, wealthy to broke, and back again as many times as he/she chooses or until the personal economic comfort zone and level of confidence is found. One of the best-kept secrets of our Free Enterprise/Capitalist system is that there are *always* opportunities for upward economic mobility. Yes, the price is steep but as our own desires stimulate action and as we emulate successful principles and people, we can dictate our finish regardless of where we start. This is the fundamental understanding that has been the magnet for the millions attracted to our shores. It is an understanding best symbolized by a gift given to our country by France in 1886, the Statue of Liberty. Inscribed on a tablet within her walls are the words:

"Give me your tired, your poor,
Your huddled masses yearning to breathe free.
The wretched refuse of your teeming shore
Send these, the homeless, tempest-tost to me,
I lift my lamp beside the golden door!"[5]

"Yearning to breathe free" embodies the spirit that has defined the American Way. It is the American Way that for more than 200 years has made and kept its promise to allow the dreams of its citizens to remain possible. It is the one country that has for 200 years consistently and predictably granted upward mobility, increased opportunities and lifestyle to each succeeding generation. Its promise has for generations, kept our nation from sliding (as many nations have) through the spectrum of "isms" into totalitarianism. Its promise gives to every "willing" American the confidence to

---

[5]   http://www.lightomega.org/worldwatch/StatueofLiberty.html

know that, regardless of his or her humble beginnings, they are free to choose their own pathway to success. With this freedom comes another important message of truth... "One who seeks to steal from or to demean the success of others, hinders his own opportunity to one day be."

As we seek to leave our legacy for future generations, it is important to remember that it will be our society's respect for the success of others that will establish our futures' scope and limits. If we fail to voice appreciation for those who have overcome to become, we stand to lose the essence of what has made our American Republic the freest society in the history of mankind. It is through encouragement and gratitude that "We the People" unleash our great "problem solving" ingenuity. It is only when we envision ourselves as the catalyst for our own solutions that we can position ourselves to partake of the forthcoming fruit of our own labor. Harriett Tubman saw herself, despite her many obstacles and human flaws, as a solution for generations of freedom-loving people. Through her personal efforts, she helped free hundreds of souls and by her example she has inspired millions and millions more. The spirit depicted by her courage, vision, and love for her fellow man, best illustrates what we call the American Way. This spirit has been displayed by many countless numbers of nameless Americans of all colors, races, religions and creeds, throughout our nation's history. Though diverse, our commonality of principles, beliefs and values has defined us as Americans.

For the future of our country and to insure a society that will be a blessing to our children, we must recapture that spirit of Harriett Tubman. It will take courage, tenacity and vision to lead our fellow Americas to the envisioned Promised

Land. Unlike the fight against slavery in the 1800s, the KKK threat of lynching throughout the early 1900s, and the quest for equal civil rights in the 50s and 60s, today's freedom adversary does not threaten with physical retribution. Instead its method of intimidation is one of ostracism, rejection and, for independent Black Americans, accusations of betrayal of their race. Today's battle will require a different level of commitment from its warriors. It will require the willingness to sacrifice acceptance, prestige, popularity and opportunities for "cheap" wealth. There is a guarantee that "friends" will be lost and enemies accumulated. For on this battlefield are blacks and whites, rich and poor, the powerful and the impotent who cannot tolerate voices that stand against the status quo. Their leadership will come from the ranks of those who embrace the ideology of Liberalism, "The Royalty Class" who have for decades profited in prominence, popularity and wealth from status quo. They have for decades discussed, hypothesized and postulated about the problems of the Black community but have yet to offer "constructive, measurable and accountable" solutions. One of American's greatest pioneers, a former slave, educator, entrepreneur, advisor to Presidents and the founder of Tuskegee University, Booker T. Washington, spoke of this class in his 1911, "My Larger Education." He referred to them as "Problem Profiteers", the definition of which has remained consistent into our new millennium.

"There is another class of colored people who make a business of keeping the troubles, the wrongs and the hardships of the Negro race before the public. Having learned that they are able to make a living out of their troubles, they have grown into the settled habit of advertising their wrongs—

partly because they want sympathy and partly because it pays. Some of these people do not want the Negro to lose his grievances, because they do not want to lose their jobs."[6]

These are the Black intellectuals and elitists, "The Royalty Black Class" who have chosen to recuse themselves from providing measurable solutions to stem the tide of hopelessness and despair within the urban Black community. They have instead opted to profit from its misery. These are those who will assuredly, on cue, demonize and demean all thought and voices that seek to break the hold of a *statistically proven* destructive ideology. The independent, free-thinking Black American is guaranteed to be their targets. Intimidation attempts will be used, that in the past have been effective in keeping in compliance anyone who dared dissent from the community "group think." But tired terms like Uncle Tom, Oreo, Turncoat, House Nigger, Sellout, and Porch Monkey are superficial and cynical, denoting elitism and intellectual laziness and will not abort this mission. For those emboldened by the spirit of Harriett Tubman, the sacrifice will be made with both purpose and honor… for like Harriett, it is our love for freedom that matters most. "I was free, they ought's to be free."

It has been both purposeful and effective on the part of the ideology of Liberalism to inject within the Black community a sense of victimization, disconnecting it from its proud past through revisionism. This strategy has had a tremendously negative impact on race relations as White Americans are tasked to take on the responsibility for the actions of other White strangers, who died hundreds of years

---

6   http://americanvision.org/5276/booker-t-washington-on-black-victimhood/

ago. In the meanwhile, this high bar of accountability is imposed on them by a class of Black Americans who refuse to take responsibility for their own actions within the last 24 hours. Because of the decades-long embrace of this ideology, many Black Americans are no longer able to envision for themselves the promise of America. They have accepted the premise that doors once closed to their ancestors remain closed today. They remain unaware of the multi-generational success stories of their own ancestry earned through tenacity, ingenuity, hard work and vision. Many Black Americans who choose to work, study and achieve are today faced with the temptation to accept a false narrative that their accomplishments are beyond the reach of others of their race. Many are made to believe that their adoption of successful habits regarding personal appearance, speech, attitude, morality and actions are "white people" actions and they have become Uncle Tom-ish. They thus proceed to categorize their success as luck, which is not only a condescending insult to their own race, but also an insult to a nation that grants like opportunities to every other race and culture.

This message of a hapless and "put upon" race has left millions of Black Americans seeing no real value in themselves and having no real pride in their "defeated and subservient" ancestry. With the acceptance of the ideology of Liberalism, millions of Black children have no interest in researching their own ancestral linage, though they can easily justify demanding personal reparation for them... victims! This false projection of a race that was unable to overcome, victims of another more powerful and dominating race, is the *Greatest of All* insults to our past great generations. It has thus been the will and the way of the ideology of Liberalism that the

Black Race, with its long proud history of accomplishments and contributions, is reduced to our nations' *Street Corner Beggar*.

It is the American way, embraced by past generations of Black Americans that has no room for elitism or eternal victimhood. It is, after all, America whose foundational Judeo-Christian tenets instruct us to "teach a man to fish today so he can feed himself and his family forever." It is a country built on the premise of freely giving a caring hand up, without an agenda of developing a dependency for a hand out. *Respect and Pity can never exist simultaneously in the relationship of equality* was the true and yet mischaracterized message of Booker T. Washington in 1900.

It is my hope that the spirit of Harriett Tubman, an eternal vision emboldened by faith, can be gleaned through the words and thoughts penned in this book. It is the spirit of love for our fellow citizens and our country that will resurrect the black community. It the spirit of confidence in the strength, will and tenacity of the Black community, as articulated by former slave, abolitionist and freedom fighter, Fredrick Douglas.

"What shall we do with the Negro?" I have had but one answer from the beginning. Do nothing with us! Your doing with us has already played the mischief with us. Do nothing with us! If the apples will not remain on the tree of their own strength, if they are worm-eaten at the core, if they are early ripe and disposed to fall, let them fall! I am not for tying or fastening them on the tree in any way, except by nature's plan, and if they will not stay there, let them fall. And if the Negro cannot stand on his own legs, let him fall also. All I ask is, give him a chance to stand on his own legs! Let him alone! [7]

So it will be within the Black Race where the solution to the problems of the Black Race will be found. It will be discovered within the broad diversity of Black men and women who, with courage and commitment, will put the welfare of their race above all else... social status, financial gains, power, party and politics. It will be the Black middle class who once again, by recapturing the spirit of empathy and by denouncing the elitist spirit of the Royalty Class Black Man, will lower the economic bridge to those willing to work, learn and earn their way to join them. It will be those willing to forgo the comfort and ease of Black "Group Think" and will embrace the simple yet powerful words of the Freedom Pioneer, Harriett Tubman....

"I was free, they ought's to be free."

---

[7] http://www.lexrex.com/enlightened/writings/douglas.htm

CHAPTER 3
WHAT HAPPENED TO ALL THE GOOD MEN?

*"The impact of a man's life will be determined
by his courage to have a vision, his wisdom to
understand and overcome life's obstacles, and his
faith to know that he is meant to be."*
                                    - Burgess Owens

As a father of five daughters, I've asked the question more
than a few times over the many years: "What has happened to
all the good men?" It is a question increasingly being asked
by millions of women throughout our country from all races
and backgrounds, but no more so than by an overwhelming
majority of Black women. The theme of this book is to expose
the progressive influence of the ideology of Liberalism on the
Black race. Because of its agnostic nature, its influence and
long-term impact are equally being felt among all cultures and
communities that it touches. Its most demonstrable imprint
is on the transformational redefinition of the role of man,
regardless of his race, creed, background or color. Nowhere
can this be seen more than within the Black American
community. The result of its many decades of acceptance has
left a vast majority of its women continually lowering their

expectations of Black manhood. Unfortunately, even with this downward recalculation, increasing numbers of Black women are still finding themselves disappointed and alone. The ideology of liberalism is tenacious and unrelenting in its demands to alter the divine nature that defines manhood.

Throughout history, men have not only found pride in their role, but have innately been anxious to fulfill it. This is particularly true within the more than 200-year-old Judeo-Christian American culture. Defined by terms such as Protector, Provider, Leader, Visionary and Server, it is a role that has enhanced man's self-esteem and given him purpose. The example he sets as a committed provider gives his family pride in carrying his name...a name respected by others. The ideology of Liberalism demands the role of supremacy and is envious of anything that threatens its place. It cannot tolerate the presence and competitive role of Manhood, which seeks independence that can only be found in self-direction, self-fulfillment and self-empowerment. Men are emboldened with confirmation that women have confidence in their ability to comfort, lead and protect. The ideology of Liberalism views this as threatening and will endeavor, at all cost, to force men into a role of subservience. With acceptance of subservience to any ideology that degrades him and subverts his responsibility, a man gives up the right to be called a Real Man.

In the Black community, the Royalty Class Black Man has acquiesced his role to the demands of the ideology of Liberalism. He once presided over a proud and vibrant community but chose, for the sake of self-aggrandizement, to abandon it. Betrayed and left without visionary leadership, the Black community has devolved into ruin. This is the consistent state of *every* urban community now overseen by the Royalty-Class Black Man and the ideology of Liberalism he is committed to.

Liberalism represents both an ideological and spiritual view of the individual. It demands of its believers an acceptance of a limited scope of personal freedoms, initiative and accountability. It is an ideology that prioritizes "Class over Race", as it depends on the prominence of two particular classes for its existence... The Ruling Class and The Dependent Class. It is the perfect storm when the narcissistic, superiority beliefs of the Rulers combine with the self-condescending inferiority beliefs of Dependents. In this potent concoction is where the godless/atheist ideology of Socialism festers. The Rulers see themselves as Godlike providers of all things and the hopeless Dependents accept them as such. Attempts to put anything in between this symbiotic relationship, i.e. education, alternative options or in particular God, is met with wrath, condemnation and anger.

Within a Liberal/Socialist society, the growth of the Ruling and Dependent Classes coincides with the diminishing presence of the working, value-based and empathic middle class. As the influence of liberalism increased throughout the late 60s, so did its impact on the Black middle class. The group that exploded during the 40s, 50s and early 60s began, by 1970 to be "squeezed from the middle," pushing families above and below the middle class lines. More families have been pushed upward, but their places have not been filled with families from the lower classes.[1] This unfortunately equates to a larger percentage of wealthy Royalty Class Black elitists who have little to no emotional empathy for the

---

[1]   http://www.pbs.org/wgbh/pages/frontline/shows/race/economics/analysis.html

Dependency class. As discussed later, this explains the elitist class's propensity, for its own self-aggrandizement to support every Liberal anti-Black policy demanded of them.

As with all other ideologies and doctrines, Liberalism/ Socialism has eternal prospective and fundamental tenets that are unalterable. It demands unquestioned, undaunted and unbridled loyalty, regardless of who or what is betrayed in the process. The Royalty Black Class dutifully assumes this role.

The American culture is unique. It is the only society in the history of mankind that was founded upon documents, like the Mayflower Compact and US Constitution, which purposely defined a roadmap to maximize fairness and freedom on behalf of the individual. It is also the only society that, from its beginning, freely allowed the co-existence of competing ideologies granting its citizens the opportunity to choose the doctrine which best aligns with their own vision and beliefs. The uniqueness of the American Way has been the freedom of its citizens to envision and pursue what is deemed to be in their own best personal interest.

For Americans historically, their self-interest has been inextricably tied to the best interest of their family, community, country and their God. It has been the 200-year history of the American Way to constantly seek for improvement and to form a closer alignment with the mission statement found within its founding documents. And though ideologies and doctrines are static and incapable of change, the individual remains uniquely capable of change. Through increased wisdom and perspective, the human experience is therefore self-directing and thus potentially always rewarding.

In the world of professional sports, with the donning of team jersey\ colors and logo, comes an indication of fan loyalty and commitment. The breaking of this bond, which could be intergenerational, takes bold actions by the team that the fan considers close to treachery. This was evidenced by the mass fan transition during the early 80s of Bay Area Raider fans to 49'er fans. Ranked as having one of the league's most loyal fan bases, many Raider fans felt betrayed by a business decision of its owner Al Davis, to move his team from Oakland to LA. It resulted in a large segment of its base switching its loyalty to the jersey and logo of the 49ers. The 49ers subsequent years of Super Bowl Championships cemented that decision. Now, many once loyal and committed Raider fans are inter-generational loyal and faithful 49er fans.

For decades the Black community has proudly worn the jersey of the ideology of Liberalism. Its deep seeded loyalty has justified an acceptance that no longer tracks the consistency of losing seasons. It no longer expects or seeks accountably from the coaches/leaders who have put forth decades of devastating, losing strategies. Its loyalty has allowed it to embrace a philosophy found nowhere else in the world within successful cultures... *"That the success of its race is dictated by the benevolence, acceptance or guilt of another race."* There was once a feeling of harmony and optimism in the segregated Black communities of the 40s, 50s and 60s, as it played a leadership role in our country's historic growth of the middle class. The pride of the era has long dissipated and been replaced by chronic hopelessness, anger and finger pointing.

Though betrayed for decades and saddled with a losing legacy, the loyalty of the Black community and desire to don the jersey of the ideology of Liberalism continues unabated. Though it has been forced to lower its standards and expectations of manhood for its young boys, total and abject loyalty is still prevalent within the Black community for the failed colors and logo of Liberalism. Its fatherless boys now rank on the top of "every" failure indicator as they increasingly turn away from their responsibility to family, to marriage commitments, and to their divine role to protect and provide for their own children. As these young men increasing fail in their educational pursuits and responsibilities to learn and apply proven success principles, they rebel with pride and arrogance at the concept of submissiveness to authority... showing an ever-deepening disrespect for women, their elders, and their race. Their lack of self-love, self-esteem and self-discipline have led to the highest percentage of murder rates nationwide with a staggering statistics of 93% of Black citizens killed by Black citizens. And yet the loyalty of the Black community and its desire to don the jersey of the ideology of Liberalism continues unabated.

As the Black community continues its well-trodden path to ruin, today's Royalty Class Black Man does nothing. With his lifestyle, prominence and popularity assured, he has long ago abdicated his responsibility to lead, protect and provide vision to the community that, in spite of it all, still trusts him. The ideology of Liberalism demands of the Royalty Class Black Man an unbridled loyalty that prioritizes it above his religion, family, race, principles, heritage and country. To these demands of subservience, he acquiesces. The ideology of Liberalism demands the suspension of all individual core principles. It is the engaged individual who is left to justify, as a Capitalist, his collusion with avowed Socialists, Communists and Marxists. As a practicing Christian, Jew or Muslim, he colludes with *rabid* anti-God atheists. As a passionate defender of Pro-Life, he colludes with passionate no-limits abortionists. As a believer in School Choice for poor Black children he must justify his collusion with Anti-Choice/Pro labor union advocates. In a show of solidarity and loyalty to the ideology of Liberalism, the Black community predictably and collectively votes for the same candidate and party as do those who are adamantly opposed to their most treasured values.

This depth of loyalty and predictability is not lost on the Royal Class Black politician. A Black member of Congress told political scientist Carol Swain that "one of the advantages, and disadvantages, of representing blacks is their shameless loyalty... you can almost get away with raping babies and be forgiven. You don't have any vigilance about your performance."[2] Total, unbridled and "shameless loyalty" is what is demanded, as the Royalty Class Black Man acquiesces. The ideology of Liberalism demands that the Black man forsake his role and responsibility as protector, provider, and leader of his family. As the overwhelming ideology of choice within the Black community, more than 70% of males who would consider themselves liberal feel totally justified deserting the mothers of their newborn children.[3] Never in the entire recorded history of the planet has there been a greater voluntary abandonment of children by their fathers than in Black America today.

For any other race, this statement alone would be embarrassing, but not so of the Royalty Class Black Man.

---

[2] Carol M. Swain, The New White Nationalism in America: Its Challenge to Integration (Cambridge University Press), 403

[3] Theatlantic.com/sexes/archive/2013/06/understanding-out-of-wedlock-births-in-black-america/277084/

The silence on this issue from the leadership of the NAACP and Black Congressional Caucus and Black Liberal media talking heads is deafening. The principles and precepts of their chosen ideology allow these males to turn their backs on the children of their own race, totally conscience-free.

THE EDUCATOR

The ideology of Liberalism demands that the Black man acquiesces, as generations of children are increasingly illiterate, chronically unemployed, hopeless and angry. It demands his silence and the perpetual support of the Civil Rights-era Royalty Class Black Politician, made popular with annual liberal media hero-worshipping. Unquestioned loyalty is expected even though the Royalty Class Politician has voted 100% for every piece of Anti-Black legislation proposed. It is this class, the ineffective and unaccountable Royalty Class Black Politician, who have enriched themselves with power, position and wealth while collaborating with the same white controlled, education labor unions that have entrapped millions of urban Black children into failure. The Royalty Class Black Man justifies the sacrifice of poor Black children on the sacred alter of Labor Union (Public) schools, as long as their children do not have to attend them. From the comfort of his secure and safe community, providing his children access to the best school systems the taxpayer money can buy, the Royalty Class Black Man acquiesces... (The topic of educational betrayal by the Royalty Black Class will be covered extensively in Chapter 11 "The NAACP Strategy: The Trojan Horse.")

THE PROTECTOR

The ideology of Liberalism demands that the Black man set aside, for the sake of the cause, the most critical of all of his manhood roles, the Ultimate Defender of his family. He is willing to disarm and recuse himself from any responsibility to protect his own family against ALL evil with "overwhelming force." The Liberal Black Man would rather position himself as a cowardly beggar, if ever called upon to defend the life and honor of own wife and children. He fails to envision himself as an empowered agent who could set aside the same amount of time he used to master his Smart phone, to learn how to use and safely store his own firearms. Predictably, as his poor urban constituents face the consequence of evil criminality in their neighborhoods, the Royalty Class Black Politician dutifully parrots the logic of his white liberal political leadership that safety rests in disarming the remaining 240 million law-abiding American gun owners. Even as statistics show that women use guns to protect themselves against sexual assault more than 200,000 times a year or that 3/5 of polled felons admitted they wouldn't mess with an armed victim, the Royalty Class Black Politician refuses to be dissuaded. John Lott, former chief economist at the United States Sentencing Commission shared statistics regarding the Stand Your Ground Laws, predicated on the legal right of citizens to carry concealed weapons. He stated that between 1997 and 2005, murder rates fell by 9% and overall violent crime fell by 11%. He added that "poor blacks who live in high crime urban areas are not only the most likely victims of crime, they are also the ones who benefit the most from Stand Your Ground Laws." It makes it easier for them to "protect themselves" when the police can't be there fast enough. Rules that make self-defense more difficult would impact blacks the most. He also added, "Blacks make up just 16.6% of Florida's population, but they account for more than 31% of the states' defendants invoking the Stand Your Ground defense. Black defendants who invoke this statue to justify their actions are acquitted eight per cent more frequently than whites who use the same defense.[4] The Justice Department data from 2013 show that, as firearm purchases were increasing, in less than two decades the gun murder rate was nearly cut in half.[5] In 2012 background checks reached 19.6 million, an annual record and an increase of 19% over 2011. Meanwhile the most violent cities in America, like Chicago and Baltimore, remain the cities with the strictest gun laws.[6] So as the murder of defenseless and innocent poor Black Americans increases where the ideology of liberalism's policies remains in place, the Royalty Class Black Politician continues to insist on disarming urban residents (victims). Consistent with this Class is the absence of their own home address in the At-Risk community where their liberal policies have been mandated.

Safely secure in his middle/upper class gated community, or surrounded by his armed security guards, the Professional Royalty Class Black Politician insists that self-protection is a threat to all other law-abiding Americans. As he promotes the abdication of the role of the father to protect himself, his family and his community, he also relinquishes

---

4   Please Stop Helping Us-Jason Riley-76
5   Emily Albert, "Gun Crime has Plunged but Americans Think It's Us" *LA Times* May 7, 2013
6   Please Stop Helping Us-Jason Riley-77

every bit of his Common Sense. He once again acquiesces to ideology, as he legislates another anti-black policy that neuters the urban man of his most important responsibility as a man… the PROTECTOR.

Why would a grown man give total strangers the responsibility to protect his own family from evil? …"Liberalism's got um."

THE PATRIOT

"Once (you) let the black man get upon his person the brass letter, U.S., let him get an eagle on his button, and a musket on his shoulder and bullets in his pocket, there is no power on earth that can deny that he has earned the right to citizenship."
- Fredrick Douglas [7]

If we as a community are to resurrect ourselves, we must demand honest answers. How do we rate as proud American citizens after 60 years of loyalty to the ideology of Liberalism? Can we look to our men today, as did past generations and apply to them the titles Defenders, Champions and Patriots? Would they accept them? If our country was in need and called on us, as it has over the last 200 years, would our community feel a connection, a bond of loyalty and gratitude? Would we feel honored to accept?

---

[7] msolsonhistory.weebly.com/uploads/5/1/2/9/5129775/alternateassignmentforglory.pdf

Black Americans from the foundation of our nation have a proven tradition of valor, commitment and patriotism to America. The question that needs to be answered is: Does the Black community still hold fast to the concept of loyalty and patriotism after decades of anti-American messaging through the liberal Rap music culture, the target messaging of the Black Community by the white liberal media outlets, BET and MSNBC, and after decades of a Labor Union controlled progressive public school system, whose founders were avowed atheists and Socialists? Could we now, 60 years after the Civil Rights Act, field the scores of intelligent, educated, patriotic, courageous legendary Black Fighters found with the 1940s Tuskegee Airmen. These young men from segregated America served with distinguished bravery, and personally envisioned a nation worthy of sacrifice for... God, Family and Country. Their valor and contribution resulted in several silver stars, 150 distinguished flying crosses, fourteen bronze stars, and 744 air medals.[8]

Today millions of Black Americans live in cities dominated by the ideology of Liberalism, including Detroit, Philadelphia, Cherry Hill, Ferguson, Baltimore, Washington DC, Newark, and others. These bastions of the ideology of Liberalism, reported on nightly news, are known for their high crime rates, low education rates and high child abandonment and abuse. More recently its anti-American sentiment has been viewed nationally as we watched young Black Americans protest and burn the American flag. Angry, uneducated and jobless these young Americans are unaware of the sacrifice of their ancestors and the opportunity presently

---

[8]   http://www.army.mil/article/12183/tuskegee-airman-looks-to-todays-soldiers/

available if they would but duplicate their drive and tenacity. Their union controlled progressive public school education has left them apathetic and clueless regarding the efforts of the Black Americans who served our country in both the Revolutionary War and the War of 1812.[9] American children are not being taught that the *first martyr* for the cause of American independence from Great Britain was an ex-slave, Crispus Attucks, killed in the Boston Massacre of 1770, or that during the Revolutionary War, more than 5,000 black soldiers and sailors fought on the American side.[10]

They are likewise unaware of America's first All-Black military unit, the 54th Regiment Massachusetts Volunteer Infantry, which served during the Civil War. These brave young Black Americans fought in Confederate territory knowing that if they were captured, per the Confederate President's dictate, they would be tortured and killed. A monument in Boston, across from the State House, honors this unit. Not only are young Black Americans not aware of their sacrifice and our country's acknowledgement, but the ideology of Liberalism has also taught them not to care.

Our young men, as they master the latest video game, have no connection to the historic 1869 All-Black Buffalo Soldiers, the five Medals of Honor earned during the Spanish- American War at the Battle of San Juan,[11] or of the 369th Infantry Regiment, which was the first Black American regiment to serve with the American Expeditionary

---

9 http://www.nps.gov/boaf/learn/historyculture/shaw.htm
10 http://history-world.org/black_americans.htm
11 https://en.wikipedia.org/wiki/Buffalo_Soldier

Forces during World War I. Nicknamed the Harlem Hellfighters, the Black Rattlers and the Men of Bronze by French, they were awarded the Croix de Guerre, France's highest military honor. The nickname "Hell Fighters" was given to them by their enemies, the Germans, due to their toughness. They never lost a man through capture, a trench or a foot of ground to the enemy. They helped change the American public's opinion on African American soldiers and helped pave the way for future African American soldiers. [12] My Grandpa Kirby, was a WWI volunteer at the age of 16, as was my dad's favorite relative, Uncle Anderson.

WWI Soldiers of the 369th (15th N.Y.) who won the Croix de Guerre for gallantry in action, 1919[13]

---

[12] wikipedia.org/wiki/369th_Infantry_Regiment_(United_States).

[13] https://en.wikipedia.org/wiki/Military_history_of_African_Americans#/media/File:369th_15th_New_York.jpg

Little do these angry and frustrated liberalized young Black men know that by stepping on the America flag, they are desecrating the sacred memories of generations of patriotic and America-loving Black men who are part of their bloodline and lineage. They demean the memory of the 332d Fighting Group (The Tuskegee Airman), the all-Black 555th Parachute Infantry Battalion, the all-black 43rd Infantry Regiment (Philippine Scouts) where my dad served, and the all-black 777th Field Artillery Battalion (Germany), where my Uncle Emiel served and was wounded.[14]

Tuskegee Airmen 332nd Fighter Pilots

There is a list of more than 70 All-black Battalions, Regiments, Brigades and Divisions, representing 125,000

---

14   http://5thplatoon.org/notable.html

men [15] who willingly served God, Family and Country during a war that saved freedom for the rest of the world. Can we find even 1% of them in the communities dominated for decades by the Royalty Black Class, and their symbiotic host, the Ideology of Liberalism?

Because of the ideology of Liberalism's innate disrespect for the American Way, it demands that all historical lessons that do not comport with its view are either negated or ignored. It neglects to teach the downfall of past great societies due to uncontrolled immigration. The Royalty Class Black Man's unbridled doctrinal loyalty makes it impossible for him to envision the intergenerational threat that uncontrolled borders pose to his country, community and eventually to his own way of life. He refuses to be convinced of the threats to his security and freedom by allowing massive entry of non-assimilating, non-law abiding and potential anti-America foreigners into his homeland. He refuses to weigh the competitive threat for jobs, education and other opportunities of non-Americans, to the Black community.

As the poor of his race suffer at the bottom of the employment rung, the Royalty Class Black Man exhibits his innate lack of empathy for those destined to suffer even more. Instead of leading and envisioning means of providing opportunity for his race, he once again acquiesces and accepts a subservient role that mandates being Visionary-Free. The ideology of Liberalism demands that the Black man suspends any pretext of pride in his own race and in his "American" heritage. As he once again prioritizes "class over race," the Royalty Black Class acquiesces.

---

[15] https://en.wikipedia.org/wiki/Military_history_of_African_Americans

THE VISIONARY

For the Royalty Class Black Man it does not matter that the abortion industry was established strategically to eliminate his race in 1910 Black Harlem. Nor does it matter that today it ranks as the number one killer of Black Americans.

As the Royalty Black Man reads the words of the unrepentant pro-KKK, pro-Nazi, pro-eugenic and racist Margaret Sanger, he intellectually and passionately justifies his loyalty to the abortionist cause. He has discovered that political and financial perks can be gained by siding with the white liberal political establishment, regardless of the impact on his community. As they honor and exalt a self-avowed racist woman who succeeded where the KKK failed, he dutifully acquiesces. It is the nature of the Royalty Class Black Man to find comfort with his acceptance by the prominent and powerful, as it was in 1930 with the abortionist Sanger's. Here is a sampling of her thoughts on the Black race:

"Human weeds," "reckless breeders," "spawning... human beings who never should have been" [16]

"Human weeds...deadweight of human waste," "[Blacks, soldiers, and Jews are a] menace to the race," "Eugenic sterilization is an urgent need. We must prevent multiplication of this bad stock." [17]

"The mass of significant Negroes still breeds carelessly and disastrously, with the result that the increase among Negroes ...is in that portion of the population least intelligent and fit." [18]

---

[16] http://www.dianedew.com/sanger.htm
[17] http://www.dianedew.com/sanger.htm
[18] The pivot of Civilization, Margaret Sanger

"Where there is no vision, the people perish" (Proverbs 29:18). These simple eight words capture the essence of today's Black community of men. In this area, the ideology of Liberalism has had it greatest success. It has succeeded in undermining the Black man's role as the Visionary of his family, community and country. It has been his lack of vision that has left his community rudderless in resolving the epidemically high dropout rate of its young men, from both high school and college. It has been his lack of vision that allowed the Free Enterprise infrastructure that produced a thriving Black middle class for more than 60 years to be turned into Petri dishes of socialism across our country. In every urban community it is predictable for its residents to wait for their elected officials to fulfill their promises to deliver more freebies. It has been the lack of vision that has allowed the Black man to remain compliant as liberal politicians disarmed and striped him of his responsibility to protect his family against ALL evil. It is due to the lack of vision that he continues to support the same professional politicians who have willingly sacrificed his children at the altar of an inept public school system. It is the lack of vision for Black Christian parishioners to remain in a church led by pastors who preach their support for anti-Christian policies and socialist anti-God politicians. Most importantly it is the lack of vision that the Black community has accepted, as the new normal, a 70% abandonment rate of its mothers and children by its self-centered, cowardly males. The effectiveness of the ideology of Liberalism resides in it ability to neuter men, which this last statistic alone has shown its success. The ideology of Liberalism has stolen from the Black Man his essence, *the empathy to Feel* and the *courage to Act*.

THE ENTREPRENEUR

The ideology of Liberalism demands that though the entrepreneurial Black man has used universal business principles to acquire success and experience the American Dream, he must downplay them. These principles work consistently regardless of the field of endeavor or who uses them. Among them are work ethics, people skills, honesty, appearance, education, respect for authority, respect for self, service, articulation, risk taking, tenacity, interracial networking, going the extra mile, endurance, accountability, timeliness, a firm handshake, a confident look into the eye, etc. The Royalty Class Black man shares these secrets only with his friends and family.

Outside of his circle of friends and family he delivers a different message: "Success in America is a matter of LUCK, with the wheel of fortune being turned by the White Race." LUCK… a word popularized by the elitist and the envious.

To the remainder of his race, he parrots the condescending message of the ideology of Liberalism, that success is no more than a matter of chance, not choice. It is here where the Black Royalty Class uses the false façade of humility to deliver his elitist message of betrayal. For it is within this message, that the deceitful web of the ideology of Liberalism/Socialism is spun. It entices entry of its victims with the attractive and trusting promise that in the benevolence of others, happiness will be ensured. In time the true purpose of this message is always revealed. It is the ideology of Liberalism/Socialism that, with sweet sophistry, entangles its victims into dependency. It is soul-degrading dependency that kills the independent, self-sufficient spirit. It leaves in its wake hopelessness, futility and the death of the human body, mind and soul. The diabolical subtlety of this strategy has played itself out within the Black community for over a century and continues unabated today. It began with the ultimate trust in a Royalty Class Black Socialist, who served as the face and voice for twenty-one wealthy white, anti-Capitalists, anti-Christian, Socialist Executive Board members of the NAACP. As will be discussed later, this model has been duplicated and continues to be implemented in some of today's more powerful Corporate Board rooms. It was understood by the NAACP White Executive Board during its 1910 beginning, that their policy and politics would not have been received within the Black community, if made transparent. Therefore, the strategy of stealth and deceit was implemented. The *Crisis* Magazine in 1910 was designed to be the delivery system for Liberal messaging, controlled by the NAACP's White Board of Directors and founders, though branded with a Black name. This gave the impression to millions that it was a Black controlled organization whose priority was to the Black community. Never, over its 100-year history, has the Black community suspected what can now be statistically substantiated. For Socialist, whether Black or White, the priority will always be their elitist "Class over Race." Though the name has changed, as has its high tech and alluring delivery system, the strategy of deceit has not. It is now the 100% White controlled BET (Black Entertainment TV) that delivers the message of Liberal/Socialist politics to the Black community. As it has done so for close to two decades, there has been no representation of the Black community sitting on its "controlling" Board of Directors. As it promotes itself as a wholly owned subsidiary of Black Entertainment Network, featuring Black news, Black history, Black headline, Black entertainment and flaunting 100% Black faces through out its website, the man behind the curtain is a 100% White owned/controlled Corporate entity, Viacom. Viacom assets include (CBS and UPN), cable television networks (MTV, VH1, Nickelodeon, MTV2, BET, Comedy Central, Nick at Nite, Noggin/The N, TV Land, CMT, and Spike TV), pay television (Showtime and The Movie Channel), motion pictures (Paramount Pictures), and television production (Spelling Entertainment, Paramount Television, and Big Ticket Entertainment), *The Oprah Winfrey Show*, *Dr. Phil, Wheel of Fortune*, and *Jeopardy!*[19] Its owner is the ultra Liberal/Socialist Democrat and founder, Sumner Redstone.

In 2007, the House Subcommittee on Commerce, Trade, and Consumer Protection held a hearing discussing the impact of the sexist, misogynistic and racist themes in the media, with an emphasis on the negative influence of Hip-Hop music and the gangster culture. Powerful corporate executives joined with Hip-Hop artists, to downplay their responsibility to the Black community. Representing the Liberals/Socialist empathy-free responsibility to their own (BET) Black customer base, Philippe P. Dauman, President and CEO of Viacom- the owner of MTV, BET and numerous other media outlets said that "ultimately the responsibility lies with parents and the consumer to avoid explicit content, such as music containing the "N," "B," and "H" words.[20]

---

19 https://en.wikipedia.org/wiki/Sumner_Redstone#Political_views

20 http://www.msmagazine.com/news/uswirestory.asp?ID=10548

Translation: *We, the caring White Liberal Elitist hidden behind the curtain of our 100% owned and controlled BET, feel totally justified to fire hose YOUR community (not OUR White targeted audience on CBS, Nickelodeon, etc.) with anti-social,* sexist, misogynistic, racist *and anti-authority FILTH ...Single Black mothers, since our ideology has already successfully eliminated the concept of Black men supporting their own children, (70% abandonment)...GOOD LUCK keeping your kids clean, educated, respectful, successful and independent thinking..*

As with the strategy of the 1910 NAACP, it is from behind the facade of Blackness that BET strategically attacks the voices of independent Black Americans, without mercy, empathy or tolerance. As the ideology of Liberalism effectively employed the Royalty Black Class, W.E.B DuBois, to demean the character and message of the successful Capitalist, Booker T. Washington, it continues to do so today as it pulls millions of unsuspecting Black Americans into its sophistry of intolerant "Group Think." Through its purchase of the "Blackness Brand," the Liberal white owned BET has covertly used its headline news releases and entertainment updates to castigate all Black Americans "who dare to think different". Labeled as disloyal Uncle Toms, this conclusion of betrayal is then embraced without ANY thought, question or debate by the BET trusting community. Due to the blind trust of its audience, the agenda of BET has never been questioned. There has been no thought as to who controls the messaging directed at the urban Black youth. Never questioned is the lack of Black ownership/management within this powerfully influential network. Viacom has, for two decades, had total unfettered access to the urban Black community. There has not been a single media organization with a greater opportunity to impact the lives of millions of Black Americans. This multibillion-dollar corporation had an opportunity to deliver new hope in a number of ways. It could have promoted quality education for its poor and neglected. It could have changed the expectations within single parent homes by promoting commitment to marriage by its male teens. It could have been an advocate for Black teen employment and delivered messaging of successful work ethic.

Instead, the wealthy white Liberal Viacom Board chose to develop a Black Brand that will haunt the Urban Black Man for generations. Viacom's vision of the Black Race can now be seen throughout our nation with the demeaning acceptance of Black thuggery. It has promoted gangster violence and the anti-social, anti-American, drug environment of Hip Hop. Its vision was seen on full display during the 2016 election cycle in the cities of Ferguson, Baltimore, Charleston and others. It was the fruition of the ideology of Liberalism as we viewed unemployed, uneducated, inarticulate, undisciplined, sloppily dressed, angry young Black men riot and loot. From behind the curtain, this same powerful white Liberal Board directs highly compensated Black employees to attack, demean, and attempt to destroy the livelihood of all independent-minded Black Americans. The targeting of these Black Christians, capitalists, patriots and Conservatives has been a strategy of stealth used to diminish the influence of freethinking Black Americans since its implementation in 1910.

The parent company, Viacom, acquired BET in 2000 for a reported $3 billion. It did not however see the value of offering BET's Black founder, Robert Johnson, an Advisory or Directorship position to support its new Black community initiative. He was employed by BET, a Division of Viacom, until 2006 when he subsequently resigned.[21] As with the NAACP during its first decades of existence, BET's direction, strategy, content and messaging for the Black community remains 100% Liberal White controlled.

This explains the vitriol, name-calling and angry demeaning of minorities who step over the line against the prescribed ideology of Liberalism. For the man behind the curtain can feel safe from his position of control. He directs his employees how and who to attack without any concern of correctly being called a racist. With the cloak of a Black name, hiding behind his façade of Black employees delivering his message, no one is even aware of his presence. Meanwhile, through this filter and support of the compliant Royalty Class Black Man the message of the Conservative Black American, i.e. independence, work ethic, morality and self-sufficiency, is translated as traitorous and Anti-Black. The suggestion that solutions can be reached through free enterprise, personable accountability, lessons through failure and trust in an omnipotent God is angrily denounced with filthy, gutter language. Suggestions to Liberalism's victims that they are capable of change and of adopting successful new habits, is considered a personal attack and sacrilegious. And as the community displays its hatred toward successful Black Americans attempting to offer a new pathway, Black and White Liberal elitists enjoy the advantages gained from a segment of Americans who simply cannot help but trust them.

---

[21] https://en.wikipedia.org/wiki/Robert_L._Johnson#Black_Entertainment_Television

THE POLITICIAN

The ideology of Liberalism demands that the Black man, though accomplished in every field of endeavor in which he has ever ventured, NOT use his leadership, thinking skills and talents in the arena of politics. In this arena alone it is demanded, "that he suspends his common sense, logic, core values and any concerns for his race as he elects Royalty Class Black Politicians whose unbridled loyalty is to his party's' white liberal political leadership." As this Royalty Black Politician is rewarded with political perks and decades of security at his elected position, he must simultaneously appear to be angry and anti-white. At a moment's notice be must be prepared to repeat his memorized white racism, black victimization and government reparations speech. He aptly parrots his party leadership's mantra of solutions for his race, often devoid of all logic and deemed nonsensical to an educated audience. The Politician Liberal Black Man is therefore relegated to run for office ONLY in Black urban, poor, uneducated and hopeless communities. Here his lack of logic is not questioned and his policies guaranteed to keep his trusting constituents voting as a monolithic, poor, uneducated and hopeless "group think" community.

22

"There is a certain class of "race-problem solvers" who don't want the patient to get well; because as long as the disease holds out, they have not only an easy means of making a living but also an easy medium through which to make themselves prominent before the public"[23]

Booker T. Washington

CHIVALRY

Manhood's divine nature and role is founded upon distinct characteristics and attributes. Among these are integrity, empathy, charity, commitment, loyalty, honesty, principled, faithfulness, vision and others. The very keystone though of his nature is Courage. Without this, he is naught. A

22 http://www.bing.com/images/search?q=booker+t+washington&view=detailv2&&id=3746EAB2F7E5B73B3C14AAA3B8F72A67D9AB4239&selectedIndex=17&ccid=e IjBRSBM&simid=608040101647155996&thid=OIP.M7888c145204c275590a753c4 f04bb4bdH0&ajaxhist=0

23 https://en.wikiquote.org/wiki/Booker_T._Washington

man of principle has the courage to stand, regardless of the price asked of him—even if he must do so alone. Before his test begins, he believes that because his cause is just, he must endure to the end—regardless of where that end might take him.

The most important deployment of courage for manhood is for the protection and care of womanhood. Throughout the history of mankind, the most attractive and admired trait of manhood is his innate courage to pay any price, including his own life, for the well-being, safety and honor of women. Chivalry, as an ideal, has been in the crosshairs of the ideology of Liberalism for decades. It has done its best to blur the line between genders, thus facilitating and encouraging the demeaning of both.

It is here where the ideology of Liberalism has prevailed in its greatest damage to the Black community. For where there are no men available to protect, defend and honor the sacred role of womanhood, there are no men. When Black males accept the role of silence and collusion, White liberal racists disrespect Black women in the vilest and most reprehensible ways.

The ideology of Liberalism's most hated and feared minority within the American populace is the successful, independent and articulate Black woman. It is with this minority segment of the Black community, in their attempts to intimidate and silence, where the despicable and ugly face of liberal white bigotry erupts. Predictably it is also here, in the shadows, where the cowardly and compliant Royal Class Black Man is found. Even though his community's youth desperately crave for positive male and female role models, the Royal Class Black Man is willing to sacrifice his race's best and finest upon the alter of his chosen political doctrine.

This minority's message of overcoming all odds, of embracing universal success ethics, of pride in race accomplishments and of the availability of opportunities throughout the American Free Enterprise system is a threat to the ideology of Liberalism. It is therefore a threat to the symbiotic relationship with the Royal Class Black Man, as he submissively colludes with liberal white racists.

As women of his race, who hold independent political views, are verbally abused and depicted in racist caricatures he remains silent. As the Liberal White man propagates the myth that success for the Black race is only possible through the benevolence of liberalism and its demeaning "black specific" policies, he remains silent. And as Black Americans speak independently of alternative solutions, the racist Liberal White man has no fear of condemnation or reprisal. As seen with the racist treatment of one of the Black Communities most respected woman, Condoleezza Rice, the Royalty Class Black man performs his duty well as he acquiesces to the ideology of Liberalism and remains silent.

Condoleezza Rice was born in the deep south, segregated Birmingham, Alabama, in 1954. She graduated from the University of Denver at the age of 16 and eventually became a Professor of political science at Stanford University. Many other honors came to her while at the university. During her tenure there she served on the National Security Council as the Soviet and Eastern Europe Affairs Advisor to President George H.W. Bush during the dissolution of the Soviet Union and German reunification. She was the distinguished Director of Stanford University Global Center for Business and the

Economy; Senior Fellow of the Institute for International Studies; Senior Fellow of the Hoover Institution and Founder of the Center for New Generation, an afterschool program created to raise high school graduation numbers. She was also a spokesperson advocating leadership roles for girls. She became Secretary of State for George W Bush, the First Black female to serve in such a capacity.[24] As such she came under attack from the liberal left.

White Liberal radio hosts Gregg "Opie" Hughes and Anthony Cumia laughed as a guest they called "Homeless Charlie" talked about wanting to rape Secretary Rice. Cumia gleefully said, "I just imagine the horror in Condoleezza Rice's face... as you held her."[25] White Liberal program director and morning host John Sylvester called Rice—then the nation's First female national security advisor—"Aunt Jemima." When asked by his critics to apologize, Sylvester said he was planning a giveaway on Friday's show of Aunt Jemima pancake mix and syrup. "I will apologize to Aunt Jemima."[26]

White Liberal comic writer, Garry Trudeau called Secretary Rice "Brown Sugar" in "Doonesbury" and Aaron McGruder suggested a boyfriend might stop her from being "hell-bent to destroy" the world in the now-defunct "The Boondocks." Ted Rall suggested she is a "house nigga" who needs "racial re-education."[27]

On the editorial pages, Jeff Danziger and Pat Oliphant drew her with accentuated black features and mimicked her,

---

24   https://en.wikipedia.org/wiki/Condoleezza_Rice
25   https://www.nationalcenter.org/P21NVAlmasiRice90507.html
26   http://www.freerepublic.com/focus/f-news/1285542/posts
27   https://www.nationalcenter.org/P21NVAlmasiRice90507.html

using poor diction as these blatant and inexcusable racist comments were advanced to Nationwide audiences.[28]

The Independent Women's Forum was one of the few National Women's organizations to take issue with this apparent collaborative attack on the portrayal of a successful, wicked and indefensible portrayals of black women. Black female role model by the racist Liberal Left. In a Nov 20004 article titled "IWF Denounces Racist Depictions of Dr. Condoleezza Rice in Popular Editorial Cartoons," they stated the following:

The Independent Women's Forum today denounced as blatantly racist several editorial cartoons featuring Dr. Condoleezza Rice, National Security Advisor and President Bush's nominee for Secretary of State. These cartoons clearly draw upon centuries of deep-rooted, wicked and indefensible portrayals of black women.

"The depiction of Dr. Condoleezza Rice by Jeff Danziger, Pat Oliphant and Garry Trudeau as an ebonics speaking, big-lipped, black mammy who just loves her 'massa' is a disturbing trend in editorial cartoons," said Michelle D. Bernard, senior vice president of the Independent Women's Forum. "These cartoons take the racism of the liberals who profess respect and adoration for black Americans to a new level. It is revolting."

Danziger, Oliphant and Trudeau, whose editorial cartoons are very popular in the United States, are also renowned all over the world. (We have linked to the cartoons in an effort to allow the public to view the negative portrayal

---

28 http://www.bing.com/images/search?q=jeff+danziger+and+pat+oliphant+and+con di+

of Dr. Rice, and by analogy, all black women as portrayed by these celebrated Liberal cartoonists: http://www.bing.com/images/search ?q=jeff+danziger+and+pat+oliphant+and+condi+)

"The most powerful woman in the United States is young, gifted and black. Given our nation's history of race-based slavery, the ensuing civil rights movement and our continual battle against race-sex based discrimination, every citizen in our nation should take pride in Dr. Rice's accomplishments," said Bernard. "She is a representation of America's past and future all at once. One must ask where is the outrage of the nation's civil rights leadership, feminist organizations, and the so-called liberals who only seem to embrace black America in election years?"

"Condoleezza Rice was the first woman ever appointed as National Security Advisor. After Secretary of State Colin Powell, Dr. Rice will be the second African American to hold both posts," said Bernard. "These cartoons are decidedly unfunny."[29]

These degrading images of Black womanhood reveal the true racist heart of the Ideology of Liberalism, as it also highlights the spineless backbone of the Royalty Class Black Man. This diatribe of Uncle Tom-ary drew the predictable response from the complicit Royal Black Class, the NAACP, the Congressional Black Congress, Al Sharpton, Jesse Jackson, Royalty Black Academia, Entertainers and media MSNBC Black talking heads.... Silence!! In the new PC age, in which saying Merry Christmas during the Christmas holidays might be taken as offensive, these comments were

---

[29] http://www.iwf.org/media/2434659/IWF-Denounces-Racist-Depictions-of-Dr-Condoleezza-Rice-in-Popular-Editorial-Cartoons

met with no outrage, no condemnation, no outcry of racism, no feminist outcry of misogyny and no dialog regarding the negative message given to Black youth, as another successful Black role model is denigrated.

More importantly, the Royal Black Class has delivered their subtle message to all: Racist White Liberals will be given carte blanche authority to besmirch your name, reputation and financial future if you dare act as an independent Black woman. Note the difference in the *Man-Up* potential of the Royal Black Class Man if we were to substitute the name of the FIRST Black Female Secretary of State, FIRST Black female Advisor and FIRST Black female selected to the National Security Council with that of the WIFE of the FIRST Black President, Michelle Obama.

It is guaranteed the Royal Black Class Man would respond like real men and demand that heads roll. Guaranteed would be the loud voices of protest, demonstration, threats of boycotts, lawsuits and demands for multiple layers of media firing. For with the Royal Black Class Man, it is not the racist verbal insult of successful members of his race that generates his most passionate ire nor is it the disrespect given by racist white men to prominent Black women, role models of his own community. Instead the Royal Class Black man saves his courage, his ideals of chivalry, to defend his most precious ideology. As is always the case with the Socialist/ Liberal elitists…. "Class over Race."

Ironically it is the same white media elitists who are committed followers of an ideology that demands "PC speak" limitation, protecting of every other minority's feeling. This includes non-Americans who are illegally in our country. The term illegal Aliens for those presently residing in our country illegally, has officially been pronounced by the ideology of Liberalism, PC police, as offensive. But for the smallest American minority however, the Black Conservative Women, the "PC Speak" limitations are abandoned to expose the true immoral, depraved and racist minds of liberalism. This interchange can be read often on the Facebook page[30] of another Black Conservative, actress, Fox contributor and author of *There Goes My Social Life: From Clueless to Conservative*, Stacey Dash. Stacey, would be a guaranteed a "darling status" by the Royal Black Class and their supportive White liberal media, if she would but only remain silent, acquiesce, empathy-free or clueless. Instead she shares conservative values of patriotism, self-empowerment, Pro-life and occasionally suggest that whining is not becoming of real men.

Recently Stacey made comments questioning the relevance of the NAACP Image Awards, BET and Black History Month. From the vantage point of concerned Black Americans recognizing a community beset with problems, it would seem reasonable to have an open and civil debate. Should there be an open discussion regarding the necessity of an All-Black NAACP Image Award? Should we support a 100% white controlled BET network and the messaging that comes with it? Why is there only one race in America who needs a Liberal defined History Month? Should we not question if these events, corporate organizations, or the month of February have any measurable impact on the Black community? Or is the true end game, self-promotion and political fund raising? The questions that arise are legitimate

---

[30] https://www.facebook.com/OfficiallyStaceyDash

ones... "Is it the desire of the Black community to assimilate as Americans or to work to separate ourselves from all other Americans?" Assimilation has, since our participation in the American Revolution, been our historic calling. Statistically the races that have best assimilated into the American culture have the highest percentage of success in our country. If this is no longer our calling than how, when, why and to what have our goals, as a race, changed? And, as important... by whom?

This question of relevance and direction evoked a response typical of the intolerant ideology of Liberalism. No more evident of this was an event for the gathering of the Royalty Class Black Entertainers during the 2016 NAACP Image Awards. Always interesting is the display of courage that comes from gang bullying, prevalent when the Royalty Black Class congregate to entertain each other, in front of a like-minded adoring crowd. Typical of the backslapping, self-praise giving and all-knowing culture of the Royalty Class, the idea of a thoughtful civil debate is not an option. Conversations with this Class quickly devolve into unreasonable/unhinged anger, personal attacks and the demeaning of any Black American who has an independent thought. The spirit of the ideology of Liberalism was on full display at the 2016 NAACP Image Awards. The host, Anthony Anderson stood tall and with total confidence that his condescending judgmental joke, questioning the Blackness of another successful Black American would receive grins, from ear to ear, from his wealthy Royalty Black Class audience.[31] As this **Black** host besmirched Conservative thinker Stacey

---

[31] http://www.nydailynews.com/entertainment/movies/anthony-anderson-mocks-stacey-dash-naacp-image-awards-article-1.2522502

Dash in front of his **All-Black** entertainers, handing out awards to **All-Black** nominees, highlighted by **All-Black** rapper groups and **All-Black** performers, televised to a predominantly **All-Black** TV audience, the relevance of her question becomes apparent. If our goal is to view ourselves ultimately as Americans can we complain about segregation if we are "demanding segregation"? Should we accept judging and separating people based on the color of their skin, ONLY if Blacks are doing the judging and separating? Last but not least, does this train of thought lead us to the goal of assimilation and acceptance or does it encourage race baiting, divisiveness and hatred? Regardless of how we answer this as a community, our choices bear consequences and leave no room to blame others.

There are three points that were instructional with Anderson's opening line of the Image Awards… "Everybody give a round of applause for Stacey Dash," followed by his condescending Uncle Tom joke. First is the predicable methodology of the ideology of Liberalism, as it seeks to intimidate anyone who dares question it. The subtle message, given to those present and to the national Black audience was that, if anyone dares to think independently and voice it publically, we're coming after you and regardless of any previous friendship, we will destroy you, your reputation and any job opportunities you seek. Know that any Black actor or actress present, with a tinge of independent thought, received the message loud and clear... *back in the closet*. Also on display was the Royal Black Class Man's false premise of courage, when REAL courage is required. It is EASY to pile on at a Black "Group Think" NAACP Image Awards. Where are the Royalty Class Black men on issues that are imperative for the welfare of the Black race, but unpopular with the Left? Where was Anderson, his tweets, jokes or comments when President Obama signed his first executive order to kick more than 2,000 Black urban kids each year out of a successful school choice program, sentencing them to failure? There will be more than 16,000 young black lives negatively impacted, in some cases destroyed, by the end of his two terms. Where were Anderson's jokes, comments and tweets when it was uncovered that Black Babies were being strategically aborted, and their body parts sold by Planned Parenthood for profit? Knowing that abortion is the #1 killer of Black Americans, a show of real courage would have been for the Black host to have raised his fist in the air pronouncing that Black Lives Do Matter.... "even those being sold for research." What Anderson understands is that uttering those last six words would have ended his career, costing him millions. The ideology of Liberalism is not at all tolerant and as the Royalty Class Black Entertainers understand well, "real courage" is a deterrent in their profession.

In 2013, the last Black TV station owner in America, out of 18 when President Obama was elected, testified before a majority House of Democrats. Noted during the hearing was the recently passed legislation and mandated regulation that was driving the Black minority owners out of business. Where were the NAACP, Anderson and the Royalty Black Class when a Black businessman was on his heels looking for support...desiring to bring positive messaging to the Black community? In 2006, there were only 18 African American-owned and operated full-power commercial TV stations—representing just 1.3 percent of all such stations.

By December 2012, those 18 had shrunk to just five. Roberts' Broadcasting, a black-owned media company, sold its three remaining full-power TV stations to ION Media Networks for nearly $8 million. Once considered a phenomenal success story in an industry known for its stunning lack of diversity, Roberts' Broadcasting was forced to declare bankruptcy in 2011.[32] Also with this lack of Black ownership was the lack of Black American presence in the Big Media Board rooms, influencing the message to the Black community.

Ownership presence in this arena has recently changed when Black Capitalist and conservative commentator Armstrong Williams purchased two TV stations. His purchase of KVMY, the MyNet affiliate in Las Vegas, and WLYH, the CW affiliate in Harrisburg, Pennsylvania, brought his total holdings to seven television stations. Out of 2,119 stations nationwide, a mere 12 have black owners, making Williams' seven the majority.[33] This example of work, risk, and vision through Black Ownership should be celebrated and emulated. Armstrong's rise in influence in this media arena should be the source of inspiration for a community whose only exposure to Black success are entertainers and professional athletes. Instead of highlighting and praising the tenacity, skills and vision of a Black American competing in the media industry, the Royalty Class Black Man remains silent. For once again it is the mantra of the ideology of liberalism that must be repeated and protected. Success in America is *luck,*

---

[32] http://newamericamedia.org/2013/12/number-of-black-owned-tv-stations-plummets-to-zero.php

[33] http://www.atlnightspots.com/armstrong-williams-largest-black-owner-tv-stations-america/

not *choice* and always, always Socialism's mantra "Class over Race".

The remarkable propensity to bully, disrespect and pile on for the sake of acceptance, defines the Royalty Class Black Man today. It is indeed a different generation from the proud Black men of the early to mid-1900s, spoken of earlier in this chapter. Those were men of principle, working to insure the progress of their entire race, not just the elitist Royalty segment. They did not require "Group Think" to find their voice of courage but were willing to stand alone, if necessary.

Last but not least, as a response to the NAACP Image Awards host Andersons' crowd-pleasing comments, was Stacey's instructional tweet. *"Well it's funny how woman who weighs 105 wet! Can get grown a-- men to act like little girls! Haha,..."*

Her response was absolutely "Spot On" and sends a message on behalf of all committed Black Conservatives throughout this country. **Translation:** *Your intimidation tactics don't work anymore, so Man-Up and find a way to build-up our race instead of tearing it down!!!*

As with Condi Rice, the depth of vitriol from the ideology of Liberalism has no concern of PC backlash or self-reflecting shame, because within this ideology there is no shame. And as the Royal Black Class is invited into the free forum of debates, their lack of critical thinking becomes apparent, as does their limited vocabulary. In frustration the Royal Class Black man reverts to his condescending and judgmental words such as: ignorant, Uncle Tom, turncoat, Oreo and a full list of others listed in Kevin Jackson's book *Race Pimping*.

It is consistently the ideology of Liberalism, not Conservatism, that thrives on disrespecting Black women. It is the liberal manifested Rap culture funneled through liberal white owned MTV and BET that depict misogyny as fun, funny, cool and in vogue. And here lies the Royalty Class Black Man's disconnect with manhood. For where there is a lack of respect and a heightened degree of cowardice in defending woman, there is in like kind a lack of Manhood presence. The answer for those who wonder where all of the good, courageous and thoughtful men have gone—the answer... "Liberalism's got um."

In kowtowing to the demands of the ideology of Liberalism, the Liberal Black man has lost the belief in the potential of his race and most important, the courage to fight for the sanctity of womanhood within. Nowhere in America has the lack of respect for its women and children been more prevalent and damaging than in the Black community. As the Royal Black Class Man acquiesced to the attraction of power, wealth and fame, he opted out as the Protector of his race. Instead, as facilitators, he aided in the ingratiation of the ideology of Liberalism's degraded view of manhood. He served as the trusted messenger of its subversive filth-laden, women degrading sub-culture through music and video that has ravished the minds and souls of today's Black youth. He opted to remain silent or, in the case of the Academic Royal Class Black Man, encouraged young black sons to accept, as normal, referencing our Black daughters in the most degrading terms. Their silence and lack of condemnation encouraged our Black daughters to accept such denigrating labels as "baby mommas." defined by the Webster dictionary as: "the mother of one or more of a man's children, especially one who is not his wife or current partner."[34]

No longer is there an expectation of respect for the Urban Black woman to be referenced as Mother or Wife, but instead "partners" to several, passing through, non-committal, sorry black males. After decades of leadership from the Royal Class Black Man, this has come to define Liberalism's degraded version of manhood… an increasing number of black boys who are totally clueless about commitment, respect, loyalty, and their responsibility to "Man-Up."

---

[34] https://en.wikipedia.org/wiki/Baby_mama

CHAPTER 4

ANTHONY, AND THE
IDEOLOGY OF LIBERALISM

*"I thought of what Daddy had said when I asked
him why he'd never gone on public assistance.
'Because they take away your manhood,' he said."*
- *Clarence Thomas*, His Grandfather's Son

(Anthony is a fictional representation of real children and real statistics, living in an environment of mandated liberal policies, imposed by the Royalty Class Black Man. These are members of the urban Black community, who by design, are failing.)

Black twenty-one-year-old Anthony now has time to think as he clutches his hands and rests his forehead against the bars of his jail cell. Most of his friends had already gone through this experience. He had been so confident that he was smart enough not to end up like them. Anthony knew enough about the system, his options and his crime that, with a high degree of confidence, he would become very familiar with these surroundings over the coming years.

As a father of at least two boys that he is aware of, Anthony was raised by a caring grandmother. He barely knew his mother who gave birth to him when she was 15 years old but had been murdered by an abusive boyfriend by the time he reached that same age. He never met his father. He had heard that he was serving a life term for actions he took in a robbery that went wrong. When he was younger he did meet his three half-brothers, all from different fathers and who were living in foster homes. Anthony is now taking time to reflect over his last 21 years. He thinks about the hope he once held of breaking free of this community and wonders how he had come to this point where his life's options and freedom had changed forever.

He remembers it like it was yesterday, his feelings as a six year old, when his grandmother told him how proud she was of his math skills and that he was a "natural born" leader. Outside of his home, those types of compliments didn't come often and he now looks back and cherishes those conversations with his grandma. He remembered that as he got older, her anticipation increased every year as she placed his name into the school voucher lotto with hopes that he might have a chance to escape the drug riddled, inner city school he attended. He was fortunate in one aspect; he was smart and his grandmother diligent. By the time he was in fourth grade he knew how to read, unlike 60% of his classmates who were functionally illiterate.[1] Anthony learned to use his reading time to escape his surroundings, in his imagination he felt unlimited in what he might one day be.

---

[1]   http://begintoread.com/research/literacystatistics.html

As they waited each year for the results of the lotto, they knew that he was competing against thousands of other black families vying for the few coveted school openings and that the odds were against him. It was indeed a euphoric moment when they received the news that he had been one of the lucky ones selected. Added to the excitement in their household that November was the result of our nation's choice of its first Black President, Barrack Hussein Obama. For his grandmother this was truly two dreams coming true at once, to have her grandson, against all odds, have the opportunity to attend one of Washington D.C.'s top private schools and to have lived to see the day that our country would elect its first black President. Anthony found in the following weeks that the school he was going to attend was the same school President Obama had chosen for his daughters, Malia and Sasha. The Sidwell Friends School had between 1,000 and 1,100 students, of which 39% were of color. The tuition for one year was $28,442.[2] He was a little excited that his presence at Sidwell would push the percentage of color closer to 40%. He also knew that this opportunity was the miracle that they were hoping for and would allow him to step away from the hopelessness of his neighborhood. He would never forget this blessing and promised his grandmother that he would work very hard to prove how much he appreciated what she had done. He made a decision that he would prepare for a good college and get a job that would allow him to buy a home for her, far away from the crime and violence that was an everyday occurrence in their neighborhood. Who knows, maybe one day he'd run for President of the United States.

---

[2]   Wikipedia.org/wiki/Sidwell Friends School

At least for now, he knew that the coming fall he would have an opportunity to say hello to President Obama's daughters.

Unfortunately, in less than six weeks of President Obama lifting his hand to take the oath of office to be President of the United States, Anthony's dreams of an education were shattered. In his State of the Union address the previous month, President Obama spoke about the importance of kids staying in school and even urged states to raise the dropout age to 18. So it was strange that he and his party would immediately pass a new $3.8 trillion budget providing no new money for a school voucher program in Washington, D.C., that is producing significantly higher graduation rates than the D.C. public school average.[3]

Neither he nor his grandmother could understand why, the Democrats and the newly elected President, who she and the community had always supported, had defunded the voucher program that had been specifically designed to help poor people like them. The local politicians had supported it because of its overwhelming graduations success rate versus those who stayed behind. Everyone he had known in the program was graduating. Most had already been accepted to schools of higher education. This was one of the reasons he was so confident that he would succeed if given the opportunity.

Why would the voucher scholarship program be one of the first programs eliminated? He and his grandmother held hope when the Republicans added an amendment to the congressional spending bill that it would save the program, but the Democratic controlled Senate voted 50 to 39 to reject it.

---

[3]   http://www.wsj.com/articles/SB10001424052970204883304577223290975405900

At the behest of the National Education Association and civil liberty groups including People for the American Way, Senate Majority Whip Richard Durbin (D-Ill.) inserted language into the $410 billion omnibus spending bill effectively terminating the program unless Congress reauthorized it.[4] The Democratic controlled House and Senate did not.

The decision was made by a President who had chosen to spend as much as $64,000 annually to put his children with the school that best met his family's needs. This was truly a confusing time for Anthony. Everything seemed upside down. How could it be that the Republicans were fighting for him and the other 2,000 plus underprivileged DC students and the Democrats were fighting against them? He was frustrated and angry but didn't know where to vent. One thing for sure, his grandma clearly felt betrayed.

Anthony was one of 216 black students who had their scholarship revoked for the 2009-2010 school year.[5] As the fall school year approached, it began to sink in that this New Year would be the same as the preceding school year. There would be metal detectors at each school entrance, the classrooms were being run by the most violent kids, many who had already been held back a couple of times, and teachers were never available before or after school to give him the extra help he sometimes needed. Not that he could blame them. His teachers and the principal were all women and many of his male classmates seemed to get increasingly disrespectful as they got older. The phase, "the inmates are running the asylum" seems to describe the atmosphere of

---

4   http://www.weeklystandard.com/not-free-to-choose/article/270807
5   Ibid

discipline and authority or the lack thereof. There was also a drug subculture that brought with it an anxiety that at any moment, there could be an eruption of violence. Whether the teachers didn't care or didn't know how to control the classroom in this setting, the end results were the same. There was no substantive teaching or learning going on. Anthony found himself daydreaming more and caring less about sitting in classes that he felt would be of no benefit to him.

Once the scholarship program was eliminated, Anthony remembered his grandmother's desperate attempts to get him into another private school. He knew that she loved him and believed in him, but he also felt that her valiant efforts had something to do with the guilt of losing her daughter, his mother, to the same system. She had watched helplessly as peer pressure, low expectations and bad decisions on her daughter's part had snowballed from becoming a mother at 15 years old to dropping out of school and eventually being killed by an abusive, alcoholic boyfriend.

They were told that one of their options was to find a friend or family member who lived in a nicer school district and who would be willing to take him in for the year. Nicer neighborhoods equated to a higher quality education. Unfortunately for Anthony, they didn't know anyone outside of his inner city community. Even if they did, he would be concerned about what could happen to his grandmother if they were caught. He had a read disturbing new account of Kelly Williams-Bolar, an Akron, Ohio, single Black mother of two daughters.

Kelly was sentenced to 10 days in jail convicted of two felony counts of falsifying records. She had used her father's address in the Copley-Fairlawn school district instead of her own Akron public housing address. According to Greatschools.org, Copley-Fairlawn schools rated 9 on a scale of 10, while Akron schools rated 4 out of 10. The school district felt it was such an offense that they paid thousands of dollars to a private investigator to follow and shoot video showing Kelly driving her children into the district. Even though her children no longer attend school in the Copley-Fairlawn District, school officials said she was cheating because her daughters received a quality education without paying taxes to fund it. "Those dollars need to stay home with our students," said the school district officials.[6]

Kelly was convicted and fined $30,000 for in essence stealing education for her daughters that she didn't pay for. The White Liberal anti-school choice Judge Patricia Cosgrove also sentenced her to 10 days in county jail, and a three-year probation requiring her to perform community service. Acknowledging the harshness of a sentence, Judge Patricia Cosgrove stated, "I felt that some punishment or deterrent was needed for other individuals who might think to defraud the various school districts."[7]

Anthony couldn't imagine how he would respond if this had happened to his grandmother. He once again was forced to reflect on the frustration they had experienced when he had been denied his educational opportunity through the DC lottery. For the rest of his life he would wonder... "What if?" As he read about this single mother, he could see that she shared a lot in common with his desperate grandmother. In

---

[6] http://abcnews.go.com/US/ohio-mom-jailed-sending-kids-school-district/story?id=12763654

[7] Ibid

his gut he also recognized a spirit that was present in both cases. It was a spirit of meanness, anger, a lack of charity and empathy for those who were powerless, like his grandmother, Kelly and him. Even without a high school degree, he knew enough about the criminal system that a felony conviction was a lifetime sentence of limited opportunities. Why would any Judge, especially a white liberal woman be so callous and heartless toward another woman, no less a single Black mother? He had always heard that liberals were the compassionate ones… this just wasn't adding up. One thing for sure, he would never take even a remote chance of seeing his grandmother go through this type of ordeal.

Anthony had also heard stories of coaches who made arrangements with athletes from other school districts to live with families in their districts so they would be eligible to play there. Unfortunately, Anthony's athletic skills did not qualify him for that option. When he was much younger, he had dreamed of playing in the NBA, but when he had run the numbers in his head he realized that the odds were heavily stacked against him. After his grandmother had exhausted all avenues, they accepted the reality that he would have to make the most of staying where he was.

Anthony was fortunate to have a good friend, Johnny, who was considered by his grandmother to be a self-starter. He and Johnny agreed that they would find jobs that would allow them to use their free time productively and help them become a little more self-sufficient. He was growing into a young man and didn't like going to his grand-mom for every dollar. Every school break, summer and holidays, they would look for a job. Consistently, he and Johnny were frustrated in their quest to find one, even though he remembered seeing non-black teenagers working at the local fast food chains. He wondered how these other teenagers were getting these jobs when it finally occurred to him that the franchise businesses were run and owned by non-black entrepreneurs and that the teenagers were of the same race/culture as the owners.

Anthony often wondered why he saw such a small number of black-owned businesses in his neighborhood— mostly barber shops or nightclub owners. He was aware of the many federal public works projects in his community over the years but they were always run by predominately white labor unions that hired a very small number of black laborers. None of these black laborers ever had the authority to hire others.

During that year of searching, he remembered walking into the office of a small contractor and offering to work for practically nothing. He was willing to do anything to prove himself and get some experience to help him decide on the right career path for him. It was obvious to him that the owner was impressed by his offer and wanted to hire him. Unfortunately, there were minimum wage laws that prevented him from doing so. Because of the wage mandate, the business owner could only afford to offer jobs to "experienced" workers. He explained that if he were to follow his heart and give Anthony the job and experience he wanted, it could potentially result in fines that could cost him his business.

Anthony felt "experienced worker" was a code for "Union worker," which took him to another level of frustration. It was impossible for him to get into a Union without connections—a White Union Worker Connections. The neighborhood that he lived in didn't give him an opportunity to be around potential White connections. If he couldn't get a recommendation that allowed him onto a long Union waiting list, how was he to get experience? So for him as a young Black teen, who was trying to do the right thing… No Union, No Experience… No Experience, No Job… No Job, No Experience… No Experience, No Job. So without the benefit of Black entrepreneurs in his neighborhood, job opportunities were almost non-existent. Anthony wondered, "so where does this end or maybe a better question, where does it begin?"

At 13 years of age, Anthony did have an opportunity to take part in a Planned Parenthood organization, Teen P.A.C.T. (Positive Actions and Choices for Teens), where he trained with other kids his age about having safe sex. He has been sexually active ever since. He worked for a few hours each week during the summer and at sixteen he was given the position of a sex educator for his peers.

During his last two years of high school Anthony began to think that it was actually good that things worked out the way that they did. As he had gotten older, he realized that the road his grandmother was directing him on was not something he was feeling any more. She talked about education, dressing to make a good first impression, good association, and clean language. But these were the actions, in his environment, of an "Uncle Tom," blacks who were "trying to act white." The last thing he wanted to do was to "act white" in front of his friends. She had encouraged him to go to church, which he had done until he was grown enough to tell her no. Besides being very observant, he realized that this was a place for ministers, children and older women. He was no longer a child and didn't plan on being either of the other two. After all he was almost a man at age sixteen. He had been sexually active for years and had learned to use his math and leaderships skills to make some cold hard cash on the streets. At his age he definitely didn't need the advice of an old lady.

Anthony's options over time had become obvious to him. Though the schoolwork was easy and most of the time, non-challenging, he didn't want to appear like he was turning on his people and trying to be white. So against the protest and deep disappointment of his grandmother, he simply stopped trying. Based on his exposure to black men who had "made it," his options where clear: win the lottery, play in the NBA or NFL, become a Civil Rights preacher/ community organizer, or get good at a profession that would take less time and not require a school degree to get plenty of cash, girls, bling/bling and respect in the neighborhood, "a gangster."

He was sure he would hit the lottery at some point in his life but he needed to do something in the meanwhile. NBA? He wasn't tall enough and had calculated the numbers— so few selected each year, for such hard work and chance. Not realistic. Civil Rights Preacher—Anthony felt that he had the leadership skills necessary to become a Civil Rights community organizer. After all, their power and prestige seemed to be based on their ability to pull the community together for a rally or a march. It did appear to him that there were limited national positions available and he wasn't sure who was in charge for determining who the black leader would be or how many were needed at any particular time. He also remembered his feelings while listening to their sermons and understood why there were not more black men sitting in the pews. He would often feel more hopeless, impotent and angry after their sermons, particularly hearing the more popular civil rights preachers. Though they spoke of Christ, His atonement and forgiveness, Anthony never felt Christ-like after leaving church. He was always reminded that somebody was at fault for his predicament and since his ancestors had been forced onto slave ships to leave their beloved Africa to come to this place, the culprit had to be the white man. That made total sense but Anthony found it a little confusing trying to understand the relationship these Civil Rights preachers had with white people. They were praised and exalted on MSNBC, CNN, ABC and CBS as black experts, smiling with white people, and getting paid "big bucks" from white people but seemed to always be angry at white people when with a crowd of black people.

What Anthony was not confused about were his feelings of desperation that he couldn't seem to shake. Once he had internalized the message though, he didn't need to sit in a church to hear more, he got it!

It would be the gangster life for him. As he began, over the months and years, to transform in dress, personality, and association he realized just how popular this persona was and how well he was accepted. He thought about how popular "gangster rap" had become within the community. There was his favorite black channel, BET, supporting the lifestyle, there were black professional athletes making millions of dollars a year yet dressing the part of gangsters. There were even rich and middle class black kids dressing and acting the part. Gangster was empowering.

He calculated the consequences. It meant that he would never again have to dress up to impress the white man. Gold teeth were in, tattoos on arms/hands, neck and face were cool, slouchy pants exposing his underwear and butt, fashioned after prison-wear, were stylish. A slang and debased ghetto language, Ebonics, was in and supported by union educators. He had read that black Oakland California educators had attempted to have this "gutter language" accepted as a bilingual replacement for their urban kids who hadn't been taught how to read or write.[8] This all proved to him that he didn't have to "act white" to make it through.

He noticed that black adults in the neighborhood, the NAACP, the Congressional Black Caucus, and nationally renowned black civil rights preachers never put down the gangster lifestyle. For Anthony and his boys, it didn't matter whether this silence was due to fear, respect or apathy. Either was OK. He knew that he was getting something that he had never received from any black male in his life: Acceptance. For Anthony, of all the options he had considered, this choice was the most desirable. He finally had family, his gang members, who unlike all the other black males in his life, he could trust to be there for him.

As Anthony rested his head against the jail cell bars considering the consequence of his crime, he could not help but think about how far he'd come from that day when his grandmother had said those simple and kind words to an impressionable six-year-old, that he would never, ever forget, that she was proud of his math skills and that he was a "natural born leader.

The tragedy of Anthony's life is that though he felt anger and hopelessness for years, he was unaware of the invisible hands of policy makers, who had over the many decades put

---

[8]   https://en.wikipedia.org/wiki/Oakland_Ebonics_resolution

impediments in his way. These roadblocks would boost his doubts in the ideals of the American Dream and confirm to him, that it was not real for people like him. Anthony and all the other unsuspecting members of his community had been living the consequences of black and white, liberal politicians, both Republican and Democratic whose insatiable appetite for wealth, power and prestige had given them self-justification to legislate and then defend decades of anti-poor/anti-black policies.

The results of these anti-poor/black legislative roadblocks could now be seen throughout the community in the tragic life of its young males, where over 25% of them would face incarceration in their lifetime.[9] With a 93% Black on Black crime rate, this environment is the more threatening than any other for a black male.[10] The real tragedy for the community, marked by illiteracy, crime, abortions, abandonment, and hopelessness is the legacy that would be guaranteed to be passed to yet another generation, fatherless boys left behind to produce another generation of irresponsible, fatherless boys.

The Anti-Poor/Black policies faced by Anthony and his grandmother have frustrated the efforts of Black Americans for generations as they have sought the American Dream. Some of these policies, known for their racist roots, go back as far as 1931 and are today supported and defended by the Royalty Class Black politicians, the NAACP and their co-partners the wealthy, White Liberal/Socialist Establishment.

---

9 https://en.wikipedia.org/wiki/Statistics_of_incarcerated_African-American_males
10 http://www.nationalreview.com/corner/394489/new-data-its-still-about-black-black-crime-heather-mac-donald

- **Davis-Bacon**—Race-based legislation enacted in 1931, for the distinct purpose of preventing black entrepreneurs and black laborers from competing against segregated white labor unions for Federal funded projects.[11] Passed during the Great Depression, negated opportunities for the Black population to take part in the Federally funded work programs that supported other communities. *Anti-Black Policy supported by Labor Unions and 100% of Democrats.*

- **Minimum Wage Laws**—Viewed as a starting wage, this Legislation increases the cost of unskilled labor and justifies the use of more expensive but "skilled worker." These laws have been statically proven to hurt most the unskilled and young labor force that need work experience to gain a foothold. They benefit most children of the middle class, who need temporary and part time income. It also increases the baseline salary of union workers when negotiating wage increases. In a statement by Arthur Laffer, "The minimum wage makes absolutely no sense whatever. I mean, honestly, it's just the teenage—black teenage—unemployment act, and this is the very group that we need to have jobs (and) not be put out of work because of the minimum wage.[12] The Results of present wage laws on the Black community-overall Black teen unemployment is 38%[13] *Anti-Black*

---

[11] https://en.wikipedia.org/wiki/Davis%E2%80%93Bacon_Act

[12] http://www.theroot.com/articles/politics/2014/01/regan_economist_minimum_wage_is_the_black_teenage_unemployment_act.html

[13] http://www.breitbart.com/big-government/2014/02/07/black-teen-unemployment-jumps-to-38/

Policy supported by Labor Unions, 100% of Democrats and Liberal Republicans.

- **Anti-School Choice Legislation**—Legislation that denies poor black children from leaving underperforming public schools. Free choice represents competition (better product) from Charter, Private, Religions non-profits and pose great threats to Teacher Unions, not desirous of competition (better product). Safe from competition and measurable accountable results, the union organization can continue to focus on increasing union member salaries, and union dues revenue while decreasing the choice of options for their customers, the poor minority student... Socialism at its best. The poor and powerless suffer, while the rich and powerful gain more wealth and power. Results: A 2006 study by The Manhattan Institute surveyed 100 of the largest school districts in the United States and found that only 48 percent of African-American males earned a diploma—that's 11 percent less than African-American females. More troubling is the research that shows on average, one out of four Black males who drop out of high school will end up incarcerated.[14] *Anti-Black Policy supported by Labor Unions and 100% of Democrats.*

- **Federal Housing and Welfare**—Legislation/Policies that began in the mid-1960s gave young and old mothers a disincentive to be self-sufficient. Policies introduced a (welfare) mindset into Black Urban families to rely on Federal Government largess instead of the traditional

---

[14] http://www.bet.com/news/national/2011/08/16/why-are-more-black-males-dropping-out-of-high-school.html

family unit that had served the Black community well throughout the early 1900s. The role for the Black male was re-defined from that of providing, securing and protecting his wife and children to that of a baby producing "freeloader." Introduced in mid-60s with free housing and weekly cash payments to mothers who remained pregnant and single, these welfare programs rapidly led to implosion of the Black family unit. In a 1965 report known as the Moynihan Report ("The Negro Family: The Case for National Action")[15] Democratic Senator Patrick Moynihan warned of the dire consequence in coming years from the exponential growth of Black families headed by government dependent single mothers. The ideology of Liberalism and the Royalty Class Black Man attacked this report viciously as racist and insulting to Black single mothers. Results have seen decades of inter-generational welfare families with children as young as 14 and 15-year old having babies. Generations of mothers who strategically remain pregnant, single and increasingly dependent on government checks with "fathers" increasingly providing irresponsible, low-life role modeling. With the community's acceptance of their babies as a commodity for securing a free lifestyle via Federal checks, came an acceptance of the devaluations of life and increase in abortions. Planned Parenthood has accommodated this devaluation of Black lives by establishing a majority of their laboratories in Urban Black neighborhoods. A new research released by Protecting Black Life (an outreach

---

15   https://en.wikipedia.org/wiki/The_Negro_Family:_The_Case_For_National_Action

of Life Issues Institute) reveals that 79% of Planned Parenthood's surgical abortion facilities are located within walking distance of African American and/or Hispanic/Latino communities.[16] The message to young Black Boys… Simply hit and Run. Result: 73% of black babies are born out of wedlock to single mothers, who are convinced that marriage and the support of a committed husband should not be expected.[17] *Anti-Black Policy supported by Labor Unions and 100% of Democrats.*

---

[16] http://www.lifenews.com/2012/10/16/79-of-planned-parenthood-abortion-clinics-target-blacks-hispanics/

[17] http://www.nbcnews.com/id/39993685/ns/health-womens_health/t/blacks-struggle-percent-unwed-mothers-rate/#.VtUOgCpVhBc

CHAPTER 5

THE BLACK FAMILY: 40 YEARS OF LIES

Reprinted by permission of City Journal and Kay Hymowitz in its entirety.

Read through the mega-zillion words on class, income mobility, and poverty in the recent *New York Times* series "Class Matters" and you still won't grasp two of the most basic truths on the subject: 1. Entrenched, multigenerational poverty is largely black; and 2. It is intricately intertwined with the collapse of the nuclear family in the inner city.

By now, these facts shouldn't be hard to grasp. Almost 70 percent of black children are born to single mothers. Those mothers are far more likely than married mothers to be poor, even after a post-welfare-reform decline in child poverty. They are also more likely to pass that poverty on to their children. Sophisticates often try to dodge the implications of this bleak reality by shrugging that single motherhood is an inescapable fact of modern life, affecting everyone from the Murphy Browns to the ghetto "baby mamas." Not so; it is a largely low-income—and disproportionately black— phenomenon. The vast majority of higher-income women wait to have their children until they are married. The truth is that we are now a two-family nation, separate and unequal—one thriving and intact, and the other struggling, broken, and far too often African-American.

So why does the *Times*, like so many who rail against inequality, fall silent on the relation between poverty and single-parent families? To answer that question—and to continue the confrontation with facts that Americans still prefer not to mention in polite company—you have to go back exactly 40 years. That was when a resounding cry of outrage echoed throughout Washington and the civil rights movement in reaction to Daniel Patrick Moynihan's Department of Labor report warning that the ghetto family was in disarray. Entitled "The Negro Family: The Case for National Action," the prophetic report prompted civil rights leaders, academics, politicians, and pundits to make a momentous—and, as time has shown, tragically wrong—decision about how to frame the national discussion about poverty.

To go back to the political and social moment before the battle broke out over the Moynihan report is to return to a time before the country's discussion of black poverty had hardened into fixed orthodoxies—before phrases like "blaming the victim," "self-esteem," "out-of-wedlock childbearing" (the term at the time was "illegitimacy"), and even "teen pregnancy" had become current. While solving the black poverty problem seemed an immense political challenge, as a conceptual matter it didn't seem like rocket science. Most analysts assumed that once the nation removed discriminatory legal barriers and expanded employment opportunities, blacks would advance, just as poor immigrants had.

Conditions for testing that proposition looked good. Between the 1954 *Brown* decision and the Civil Rights Act of 1964, legal racism had been dismantled. And the economy was humming along; in the first five years of the sixties, the economy generated 7 million jobs. Yet those most familiar with what was called "the Negro problem" were getting nervous. About half of all blacks had moved into the middle class by the mid-sixties, but now progress seemed to be stalling. The rise in black income relative to that of whites, steady throughout the fifties, was sputtering to a halt. More blacks were out of work in 1964 than in 1954. Most alarming, after rioting in Harlem and Paterson, New Jersey, in 1964, the problems of the northern ghettos suddenly seemed more intractable than those of the George Wallace South.

Moynihan, then assistant secretary of labor and one of a new class of government social scientists, was among the worriers, as he puzzled over his charts. One in particular caught his eye. Instead of rates of black male unemployment and welfare enrollment running parallel as they always had, in 1962 they started to diverge in a way that would come to be called "Moynihan's scissors." In the past, policymakers had assumed that if the male heads of household had jobs, women and children would be provided for. This no longer seemed true. Even while more black men—though still "catastrophically" low numbers—were getting jobs, more black women were joining the welfare rolls. Moynihan and his aides decided that a serious analysis was in order.

Convinced that "the Negro revolution... a movement for equality as well as for liberty," was now at risk, Moynihan wanted to make several arguments in his report. The first was empirical and would quickly become indisputable: single-parent families were on the rise in the ghetto. But other points were more speculative and sparked a partisan dispute that has lasted to this day. Moynihan argued that the rise in single-mother families was not due to a lack of jobs but rather to a destructive vein in ghetto culture that could be traced back to slavery and Jim Crow discrimination. Though black sociologist E. Franklin Frazier had already introduced the idea in the 1930s, Moynihan's argument defied conventional social-science wisdom. As he wrote later, "The work began in the most orthodox setting, the U.S. Department of Labor, to establish at some level of statistical conciseness what 'everyone knew': that economic conditions determine social conditions. Whereupon, it turned out that what everyone knew was evidently not so."

But Moynihan went much further than merely overthrowing familiar explanations about the cause of poverty. He also described, through pages of disquieting charts and graphs, the emergence of a "tangle of pathology," including delinquency, joblessness, school failure, crime, and fatherlessness that characterized ghetto—or what would come to be called underclass—behavior. Moynihan may have borrowed the term "pathology" from Kenneth Clark's The Dark Ghetto, also published that year. But as both a descendant and a scholar of what he called "the wild Irish slums"—he had written a chapter on the poor Irish in the classic Beyond the Melting Pot—the assistant secretary of labor was no stranger to ghetto self-destruction. He knew the dangers it posed to "the basic socializing unit" of the family. And he suspected that the risks were magnified in the case of blacks, since their "matriarchal" family had the effect of abandoning men, leaving them adrift and "alienated."

More than most social scientists, Moynihan, steeped in history and anthropology, understood what families do. They "shape their children's character and ability," he wrote. "By and large, adult conduct in society is learned as a child." What children learned in the "disorganized home[s]" of the ghetto, as he described through his forest of graphs, was that adults do not finish school, get jobs, or, in the case of men, take care of their children or obey the law. Marriage, on the other hand, provides a "stable home" for children to learn common virtues. Implicit in Moynihan's analysis was that marriage orients men and women toward the future, asking them not just to commit to each other but to plan, to earn, to save, and to devote themselves to advancing their children's prospects. Single mothers in the ghetto, on the other hand, tended to drift into pregnancy, often more than once and by more than one man, and to float through the chaos around them. Such mothers are unlikely to "shape their children's character and ability" in ways that lead to upward mobility. Separate and unequal families, in other words, meant that blacks would have their liberty, but that they would be strangers to equality. Hence Moynihan's conclusion: "a national effort towards the problems of Negro Americans must be directed towards the question of family structure."

Astonishingly, even for that surprising time, the Johnson administration agreed. Prompted by Moynihan's still-unpublished study, Johnson delivered a speech at the Howard University commencement that called for "the next and more profound stage of the battle for civil rights." The president began his speech with the era's conventional civil rights language, condemning inequality and calling for more funding of medical care, training, and education for

Negroes. But he also broke into new territory, analyzing the family problem with what strikes the contemporary ear as shocking candor. He announced: "Negro poverty is not white poverty." He described "the breakdown of the Negro family structure," which he said was "the consequence of ancient brutality, past injustice and present prejudice." "When the family collapses, it is the children that are usually damaged," Johnson continued. "When it happens on a massive scale, the community itself is crippled."

Johnson was to call this his "greatest civil rights speech," but he was just about the only one to see it that way. By that summer, the Moynihan report that was its inspiration was under attack from all sides. Civil servants in the "permanent government" at Health, Education, and Welfare (HEW) and at the Children's Bureau muttered about the report's "subtle racism." Academics picked apart its statistics. Black leaders like Congress of Racial Equality (CORE) director Floyd McKissick scolded that, rather than the family, "[i]t's the damn system that needs changing."

In part, the hostility was an accident of timing. Just days after the report were leaked to Newsweek in early August, L.A.'s Watts ghetto exploded. The televised images of the South Central Los Angeles rioters burning down their own neighborhood collided in the public mind with the contents of the report. Some concluded that the "tangle of pathology" was the administration's explanation for urban riots, a view quite at odds with civil rights leaders' determination to portray the violence as an outpouring of black despair over white injustice. Moreover, given the fresh wounds of segregation, the persistent brutality against blacks, and the ugly tenaciousness of racism, the fear of white backsliding and the sense of injured pride that one can hear in so many of Moynihan's critics are entirely understandable.

Less forgivable was the refusal to grapple seriously—either at the time or in the months, years, even decades to come—with the basic cultural insight contained in the report: that ghetto families were at risk of raising generations of children unable to seize the opportunity that the civil rights movement had opened up for them. Instead, critics changed the subject, accusing Moynihan—wrongfully, as any honest reading of "The Negro Family" proves—of ignoring joblessness and discrimination. Family instability is a "peripheral issue," warned Whitney Young, executive director of the National Urban League. "The problem is discrimination." The protest generating the most buzz came from William Ryan, a CORE activist, in "Savage Discovery: The Moynihan Report," published in The Nation and later reprinted in the NAACP's official publication. Ryan, though a psychologist, did not hear Moynihan's point that as the family goes, so go the children. He heard code for the archaic charge of black licentiousness. He described the report as a "highly sophomoric treatment of illegitimacy" and insisted that whites' broader access to abortion, contraception, and adoption hid the fact that they were no less "promiscuous" than blacks. Most memorably, he accused Moynihan of "blaming the victim," a phrase that would become the title of his 1971 book and the fear-inducing censor of future plain speaking about the ghetto's decay.

That Ryan's phrase turned out to have more cultural staying power than anything in the Moynihan report is a tragic emblem of the course of the subsequent discussion about the ghetto family. For white liberals and the black establishment, poverty became a zero-sum game: either you believed, as they did, that there was a defect in the system, or you believed that there was a defect in the individual. It was as if critiquing the family meant that you supported inferior schools, even that you were a racist. Though "The Negro Family" had been a masterpiece of complex analysis that implied that individuals were intricately entwined in a variety of systems—familial, cultural, and economic—it gave birth to a hardened, either/or politics from which the country has barely recovered.

By autumn, when a White House conference on civil rights took place, the Moynihan report, initially planned as its centerpiece, had been disappeared. Johnson himself, having just introduced large numbers of ground troops into Vietnam, went mum on the subject, steering clear of the word "family" in the next State of the Union message. This was a moment when the nation had the resources, the leadership (the president had been overwhelmingly elected, and he had the largest majorities in the House and Senate since the New Deal), and the will "to make a total… commitment to the cause of Negro equality," Moynihan lamented in a 1967 postmortem of his report in *Commentary*. Instead, he declared, the nation had disastrously decided to punt on Johnson's "next and more profound stage in the battle for civil rights." "The issue of the Negro family was dead."

Well, not exactly. Over the next 15 years, the black family question actually became a growth industry inside academe, the foundations, and the government. But it wasn't the same family that had worried Moynihan and that in the real world continued to self-destruct at unprecedented rates. Scholars invented a fantasy family—strong and healthy, a poor man's Brady Bunch—whose function was not to reflect truth but to soothe injured black self-esteem and to bolster the emerging feminist critique of male privilege, bourgeois individualism, and the nuclear family. The literature of this period was so evasive, so implausible, so far removed from what was really unfolding in the ghetto, that if you didn't know better, you might conclude that people actually *wanted* to keep the black family separate and unequal.

Consider one of the first books out of the gate, *Black Families in White America*, by Andrew Billingsley, published in 1968 and still referred to as "seminal." "Unlike Moynihan and others, we do not view the Negro as a causal nexus in a 'tangle of pathologies' which feeds on itself," he declared. "[The Negro family] is, in our view, an absorbing, adaptive, and amazingly resilient mechanism for the socialization of its children and the civilization of its society." Pay no attention to the 25 percent of poor ghetto families, Billingsley urged. Think instead about the 75 percent of black middle-class families—though Moynihan had made a special point of exempting them from his report.

Other black pride–inspired scholars looked at female-headed families and declared them authentically African and therefore a *good* thing. In a related vein, Carol Stack published *All Our Kin*, a 1974 HEW-funded study of families in a Midwestern ghetto with many multigenerational female households. In an implicit criticism of American individualism, Stack depicted "The Flats," as she dubbed her setting, as a vibrant and cooperative urban village, where mutual aid—including from sons, brothers, and uncles, who provided financial support and strong role models for children—created "a tenacious, active, lifelong network."

In fact, some scholars continued, maybe the nuclear family was really just a toxic white hang-up, anyway. No one asked what nuclear families did, or how they prepared children for a modern economy. The important point was simply that they were not black. "One must question the validity of the white middle-class lifestyle from its very foundation because it has already proven itself to be decadent and unworthy of emulation," wrote Joyce Ladner (who later became the first female president of Howard University) in her 1972 book *Tomorrow's Tomorrow*. Robert Hill of the Urban League, who published *The Strengths of Black Families* that same year, claimed to have uncovered science that proved Ladner's point: "Research studies have revealed that many one-parent families are more intact or cohesive than many two-parent families: data on child abuse, battered wives and runaway children indicate higher rates among two-parent families in suburban areas than one-parent families in inner city communities." That science, needless to say, was as reliable as a deadbeat dad.

Feminists, similarly fixated on overturning the "oppressive ideal of the nuclear family," also welcomed this dubious scholarship. Convinced that marriage was the main arena of male privilege, feminists projected onto the struggling single mother an image of the "strong black woman" who had always had to work and who was "superior in terms of [her] ability to function healthily in the world," as Toni Morrison put it. The lucky black single mother could also enjoy more equal relationships with men than her miserably married white sisters.

If black pride made it hard to grapple with the increasingly separate and unequal family, feminism made it impossible. Fretting about single-parent families was now not only racist but also sexist, an effort to deny women their independence, their sexuality, or both. As for the poverty of single mothers, that was simply more proof of patriarchal oppression. In 1978, University of Wisconsin researcher Diana Pearce introduced the useful term "feminization of poverty." But for her and her many allies, the problem was not the crumbling of the nuclear family; it was the lack of government support for single women and the failure of business to pay women their due.

With the benefit of embarrassed hindsight, academics today sometimes try to wave away these notions as the justifiably angry, but ultimately harmless, speculations of political and academic activists. "The depth and influence of the radicalism of the late 1960s and early 1970s are often exaggerated," historian Stephanie Coontz writes in her new book, *Marriage, a History: From Obedience to Intimacy, or How Love Conquered Marriage*. This is pure revisionism. The radical delegitimizing of the family was so pervasive that even people at the center of power joined in. It made no difference that so many of these cheerleaders for single mothers had themselves spent their lives in traditional families and probably would rather have cut off an arm than seen their own unmarried daughters pushing strollers.

Take, for instance, Supreme Court Justice William Brennan, who wrote a concurring assent in the 1977 *Moore* v. *City of East Cleveland* decision. The case concerned a woman and her grandson evicted from a housing project following a city ordinance that defined "family" as parents—or parent—and their own children. Brennan did not simply agree that the court should rule in favor of the grandmother—a perfectly reasonable position. He also assured the court that "the extended family has many strengths not shared by the nuclear family." Relying on Robert Hill's "science," he declared that delinquency, addiction, crime, "neurotic disabilities," and mental illness were more prevalent in societies where "autonomous nuclear families prevail," a conclusion that would have bewildered the writers of the Constitution that Brennan was supposedly interpreting.

In its bumbling way and with far-reaching political consequences, the executive branch also offered warm greetings to the single-parent family. Alert to growing apprehension about the state of the American family during his 1976 presidential campaign, Jimmy Carter had promised a conference on the subject. Clearly less concerned with conditions in the ghetto than with satisfying feminist advocates, the administration named a black single (divorced) mother to lead the event, occasioning an outcry from conservatives. By 1980, when it finally convened after numerous postponements, the White House Conference on the Family had morphed into the White House Conference on Families, to signal that all family forms were equal.

Instead of the political victory for moderate Democrats that Carter had expected, the conference galvanized religious conservatives. Later, conservative heavyweight Paul Weyrich observed that the Carter conference marked the moment when religious activists moved in force into Republican politics. Doubtless they were also more energized by their own issues of feminism and gay rights than by what was happening in the ghetto. But their new rallying cry of "family values" nonetheless became a political dividing line, with unhappy fallout for liberals for years to come.

Meanwhile, the partisans of single motherhood got a perfect chance to test their theories, since the urban ghettos were fast turning into nuclear-family-free zones. Indeed, by 1980, 15 years after "The Negro Family," the out-of-wedlock birthrate among blacks had more than doubled, to 56 percent. In the ghetto, that number was considerably higher, as high as 66 percent in New York City. Many experts comforted themselves by pointing out that white mothers were also beginning to forgo marriage, but the truth was that only 9 percent of white births occurred out of wedlock.

And how was the black single-parent family doing? It would be fair to say that it had not been exhibiting the strengths of kinship networks. According to numbers crunched by Moynihan and economist Paul Offner, of the black children born between 1967 and 1969, 72 percent received Aid to Families with Dependent Children before the age of 18. School dropout rates, delinquency, and crime, among the other dysfunctions that Moynihan had warned about, were rising in the cities. In short, the 15 years since the report was written had witnessed both the birth of millions of fatherless babies and the entrenchment of an underclass.

Liberal advocates had two main ways of dodging the subject of family collapse while still addressing its increasingly alarming fallout. The first, largely the creation of Marian Wright Edelman, who in 1973 founded the Children's Defense Fund, was to talk about children not as the offspring of individual mothers and fathers responsible for rearing them, but as an oppressed class living in generic, nebulous, and never-to-be-analyzed "families." Framing the problem of ghetto children in this way, CDF was able to mount a powerful case for a host of services, from prenatal care to day care to housing subsidies, in the name of children's developmental needs, which did not seem to include either a stable domestic life or, for that matter, fathers. Advocates like Edelman might not have viewed the collapsing ghetto family as a welcome occurrence, but they treated it as a kind of natural event, like drought, beyond human control and judgment. As recently as a year ago, marking the 40th anniversary of the Civil Rights Act, CDF announced on its website: "In 2004 it is morally and economically indefensible that a black preschool child is three times as likely to depend solely on a mother's earnings." This may strike many as a pretty good argument for addressing the prevalence of black single-mother families, but in CDF-speak it is a case for federal natural-disaster relief.

The Children's Defense Fund was only the best-known child-advocacy group to impose a gag rule on the role of fatherless families in the plight of its putative constituents. The Carnegie Corporation followed suit. In 1977, it published a highly influential report by Kenneth Keniston called *All Our Children: The American Family Under Pressure*. It makes an obligatory nod toward the family's role in raising children, before calling for a cut in unemployment, a federal job guarantee, national health insurance, affirmative action, and a host of other children's programs. In a review in *Commentary*, Nathan Glazer noted ruefully that *All Our Children* was part of a "recent spate of books and articles on the subject of the family [that] have had little if anything to say about the black family in particular and the matter seems to have been permanently shelved." For that silence, children's advocates deserve much of the credit—or blame.

The second way not to talk about what was happening to the ghetto family was to talk instead about teen pregnancy.

In 1976 the Alan Guttmacher Institute, Planned Parenthood's research arm, published "Eleven Million Teenagers: What Can Be Done About the Epidemic of Adolescent Pregnancy in the United States?" It was a report that launched a thousand programs. In response to its alarms, HEW chief Joseph Califano helped push through the 1978 Adolescent Health Services and Pregnancy Prevention and Care Act, which funded groups providing services to pregnant adolescents and teen moms. Nonprofits, including the Center for Population Options (now called Advocates for Youth), climbed on the bandwagon. The Ford and Robert Wood Johnson Foundations showered dollars on organizations that ran school-based health clinics, the Charles Stewart Mott Foundation set up the Too Early Childbearing Network, the Annie E. Casey Foundation sponsored "A Community Strategy for Reaching Sexually Active Adolescents," and the Carnegie, Ford, and William T. Grant Foundations all started demonstration programs.

There was just one small problem: *there was no epidemic of teen pregnancy*. There was an *out-of-wedlock* teen-pregnancy epidemic. Teenagers had gotten pregnant at even higher rates in the past. The numbers had reached their zenith in the 1950s, and the "Eleven Million Teenagers" cited in the Guttmacher report actually represented a decline in the rate of pregnant teens. Back in the day, however, when they found out they were pregnant, girls had either gotten married or given their babies up for adoption. Not this generation. They were used to seeing children growing up without fathers, and they felt no shame about arriving at the maternity ward with no rings on their fingers, even at 15.

In the middle-class mind, however, no sane girl would want to have a baby at 15—not that experts mouthing rhetoric about the oppressive patriarchal family would admit that there was anything wrong with that. That middle-class outlook, combined with post-Moynihan mendacity about the growing disconnect between ghetto childbearing and marriage, led the policy elites to frame what was really the broad cultural problem of separate and unequal families as a simple lack-of-reproductive-services problem. Ergo, girls "at risk" must need sex education and contraceptive services.

But the truth was that underclass girls often *wanted* to have babies; they didn't see it as a problem that they were young and unmarried. They did not follow the middle-class life script that read: protracted adolescence, college, first job, marriage—and only then children. They did not share the belief that children needed mature, educated mothers who would make their youngsters' development the center of their lives. Access to birth control couldn't change any of that.

At any rate, failing to define the problem accurately, advocates were in no position to find the solution. Teen pregnancy not only failed to go down, despite all the public attention, the tens of millions of dollars, and the birth control pills that were thrown its way. *It went up*—peaking in 1990 at 117 pregnancies per 1,000 teenage girls, up from 105 per 1,000 in 1978, when the Guttmacher report was published. About 80 percent of those young girls who became mothers were single, and the vast majority would be poor.

Throughout the 1980s, the inner city—and the black family—continued to unravel. Child poverty stayed close to 20 percent, hitting a high of 22.7 percent in 1993. Welfare dependency continued to rise, soaring from 2 million families in 1970 to 5 million by 1995. By 1990, 65 percent of all black children were being born to unmarried women.

In ghetto communities like Central Harlem, the number was closer to 80 percent. By this point, no one doubted that most of these children were destined to grow up poor and to pass down the legacy of single parenting to their own children.

The only good news was that the bad news was so unrelentingly bad that the usual bromides and evasions could no longer hold. Something had to shake up what amounted to an ideological paralysis, and that something came from conservatives. Three thinkers in particular—Charles Murray, Lawrence Mead, and Thomas Sowell—though they did not always write directly about the black family, effectively changed the conversation about it. First, they did not flinch from blunt language in describing the wreckage of the inner city, unafraid of the accusations of racism and victim blaming that came their way. Second, they pointed at the welfare policies of the 1960s, not racism or a lack of jobs or the legacy of slavery, as the cause of inner-city dysfunction, and in so doing they made the welfare mother the public symbol of the ghetto's ills. (Murray in particular argued that welfare money provided a disincentive for marriage, and, while his theory may have overstated the role of economics, it's worth noting that he was probably the first to grasp that the country was turning into a nation of separate and unequal families.) And third, they believed that the poor would have to change their behavior instead of waiting for Washington to end poverty, as liberals seemed to be saying.

By the early 1980s the media also had woken up to the ruins of the ghetto family and brought about the return of the repressed Moynihan report. Declaring Moynihan "prophetic," Ken Auletta, in his 1982 *The Underclass*, proclaimed that "one cannot talk about poverty in America, or about the underclass, without talking about the weakening family structure of the poor." Both the *Baltimore Sun* and the *New York Times* ran series on the black family in 1983, followed by a 1985 *Newsweek* article called "Moynihan: I Told You So" and a 1986 CBS documentary, *The Vanishing Black Family*, produced by Bill Moyers, a onetime aide to Lyndon Johnson, who had supported the Moynihan report. The most symbolic moment came when Moynihan himself gave Harvard's prestigious Godkin lectures in 1985 in commemoration of the 20th anniversary of "The Negro Family."

For the most part, liberals were having none of it. They piled on Murray's 1984 *Losing Ground*, ignored Mead and Sowell, and excoriated the word "underclass," which they painted as a recycled and pseudoscientific version of the "tangle of pathology." But there were two important exceptions to the long list of deniers. The first was William Julius Wilson. In his 1987 *The Truly Disadvantaged*, Wilson chastised liberals for being "confused and defensive" and failing to engage "the social pathologies of the ghetto." "The average poor black child today appears to be in the midst of a poverty spell which will last for almost two decades," he warned. Liberals have "to propose thoughtful explanations for the rise in inner city dislocations." Ironically, though, Wilson's own "mismatch theory" for family breakdown— which hypothesized that the movement of low-skill jobs out of the cities had sharply reduced the number of marriageable black men—had the effect of extending liberal defensiveness about the damaged ghetto family. After all, poor single mothers were only adapting to economic conditions. How could they do otherwise?

The research of another social scientist, Sara McLanahan, was not so easily rationalized, however. A divorced mother herself, McLanahan found Auletta's depiction of her single-parent counterparts in the inner city disturbing, especially because, like other sociologists of the time, she had been taught that the Moynihan report was the work of a racist—or, at least, a seriously deluded man. But when she surveyed the science available on the subject, she realized that the research was so sparse that no one knew for sure how the children of single mothers were faring. Over the next decade, McLanahan analyzed whatever numbers she could find, and discovered—lo and behold—that children in single-parent homes were not doing as well as children from two-parent homes on a wide variety of measures, from income to school performance to teen pregnancy.

Throughout the late eighties and early nineties, McLanahan presented her emerging findings, over protests from feminists and the Children's Defense Fund. Finally, in 1994 she published, with Gary Sandefur, *Growing Up with a Single Parent*. McLanahan's research shocked social scientists into re-examining the problem they had presumed was not a problem. It was a turning point. One by one, the top family researchers gradually came around, concluding that McLanahan—and perhaps even Moynihan—was right.

In fact, by the early 1990s, when the ghetto was at its nadir, public opinion had clearly turned. No one was more attuned to this shift than triangulator Bill Clinton, who made the family a centerpiece of his domestic policy.

In his 1994 State of the Union Address, he announced: "We cannot renew our country when, within a decade, more than half of our children will be born into families where there is no marriage." And in 1996, despite howls of indignation, including from members of his own administration (and mystifyingly, from Moynihan himself), he signed a welfare-reform bill that he had twice vetoed—and that included among its goals increasing the number of children living with their two married parents.

So, have we reached the end of the Moynihan report saga? That would be vastly overstating matters. Remember: *70 percent of black children are still born to unmarried mothers*. After all that ghetto dwellers have been through, why are so many people still unwilling to call this the calamity it is? Both NOW and the National Association of Social Workers continue to see marriage as a potential source of female oppression. The Children's Defense Fund still won't touch the subject. Hip-hop culture glamorizes ghetto life: " 'cause nowadays it's like a badge of honor/to be a baby mama" go the words to the current hit "Baby Mama," which young ghetto mothers view as their anthem. Seriously complicating the issue is the push for gay marriage, which dismissed the formula "children growing up with their own married parents" as a form of discrimination. And then there is the American penchant for to-each-his-own libertarianism. In opinion polls, a substantial majority of young people say that having a child outside of marriage is okay—though, judging from their behavior, they seem to mean that it's okay, not for them, but for other people. Middle- and upper-middle-class Americans act as if they know that marriage provides a structure that protects children's development. If only they were willing to admit it to their fellow citizens.

All told, the nation is at a cultural inflection point that portends change. Though they always cautioned that "marriage is not a panacea," social scientists almost uniformly accept the research that confirms the benefits for children growing up with their own married parents. Welfare reform and tougher child-support regulations have reinforced the message of personal responsibility for one's children. The Bush administration unabashedly uses the word "marriage" in its welfare policies. There are even raw numbers to support the case for optimism: teen pregnancy, which finally started to decline in the mid-nineties in response to a crisper, teen-pregnancy-is-a-bad-idea cultural message, is now at its lowest rate ever.

And finally, in the ghetto itself there is a growing feeling that mother-only families don't work. That's why people are lining up to see an aging comedian as he voices some not-very-funny opinions about their own parenting. That's why so many young men are vowing to be the fathers they never had. That's why there has been an uptick, albeit small, in the number of black children living with their married parents.

If change really is in the air, it's taken 40 years to get here—40 years of inner-city misery for the country to reach a point at which it fully signed on to the lesson of Moynihan's report. Yes, better late than never; but you could forgive lost generations of ghetto men, women, and children if they found it cold comfort.[1]

---

[1]   http://www.city-journal.org/html/15_3_black_family.html

CHAPTER 6

THE EARLY BLACK EDUCATOR:
UNSUNG HEROES

As I have reflected upon my formative years and the life lessons that would guide my path into adulthood, I remember with clarity teachers whose love for their profession left an indelible mark. Among others was Mrs. Wright, my fourth grade teacher, Mrs. Weaver, my fifth grade teacher, and my music teacher, Mrs. Sherman.

I have known instinctively through the years that the foundation for my success, respect for my elders and many of other life skill habits, were reinforced in their classrooms. It was their commitment to us and relationship with our parents that gave us the incentive to be both accountable and disciplined. A "bad attitude" comment on my report card would bring grave consequences at home, with no questions asked as to whether the teacher was right or not. They were the adults and that was enough to end any protest. I grew up feeling empowered due to the high expectations of my elders.

Adam Fairclough's lecture, called "Black Teachers and the Struggle for Racial Equality," confirmed my recollections as I read it.[1] He gives long overdue credit to those educators

---

[1] http://www.h-net.org/reviews/showrev.php?id=6156

who, because of their dedication and love for teaching, were the true unsung heroes of that era. Being the son of two educators, I experienced firsthand the commitment of that generation to give knowledge and teach critical thinking to all who were seeking, in an effort to uplift their race.

Unfortunately, it was this era of committed teachers, and the millions of black children over the last two generations, who were harmed by the pursuit of "integration at all cost" by the NAACP and the Royalty Class Black Man. Justice Clarence Thomas addressed the fine line that separates the desire for equal opportunity and the Royalty Black Class belief that proximity to the white race would elevate the black race.

"I think segregation is bad, I think it's wrong, it's immoral. I'd fight against it with every breath in my body, but you don't need to sit next to a white person to learn how to read and write. The NAACP needs to say that."
- Clarence Thomas, Supreme Court Justice[2]

Fairclough stated, "During the grim years of Jim Crow, black teachers had to work within the confines of segregation and were unable to furnish overt political leadership. Yet in resisting the basic ideas of white supremacy—racism and inequality—they helped to undermine the Jim Crow regime. By insisting upon the sanctity of knowledge and the innate humanity of black children, they performed political work

---

[2]   http://www.definition-of.net/I+think+segregation+is+bad,+I+think+it's+wrong,+it-quote

of the most far-reaching kind."[3] Fairclough considered the role of black teachers during the Jim Crow era and noted appropriately that education "has been one of the most important political battlefields in the South, and black teachers were at the center of that battlefield. Southern whites sought to control them, fearful that educated blacks would lead movements for equality."[4]

He argued that black teachers during the Jim Crow era labored under extraordinary burdens. Faced with a dearth of material resources, they had a constant need to placate whites in order to secure both private and public funds for their schools. At the same time, black educators were expected to fulfill an array of roles beyond that of schoolteacher, "public health workers, Sunday school teachers, home visitors, agricultural experts, fundraisers, adult literacy teachers, racial diplomats, moral examples, all-around pillars of the community, and general uplifters of the race"[5]

Notwithstanding those varied demands, Fairclough argues that black teachers played a crucial role in helping southern blacks resist the crush of white supremacist bile through education and nurture. Citing Charles Johnson, he concluded that "the white South failed to construct a true 'caste system' because black people never internalized racist values" in significant measure because of the work of black teachers.[6]

"Black college presidents resorted to evasions and compromises, some of them humiliating. But the benefits of

---

3   http://www.h-net.org/reviews/showrev.php?id=6156(p. 67).

4   Ibid (pp. 1-2).

5   www.h-net.org/reviews/showrev.php?id=6156(p. 14)

6   Ibid (p. 19)

what they wrought outweighed the costs. Most obviously, they increased the educational opportunities available to southern black youth. The number of black college students steadily increased, from 12,000 in 1928 to 37,000 in 1941 and 74,000 in 1950."[7]

The NAACP criticized the fact that this enrollment growth took place in the context of segregated institutions, but Fairclough responded that these colleges made available to black youth that which was simply unavailable in racially mixed settings. Moreover, Fairclough argued, "black colleges provided intellectual space for staff and students to develop a critique of white supremacy."[8] In short, black colleges provided the nurture, training, and encouragement for the next generation of black youth to challenge the racial status quo.

Fairclough does concede that black college presidents frequently were forces of resistance during the civil rights era, as many chose to expel, rather than support, those student protesters who challenged Jim Crow. He, however, defended these actions as pragmatic: "was their desire to save black colleges so worthy of condemnation?" Those institutions were part of the sinew, brains, and soul of the black community.[9]

NAACP representatives claimed that black teachers became "a major foe of school desegregation" after Brown. Fairclough notes that many black teachers did oppose racial segregation, voting for example, to abolish separate black teacher organizations during the 1960s.[10] He argued that

---

[7]   Ibid (pp. 35-36).

[8]   Ibid (p. 36)

[9]   www.h-net.org/reviews/showrev.php?id=6156(p. 40)

[10]   www.h-net.org/reviews/showrev.php?id=6156(p. 40)

black teachers nevertheless played an important role in the civil rights movement by providing a strong education for black children and by insisting on greater resources for black schools. They also understood the impact of integration on their careers as their concerns later proved true. Integration hit those within the Black American community hardest, with the dismissal of its teachers and principals. Fairclough said "it would result in shutting down black schools, phasing out black colleges, and abolishing thousands of jobs."[11]

If Booker T. Washington's message of self-sufficiency and self-value had not been so effectively denigrated by the NAACP and W.E.B DuBois, the quest for the use of another race's property would have been weighed against the impact on the future education and of its own children. The desire to have black children sitting next to whites, at all cost, would result in them spending hours on buses, traveling out of their own environment of supportive parents and teachers to an environment where this support group would be absent.

Consistent in this transition of school desegregation, conceived by the white founders of the NAACP, was the acceptance of a perceived value of each community. It was a devalued appraisal for black property and human resources, and the equivalent elevated appraisal for white property and resources that was accepted as a baseline. The black community and generations of their children would ultimately pay the price to accommodate the vision of the NAACP and the Royalty Class Black Man.

---

[11] http://www.h-net.org/reviews/showrev.php?id=6156(p. 63)

CHAPTER 7

SOCIALISM VS. CAPITALISM: WHICH IS THE MORAL SYSTEM?

"The first battlefield is the rewriting of history."
- Karl Marx, Socialist and author of the
Communist Manifesto[2]

"The goal of Socialism is Communism"
- Vladmir Lenin

---

[1] http://www.bing.com/images/search?q=karl+marx&view=detailv2&&id=ADC983A
     21D9975EBD76BEE64255F691AD743F214&selectedIndex=7&ccid=TkzaYQfB&s
     imid=608038632767750636&thid=OIP.M4e4cda6107c1e841a432cbfeadb325fbo2&
     ajaxhist=0

[2] https://en.wikipedia.org/wiki/The_Communist_Manifesto

Socialist founder Karl Marx viewed Christianity as a trap that tricks people into willingly falling into it and an element that promotes capitalism. The Christian bible encourages subservience through teachings such as "the first shall be last and the last shall be first," and "turn the other cheek." A core concept of the bible is that there is an afterlife in which the immortal souls of people will be rewarded or punished according to how they acted during their life. Teachings such as these discourage revolution, in part because of morally dubious acts that revolutions involve like killing and "stealing" of property, and partly because the importance of what one has during their life is significantly less if there are much greater rewards in an afterlife. The ultimate consequence of these teachings is that the lower classes are repressed by their own hand and refuse to rise up and free themselves."[3]

C. Bradley Thompson
Reprinted with permission in its entirety.

Throughout history there have been two basic forms of social organization: collectivism and individualism. In the twentieth-century collectivism has taken many forms: socialism, fascism, Nazism, welfare-statism and communism are its more notable variations. The only social system commensurate with individualism is laissez-faire capitalism.

The extraordinary level of material prosperity achieved by the capitalist system over the course of the last two-hundred years is a matter of historical record. But very few

---

[3]   http://evolutionrevolutionatrhodes.blogspot.com/2010/04/marx-and-nietzsche-chris-tianity-as.html

people are willing to defend capitalism as morally uplifting. It is fashionable among college professors, journalists, and politicians these days to sneer at the free-enterprise system. They tell us that capitalism is base, callous, exploitative, dehumanizing, alienating, and ultimately enslaving.

The intellectuals' mantra runs something like this: In theory socialism is the morally superior social system despite its dismal record of failure in the real world. Capitalism, by contrast, is a morally bankrupt system despite the extraordinary prosperity it has created. In other words, capitalism at best, can only be defended on pragmatic grounds. We tolerate it because it works.

Under socialism a ruling class of intellectuals, bureaucrats and social planners decide what people want or what is good for society and then use the coercive power of the State to regulate, tax, and redistribute the wealth of those who work for a living. In other words, socialism is a form of legalized theft. The morality of socialism can be summed-up in two words: envy and self-sacrifice. Envy is the desire to not only possess another's wealth but also the desire to see another's wealth lowered to the level of one's own. Socialism's teaching on self-sacrifice was nicely summarized by two of its greatest defenders, Hermann Goering and Benito Mussolini. The highest principle of Nazism (National Socialism), said Goering, is:

"Common good comes before private good." Fascism, said Mussolini, "is a life in which the individual, through the sacrifice of his own private interests... realizes that completely spiritual existence in which his value as a man lies."

Socialism is the social system, which institutionalizes envy and self-sacrifice: It is the social system, which uses compulsion and the organized violence of the State to expropriate wealth from the producer class for its redistribution to the parasitical class.

Despite the intellectuals' psychotic hatred of capitalism, it is the only *moral* and *just* social system. Capitalism is the only moral system because it requires human beings to deal with one another as traders–that is, as free moral agents trading and selling goods and services on the basis of mutual consent. Capitalism is the only just system because the sole criterion that determines the value of thing exchanged is the free, voluntary, universal judgment of the consumer. Coercion and fraud are anathema to the free-market system. It is both moral and just because the degree to which man rises or falls in society is determined by the degree to which he uses his mind. Capitalism is the only social system that rewards merit, ability and achievement, regardless of one's birth or station in life.

Yes, there are winners and losers in capitalism. The winners are those who are honest, industrious, thoughtful, prudent, frugal, responsible, disciplined, and efficient. The losers are those who are shiftless, lazy, imprudent, extravagant, negligent, impractical, and inefficient.

Capitalism is the only social system that rewards virtue and punishes vice. This applies to both the business executive and the carpenter, the lawyer and the factory worker. But how does the entrepreneurial mind work? Have you ever wondered about the mental processes of the men and women who invented penicillin, the internal combustion engine, the airplane, the radio, the electric light, canned food, air conditioning, washing machines, dishwashers, computers, etc.?

What are the characteristics of the entrepreneur? The entrepreneur is that man or woman with unlimited drive, initiative, insight, energy, daring creativity, optimism and ingenuity. The entrepreneur is the man who sees in every field a potential garden, in every seed an apple. Wealth starts with ideas in people's heads. The entrepreneur is therefore above all else a man of the mind. The entrepreneur is the man who is constantly thinking of new ways to improve the material or spiritual lives of the greatest number of people.

And what are the social and political conditions, which encourage or inhibit the entrepreneurial mind? The free-enterprise system is not possible without the sanctity of private property, the freedom of contract, free trade and the rule of law. But the one thing that the entrepreneur value over all others is freedom–the freedom to experiment, invent and produce. The one thing that the entrepreneur dreads is government intervention. Government taxation and regulation are the means by which social planners punish and restrict the man or woman of ideas.

Welfare, regulations, taxes, tariffs, minimum-wage laws are all immoral because they use the coercive power of the state to organize human choice and action; they're immoral because they inhibit or deny the freedom to choose how we live our lives; they're immoral because they deny our right to live as autonomous moral agents; and they're immoral because they deny our essential humanity. If you think this is hyperbole, stop paying your taxes for a year or two and see what happens.

The requirements for success in a free society demand that ordinary citizens order their lives in accordance with certain virtues–namely, rationality, independence, industriousness, prudence, frugality, etc. In a free, capitalist society individuals must choose for themselves how they will order their lives and the values they will pursue. Under socialism, most of life's decisions are made for you.

Both socialism and capitalism have incentive programs. Under socialism there are built-in incentives to shirk responsibility. There is no reason to work harder than anyone else because the rewards are shared and therefore minimal to the hard-working individual; indeed, the incentive is to work less than others because the immediate loss is shared and therefore minimal to the slacker. Under capitalism, the incentive is to work harder because each producer will receive the total value of his production–the rewards are not shared. Simply put: socialism rewards sloth and penalizes hard work while capitalism rewards hard work and penalizes sloth.

According to socialist doctrine, there is a limited amount of wealth in the world that must be divided equally between all citizens. One person's gain under such a system is another's loss.

According to the capitalist teaching, wealth has an unlimited growth potential and the fruits of one's labor should be retained in whole by the producer. But unlike socialism, one person's gain is everybody's gain in the capitalist system. Wealth is distributed unequally but the ship of wealth rises for everyone.

Sadly, America is no longer a capitalist nation. We live under what is more properly called a mixed economy–that is, an economic system that permits private property, but only at the discretion of government planners. A little bit of capitalism and a little bit of socialism.

When government redistributes wealth through taxation, when it attempts to control and regulate business production and trade, who are the winners and losers? Under this kind of economy, the winners and losers are reversed: the winners are those who scream the loudest for a handout and the losers are those quiet citizens who work hard and pay their taxes.

As a consequence of our sixty-year experiment with a mixed economy and the welfare state, America has created two new classes of citizens. The first is a debased class of dependents whose means of survival is contingent upon the forced expropriation of wealth from working citizens by a professional class of government social planners. The forgotten man and woman in all of this is the quiet, hardworking, law-abiding, taxpaying citizen who minds his or her own business but is forced to work for the government and their serfs.

The return of capitalism will not happen until there is a moral revolution in this country. We must rediscover and then teach our young the virtues associated with being free and independent citizens. Then and only then, will there be social justice in America.

C. Bradley Thompson is Assistant Professor of Political Science at Ashland University and Coordinator of Publications and Special Programs at the John M. Ashbrook Center for Public Affairs.

"American Exceptionalism defines the boundless opportunities to serve, to resolve and offer solutions in an economic system that rewards such activities, without limits. The economic pillar of free enterprise is predicated on freedoms that unleash man's creativity and that reward his ingenuity and tenacity.

In the early 1900s the black community stood at a crossroad. Given two options, one would lead toward American Exceptionalism. The other, delivered through strategy and stealth, pulled it away from capitalism's moorings, leading to decades of dependency and big government socialism. To right the ship, it will be necessary to better understand the empowerment of Capitalism, the compassion of the American culture and the morality intrinsically imbedded within both. "

- Burgess Owens

CHAPTER 8

BOOKER T. WASHINGTON &
W.E.B. DuBois:
A BLACK HISTORY MONTH MOMENT

First published on February 26, 2002
A Different Drummer/Toogood Reports

Reprinted by permission of Nicholas Stix in its entirety.

Every year, during Black History Month, we celebrate the triumphs of Martin Luther King Jr., and retell the Gospel According to the Civil Rights Movement. And yet another, politically incorrect black history, once much better known, goes untold. To the degree that that history is silenced or revised out of existence, black American history, and hence American history, is both diminished, and falsified.

One such politically incorrect hero was Booker Taliaferro Washington (1856-1915). Washington, born into slavery in Virginia to an illiterate but immensely practical and supportive mother, rose to become the unofficial leader of Negro (the term used until well into the 1970s) America.

Upon being emancipated, little Booker Washington (then unaware of his middle name) lacked access to a school, didn't know anyone who knew how to read, and for obvious reasons, did not ask any white folks to teach him to read. So, he taught himself! Washington used the same kind of classic, "blue-back," Webster's spelling book that Frederick Douglass (1817-1895) had used. Eventually, Booker T., still a little boy, was able to attend school, when he wasn't working in the local salt mine to help support his mother, stepfather, and siblings.

Eventually, Washington was able to attend Virginia's Hampton Institute, one of America's first black colleges. Traveling by stagecoach, hitching rides on wagons, and traveling by foot; going days at a time without eating or sleeping; and in Richmond, Virginia, finding work unloading a ship's cargo of pig iron, while sleeping nights under a wooden sidewalk, it took weeks for Washington—who could not bathe or change clothes—to reach Hampton. At Hampton—today Hampton University—the penniless young man earned his keep doing janitorial work for the school. The plucky workhorse not only graduated from Hampton, but was asked to stay on as a teacher.

Soon thereafter, in 1881, the 24-year-old Washington was asked to found the Tuskegee Institute in the Alabama backwoods. Starting with the burnt-out husk of a plantation "big house," Washington built the buildings that for a generation made Tuskegee—today Tuskegee University—America's most influential black institution of higher education. Washington built Tuskegee the old-fashioned way—with his own bare hands. Possessing perhaps enough money to contract to have an outhouse built, Washington told his students that they would have to help him erect the school's buildings. Seeing as he had neither bricks nor money with which to buy them, Washington resolved to build a brick-baking kiln. This shocked his students, many of whom had gone to Tuskegee to escape such "common" labor. The first kiln collapsed on its maiden firing. A second attempt resulted in… abject failure. The third go-round, too. Fortunately for Tuskegee, Washington did not believe in "three strikes and you're out." While all around him wallowed in despair, Booker T. built a fourth kiln, AND IT WORKED! Not only were all of Tuskegee's early buildings built by Tuskegee students and faculty using the bricks they had baked, but when word got around in the neighboring region as to the superior quality of Tuskegee bricks, white businesses got in line to buy them. Tuskegee became the biggest local supplier of bricks.

Tuskegee also has a central place in American literary history. One of its most famous alumni, Ralph Ellison (1914-1994), depicted Tuskegee in several early chapters of his seminal novel, Invisible Man. Referred to always as "The Founder," Washington's shadow loomed large over the often surreal proceedings.) With Washington's successful, 1895 Atlanta Exposition Address before a mixed (if physically segregated) crowd, and the 1901 publication of his inspirational memoir, Up from Slavery, as told to white ghostwriter Max Bennett Thrasher, he became the unofficial leader of black America. Washington's doctrine of self-reliance involved asking little of whites, and saw blacks gaining economic success, and eventually the respect of whites, through their own businesses.

Based on his ability to placate white and black audiences alike, Washington became known as "the Wizard of Tuskegee." Nowhere was that talent more in evidence than in his Atlanta address, where many of his critics and supporters alike had expected him to offend one or both of the races. Instead, Washington propounded the accommodationist doctrine, which the vast majority of Americans of both races accepted, that "In all things that are purely social we can be as separate as the fingers, yet one as the hand in all things essential to mutual progress."

While Washington was an accommodationist, he was anything but the "Uncle Tom" that his detractors paint him as having been. Consider the following words from *Up from Slavery*:

I do not believe that any state should make a law that permits an ignorant and poverty-stricken white man to vote, and prevents a black man in the same condition from voting. Such a law is not only unjust, but it will react, as all unjust laws do, in time; for the effect of such a law is to encourage the Negro to secure education and property, and at the same time it encourages the white man to remain in ignorance and poverty. I believe that in time, through the operation of intelligence and friendly race relations, all cheating at the ballot-box in the South will cease. It will become apparent that the white man who begins by cheating a Negro out of his ballot soon learns to cheat a white man out of his, and that the man who does this ends his career of dishonesty by the theft of property or by some equally serious crime. In my opinion, the time will come when the South will encourage all of its citizens to vote. It will see that it pays better, from every standpoint, to have healthy, vigorous life than to have that political stagnation which always results when one-half of the population has no share and no interest in the Government.

As a rule, I believe in universal, free suffrage, but I believe that in the South we are confronted with peculiar conditions that justify the protection of the ballot in many of the states, for a while at least, either by an educational test, a property test, or by both combined; but whatever tests are required, they should be made to apply with equal and exact justice to both races.

His public persona notwithstanding, Washington also secretly funded civil rights lawsuits. Note, however, that in Washington's day, such lawsuits were a serious matter, and not the routinely frivolous exercises in extortion they have in recent years become.

Washington's philosophy, which many whites found unthreatening, and thus pleasing, was anathema to the founder of the civil rights movement, W.E.B. DuBois (1868-1963). In 1903, in DuBois' literary masterpiece, *The Souls of Black Folk*, he fired his first salvo against Washington. A socialist (and later, communist) who in 1909 was the sole black co-founder of the National Association for the Advancement of Colored People (NAACP), DuBois believed that black progress lay in the government immediately granting them full political rights, and providing them with social welfare programs. DuBois' model was the Reconstruction-era (1865-1877) federal Freedmen's Bureau in the South.

DuBois also favored giving blacks a classical education, which Washington had derided as a waste of time for people who did not know how to earn a living. DuBois obsessively attacked, as a pedagogy for Uncle Toms (though without using that phrase), the vocational ideal with which Washington was inextricably linked. As long as Washington was alive, DuBois' attacks on any educational notions favoring vocational over classical education were also thinly veiled, personal attacks on Washington. Consider a famous DuBois quote from 1908:

But if… the standards of a great Negro college are to be set by schools of lower and different object, whither are the ideals of this University falling? If you find that you cannot give technical courses of college grade, then give high-school courses or kindergarten courses and call them by their right names. There may often be excuse for doing things poorly in this world, but there is never any excuse for calling a poorly done thing, well done.

The times are perilous. A stubborn determination at this time on the part of the Negro race, to uphold its ideals, keep its standards, and unceasingly contend for its rights, means victory; and victory a great deal sooner than any of you imagine. But a course of self-abasement and surrender, of lowering of ideals and neglecting of opportunity—above all, a philosophy of lying in word or deed for the sake conciliation or personal gain, means indefinite postponement of the true emancipation of the Negro race in America, for the simple reason that such a race is not fit to be freed.

Such attacks ceased with Washington's death in 1915, and DuBois' subsequent ascendance. As reported in 1993 by Stephen G. Thompkins of the Memphis Commercial Appeal, and in 1995, by Tony Brown in *Black Lies, White Lies: The Truth According to Tony Brown*, during World War I, DuBois offered his services to the U.S. Army's Military Intelligence Division (MID) to spy on prominent blacks. MID offered DuBois a position, but withdrew its offer, when the story was leaked to the public.

DuBois, who loved the centralized, unlimited power of the totalitarian state, praised Hitler's National Socialism in pre-war Germany, and embraced Stalin's Soviet Union.

W.E.B. DuBois was one of America's most brilliant thinkers, and surely would have beaten Booker T. Washington in an IQ test. Indeed, DuBois' vision of a black university, and the educated, black opinion-makers (who would comprise what he called "the talented tenth") those universities would produce, was beyond the means of the greatest white universities, and all but a handful of the most brilliant whites of his day. The more humble Washington, however, possessed that unquantifiable virtue that DuBois sorely lacked: Wisdom. Washington's notions were educationally, economically, and politically of much greater benefit to the blacks of his day, and beyond.

Since DuBois' followers control the writing of history textbooks, and the media's coverage of black affairs, we get a sanitized version of his place in American history, and often as not, no version at all of Washington's. In spite of the DuBoisians' alternate neglect and disrespect of Washington, Washington's memoir, *Up from Slavery*, has continuously been in print since its 1901 publication, and is available in cheap paperback editions. (My favorite version is the Penguin Classics version, which has an introduction by historian Louis R. Harlan). More recently, Louis R. Harlan wrote a splendid, two volume biography of Washington, *Booker T. Washington: The Making of a Black Leader, 1856-1901,* and *Booker T. Washington: The Wizard of Tuskegee, 1901-1915.*

THE BLACK AMERICAN PIONEER AND HERO:
BOOKER T. WASHINGTON

April 5, 1856 – November 14, 1915) Booker T. Washington was an American political leader, educator and author of African ancestry, most famous for his tenure as President of Tuskegee University (1880–1915).[1]

Born a slave on a small farm in the Virginia backcountry, Booker T. Washington worked in the salt furnaces and coalmines of West Virginia as a child.

"I cannot recall a single instance during my childhood or early boyhood when our entire family sat down to the table together, and God's blessing was asked, and the family ate a meal in a civilized manner. On the plantation in Virginia, and even later, meals were gotten to the children very much as

[1]   https://en.wikiquote.org/wiki/Booker_T._Washington

dumb animals get theirs. It was a piece of bread here and a scrap of meat there. It was a cup of milk at one time and some potatoes at another."

After teaching himself to read and working several years to earn and save money, he made his way east to Hampton Institute, a school established to educate freedmen. There he worked as a janitor to pay for his studies. He attended Wayland Seminary in Washington, D.C. in 1878 but left after 6 months.[2] In 1881, Washington founded Tuskegee Normal and Industrial Institute on the Hampton model in the Black Belt of Alabama. Starting with a broken down building, he used his ability to win the trust of white Southerners and Northern philanthropists to make Tuskegee into a model school of industrial education.[3]

American historian, C. Vann Woodward concluded of Booker T. Washington.., "The businessman's gospel of free enterprise, competition, and laissez faire never had a more loyal exponent.

Washington called for black progress through education and entrepreneurship, rather than trying to challenge directly the Jim Crow segregation and the disenfranchisement of black voters in the South. His strong support in the black community was rooted in its widespread realization that frontal assaults on white supremacy were impossible, and the best way forward was to concentrate on building up the economic and social structures inside segregated communities. Washington mobilized a nationwide coalition of middle-class blacks, church leaders, and white philanthropists and politicians,

---

2   https://en.wikipedia.org/wiki/Booker_T._Washington#Tuskegee_Institute
3   http://www.pbs.org/wnet/jimcrow/stories_people_booker.html

with a long-term goal of building the community's economic strength and pride by a focus on self-help and schooling. Secretly he also supported court challenges to segregation and passed on funds raised for this purpose, like his substantial privately contributions for legal challenges to segregation and disfranchisement, such as the case of Giles v. Harris, which was heard before the United States Supreme Court in 1903.[4]

_____

4 https://en.wikipedia.org/wiki/Booker_T._Washington#Honors_and_memorials

Education throughout the Rural South

State and local governments gave little money to black schools, but white philanthropists proved willing to invest heavily. Washington encouraged them and directed millions of their money to projects all across the South that Washington thought best reflecting his self-help philosophy. Washington associated with the richest and most powerful businessmen and politicians of the era. He became a conduit for funding countless small southern rural schools, which continued many years after his death. Along with rich white men, the black Americans helped their communities directly by donating time, money, and labor to their schools in a sort of matching fund.[6]

---

5   http://www.bing.com/images/search?q=early+1900+university+of+tuskegee&view=detailv2&qft=+filterui%3alicense-L2_L3_L4&id=A811AD170A764614DBE623E8BAC42DBAA88F1597&selectedIndex=0&ccid=M75mhvzk&simid=608018055576422543&thid=OIP.M33be6686fce43ca1884cfdaa11aa525ao0&ajaxhist=0

6   https://en.wikipedia.org/wiki/Booker_T._Washington#Wealthy_friends_and_benefactors

America's first National Business Network

1900: In an effort to inspire the "commercial, agricultural, educational, and industrial advancement" of African Americans, Washington founded the National Negro Business League (NNBL) in 1900.

American Best Selling Author

Washington's second autobiography, *Up From Slavery*, was published in 1901 and became a national bestseller. It had a major effect on the African-American community, its friends and allies.[7]

Advisor to American Presidents

Washington was an advisor to Presidents William Howard Taft and Theodore Roosevelt. On October 1901 President Roosevelt invited him to dine with him and his family at the White House; he was the first African American to be invited there by a President.

President and Founder of Tuskegee University

- Home of Inventor: Grover Washington- former Slave best known for developing crop-rotation methods for conserving nutrients in soil, multiple agricultural-based patents and for discovering hundreds of new uses for crops such as the peanut.
- Home of the WWII pilots, the Tuskegee Airman: For Valor and Contribution
  - ○ Several Silver Stars

---

7   https://en.wikipedia.org/wiki/Booker_T._Washington#Up_from_Slavery_to_the_White_House

- ◦ 150 Distinguished Flying Cross
- ◦ 14 Bronze Stars
- ◦ 744 Air Medals
- Home of millions of Tuskegee graduates, contributors in every façade of America's progress and world influence since 1881.

Honors and Memorials

- Honorary master's degree from Harvard University in 1896 and an honorary doctorate from Dartmouth College in 1901.
- On April 7, 1940, Washington became the first African American to be depicted on a United States postage stamp.
- First coin to feature an African American, the Booker T. Washington Memorial Half Dollar (From 1946 to 1951). He was also depicted on a U.S. Half Dollar from 1951–1954.[8]
- In 1942, the Liberty ship, Booker T. Washington, was named in his honor...the first major ocean going vessel to be named after an African American.
- On April 5, 1956, the hundredth anniversary of Washington's birth, the house where he was born in Franklin County, Virginia, was designated as the Booker T. Washington National Monument.
- A state park in Chattanooga, Tennessee, was named in his honor, as was a bridge. spanning the Hampton River adjacent to his alma mater, Hampton University.

---

[8] https://en.wikipedia.org/wiki/Booker_T._Washington#Honors_and_memorials

- At his death Tuskegee's endowment exceeded $1.5 million.[9]

At the center of the campus at Tuskegee University, the Booker T. Washington Monument, called Lifting the Veil, was dedicated in 1922. The inscription at its base reads:

"He lifted the veil of ignorance from his people and pointed the way to progress through education and industry."

---

9   https://en.wikipedia.org/wiki/Booker_T._Washington#Honors_and_memorials

Booker T. Washington Quotes:

"Excellence is to do a common thing in an uncommon way."

"You can't hold a man down without staying down with him. If you want to lift yourself up, lift up someone else."

"Success in life is founded upon attention to the small things rather than to the large things; to the every day things nearest to us rather than to the things that are remote and uncommon."

"Success is to be measured not so much by the position that one has reached in life as by the obstacles which one has overcome while trying to succeed."

"There is no power on earth that can neutralize the influence of a high, simple and useful life."

"Men may make laws to hinder and fetter the ballot, but men cannot make laws that will bind or retard the growth of manhood."

"We went into slavery a piece of property; we came out American citizens. We went into slavery pagans; we came out Christians. We went into slavery without a language; we came out speaking the proud Anglo-Saxon tongue. We went into slavery with slave chains clanking about our wrists; we came out with the American ballot in our hands."

"Progress, progress is the law of nature; under God it shall be our eternal guiding star."[10]

"Character, not circumstances, makes the man."[11]

"I think I have learned that the best way to lift one's self up is to help someone else."[12]

"There is no power on earth that can neutralize the influence of a high, pure, simple and useful life."[13]

"The world cares very little what you or I know, but it does care a great deal about what you or I do."[14]

"Of all forms of slavery there is none that is so harmful and degrading as that form of slavery, which tempts one human being to hate another by reason of his race or color. "

"I would permit no man, no matter what his colour might be, to narrow and degrade my soul by making me hate him."[15]

---

[10] "The Problems of the Colored Race in the South," lecture, Hamilton Club, Chicago (10 December 1895)

[11] "Democracy and Education", speech, Institute of Arts and Sciences, Brooklyn NY (30 September 1896)

[12] The Story of My Life and Work, vol. I (1900), ch. XV: Cuban Education and the Chicago Peace Jubilee   Address

[13] "The Virtue of Simplicity," from Character Building: Being Addresses Delivered on Sunday Evenings to the Students of Tuskegee Institute (1902), p. 41

[14] Address to the African Methodist Episcopal Zion Church, Boston, Massachusetts (30 July 1903), printed in "Account of the Boston Riot," Boston Globe (31 July 1903)

[15] Charm and Courtesy in Conversation (1904) by Frances Bennett Callaway, p. 153

"No race can prosper till it learns that there is as much dignity in tilling a field as in writing a poem. It is at the bottom of life we must begin, and not at the top."[16]

"I pity from the bottom of my heart any nation or body of people that is so unfortunate as to get entangled in the net of slavery. I have long since ceased to cherish any [spirit]] of bitterness against the Southern white people on account of the enslavement of my race. No one section of our country was wholly responsible for its introduction, and, besides, it was recognized and protected for years by the General Government. Having once got its tentacles fastened on to the economic and social life of the Republic, it was no easy matter for the country to relieve itself of the institution. Then, when we rid ourselves of prejudice, or racial feeling, and look facts in the face, we must acknowledge that, notwithstanding the cruelty and moral wrong of slavery, the ten million Negroes inhabiting this country, who themselves or whose ancestors went through the school of American slavery, are in a stronger and more hopeful condition, materially, intellectually, morally, and religiously, than is true of an equal number of black people in any other portion of the globe. This is so to such an extent that Negroes in this country, who themselves or whose forefathers went through the school of slavery, are constantly returning to Africa as missionaries to enlighten those who remained in the fatherland. This I say, not to justify slavery — on the other hand, I condemn it as an institution, as we all know that in America it was established for selfish and financial reasons, and not from a missionary motive — but to

---

[16]   Chapter XIV: The Atlanta Exposition Address

call attention to a fact, and to show how Providence so often uses men and institutions to accomplish a purpose". [17]

"I have learned that success is to be measured not so much by the position that one has reached in life as by the obstacles which he has overcome while trying to succeed. Looked at from this standpoint, I almost reached the conclusion that often the Negro boy's birth and connection with an unpopular race is an advantage, so far as real life is concerned. With few exceptions, the Negro youth must work harder and must perform his tasks even better than a white youth in order to secure recognition. But out of the hard and unusual struggle through which he is compelled to pass, he gets a strength, a confidence, that one misses whose pathway is comparatively smooth by reason of birth and race."[18]

"I learned the lesson that great men cultivate love, and that only little men cherish a spirit of hatred. I learned that assistance given to the weak makes the one who gives it strong; and that oppression of the unfortunate makes one weak."[19]

"No man who continues to add something to the material, intellectual, and moral well-being of the place in which he lives is long left without proper reward."[20]

"Nothing ever comes to me, that is worth having, except as the result of hard work." [21]

---

[17] Up From Slavery (1901) Chapter I: A Slave Among Slaves

[18] Ibid. Chapter II: Boyhood Days

[19] Ibid. Chapter XI: Making Their Beds Before They Could Lie On Them

[20] Ibid. Chapter XVI: Europe

[21] Ibid. Chapter XII: Raising Money

"My whole life has largely been one of surprises. I believe that any man's life will be filled with constant, unexpected encouragements of this kind if he makes up his mind to do his level best each day of his life — that is, tries to make each day reach as nearly as possible the high-water mark of pure, unselfish, useful living."[22]

"I am afraid that there is a certain class of race-problem solvers who don't want the patient to get well, because as long as the disease holds out they have not only an easy means of making a living, but also an easy medium through which to make themselves prominent before the public. My experience is that people who call themselves "The Intellectuals" understand theories, but they do not understand things. I have long been convinced that, if these men could have gone into the South and taken up and become interested in some practical work which would have brought them in touch with people and things, the whole world would have looked very different to them. Bad as conditions might have seemed at first, when they saw that actual progress was being made, they would have taken a more hopeful view of the situation."[23]

---

22 Ibid. Chapter XVII: Last Words
23 *My Larger Education* Ch.V: The Intellectuals and the Boston Mob (pg. 118)

CHAPTER 9

THE TIP OF THE SPEAR:
W.E.B. DuBois

*"The Negro race, like all races, is going to be
saved by its exceptional men. The problem of
education, then, among Negroes must first of all
deal with the Talented Tenth; it is the problem of
developing the 'Best of this Race' that they may
guide the Mass away from the contamination and
death of the Worst, in their own and other races.*

*"Can the masses of the Negro people be in any
possible way more quickly raised than by the
effort and example of this aristocracy of talent
and character? Was there ever a nation on God's
fair earth civilized from the bottom upward?
Never; it is, ever was and ever will be from the top
downward that culture filters. The Talented Tenth
rises and pulls all that are worth the saving up to
their vantage ground."*

- W.E.B DuBois, 1903

The concept of the Talented Tenth was introduced in 1903
by W.E.B DuBois. It has impacted the progress of the black

community and the inter-racial relationship between Black and White Americans in ways that will forever be hard to fathom. This group today is referred to as the Royalty Black Class. To understand the degree of influence of this small but powerful group, it will be instructional to understand DuBois's background and the ideology of those of influence within his small inner circle. As we explore and understand the philosophy, policies and practices that he introduced into the Black community, viewed through the eyes of history, DuBois will possibly be considered one of the Black communities most successful adversaries.

W.E.B DuBois: "The Man, The Savior"

Socialism is a theory that advocates the vesting of ownership and control of the means of production, distribution and capital to a selected few. For this power to remain in the hands of the selected few (bureaucrats), the populist must remain subservient, ignorant and dependent. As centralized bureaucracy empowers itself, it must devalue the merit of individualism. It will, due to its nature, inevitably devolve into a system of tyranny and oppression. Synonyms: Communist, Marxist, Liberal, Progressive.

> *"The Soviet Union does not allow any church of any kind to interfere with education, and religion is not taught in public schools. It seems to me that this is the greatest gift of the Russian Revolution to the modern world. Most educated modern men no longer believe in religious dogma. Many folk*

follow religious ceremonies and services and allow their children to learn fairy tales and so-called religious truth, which in time the children come to recognize as conventional lies told by their parents and teachers for the children's good. One can hardly exaggerate the moral disaster of the custom. We have to thank the Soviet Union for the courage to stop it."

W.E.B. DuBois[1]

DuBois joined the Socialist party in his 20s. In 1917, he "hailed the Russian Revolution" and in 1926 and 1936 he made pilgrimages to the Soviet Union, where he especially liked "the racial attitudes of the Communists."[2] By the end of his life he was an atheist, communist and had renounced his American Citizenship.

In *W.E.B. DuBois: New Negro Leader in Time of Crisis,* Francis L. Broderick documents the journey that would lead DuBois to develop and later articulate the Talented Tenth philosophy... At Harvard his professors included William James, George Santayana, and the historian A. B. Hart. James was influenced by Charles Darwin's theory of natural selection and Santayana, an Agnostic, also studied under James.[3]

In 1892, after two years of graduate study at Harvard, DuBois went abroad on a grant. His travels included England, France, Italy and Germany. He visited Vienna, Cracow and

---

[1]   The Autobiography of W.E. Burghardt Du Bois (1968), Ch. IV : The Soviet Union

[2]   http://www.knology.net/~bilrum/NAACP.htm

[3]   https://en.wikipedia.org/wiki/George_Santayana

Budapest. "I was transplanted and started into realization of the real centers of modern civilization and into a momentary escape from my own social patterns." He went to the theater every week and symphony now and again… and art galleries. As he sailed down the Rhine, a German family took him under its wing and a young Fraulein may have fallen in love with him. Even in student beer halls he was an as welcome as any other foreigner. His exotic color was a cause for comment, though never a barrier.[4]

He made a long analysis of German socialism, which later apparently served as a lecture. At the University of Berlin, Heinrich von Treitschke lectured on the superiority of the Anglo-Saxon race and snarled at the backwardness of colored people. While under his tutorage, DuBois was also exposed to anti-Semitism. Treitschke was one of the few important public figures who supported anti-Semitic attacks, which became prevalent from 1878 onwards, and National Socialism of which he was an advocate.[5]

At the core of National Socialism was the Nationalism advocated by the historian Heinrich von Treitschke. A basic theme was Social Darwinism, in which individuals and nations are both subject to a continuous struggle for life. In this struggle, race is the center of life and all other elements are rated with reference to it. National Socialism claimed that keeping the blood and the race pure is a nation's noblest task. It proclaimed the Germanic race as the new 'icorpus mysticum' on which the salvation of the Aryan race and consequently that of the world depended.

---

[4]   web dubois-New Negro Leader in Time of Crisis.. Francis L. Broderick.

[5]   http://en.wikipedia.org/wiki/Heinrich_von_Treitschke#Historian

Accordingly, Nazis policies "figured solely as an expedient intended to improve the Germanic race genetically and to protect it against racial interbreeding which according to the National Socialists, always entails the doctrine of the higher race."[6]

Heinrich von Treitschke greeted DuBois cordially on a casual meeting before vacation time. Those months abroad made DuBois realize that "white folk were human." According to Broderick, the interlude at Berlin reinforced DuBois's conviction that intellectuals were above color prejudice.[8] Unfortunately it does not appear that his intellectual prowess would keep him from absorbing some of the anti-Semitism he was exposed to on his trip abroad. In his "Diary of my steerage trip across the Atlantic (summer of 1895) he says that he had seen the aristocracy of the Jewish race and the "low mean cheating pobel" but he had seldom seen "the ordinary good hearted intentioned man." He found two congenial Jews on the trip, but he shunned the rest- "There is in them all the slyness that lack of straight-forward openheartedness which goes straight against me."[7]

It is easy to conclude that for young DuBois, due to his liberal teaching and indoctrination at Harvard and University of Berlin, that both evolution and eugenics had become core tenets of his belief system. These tenets he would later apply to the "lesser evolved" masses of his race and the "crème le d cream" intellectuals, the Talented Tenth. As documented by Broderick, DuBois, at 25 years old, would take stock in his future. In his diary he would speculate his place in the

6   http://www.ssnp.com/new/ssnp/en/ssnp_001.htm
7   W. E. B. Du Bois, Negro leader in a time of crisis by Francis L Broderick

modern world. His comments seem to allude to a perception of self as a potential Savior of his race.

"I am glad I am living, I rejoice as a strong man to run a race, and I am strong- it is egotism is assurance-or is it the silent call of the world spirit that makes me feel that I am royal and that beneath my scepter a world of kings shall bow. The hot dark blood of that black forefather born king of men- is beating at my heart and I know that I am either a genius or a fool…. This I do know: be the Truth what it may I will seek it on pure assumption that it is worth seeking-and Heaven nor Hell, God nor Devil shall turn me from my purpose till I die."[8]

DuBois saw himself as a "strong man destined to run a race… a royal to which a world of kings shall bow." Like those who share his elitist philosophy today, he felt that his wisdom and intelligence when matched with others like him, would be capable of raising his race, i.e. "all that are worth the saving" up to their vantage ground. Based on his decades of obsessions with integration this vantage point appears to be preparation for racial acceptance and race-nullification. It was his panacea to develop the "Best of this Race" that they may guide the Mass away from the contamination and death of the Worst, in their own and other races.

DuBois view of the lowly state of the masses of his race explains his exerted efforts to undermine the works of a former self-taught slave and founder of Tuskegee University. Unlike DuBois, Booker T. Washington embraced a vision for his race that "the masses," were capable of lifting themselves up through self-reliance and the individual empowerment

---

[8]   W. E. B. Du Bois, Negro leader in a time of crisis by Francis L Broderick

of capitalism. He proved the practicality of doing so by establishing this culture at Tuskegee University. His stance against forced integration stood as a dichotomy to DuBois. He felt that his people were better served by "commanding" respect with an offering of valued products, services and a moral populace versus "demanding" respect via laws and mandates...

The white socialist "friends of DuBois" who had devised a new concept of forced integration, now only needed a trusted messenger to deliver their message to the Black community. Awarded the role as editor of the NAACP's "The Crisis," DuBois was in 1910 the best man suited for the job.

CHAPTER 10

THE TALENTED TENTH:
ROYALTY CLASS BLACK MAN

"My own panacea of earlier day was flight of class from mass through the development of the Talented Tenth."

- W.E.B. DuBois, Dusk of Dawn

"The Negro race, like all races, is going to be saved by its exceptional men. The problem of education, then, among Negroes must first of all deal with the Talented Tenth; it is the problem of developing their 'Best of this Race' that they may guide the mass away from the contamination and death of the Worst, in their own and other races."

- W.E.B DuBois[1]

Identified by W.E.B DuBois in early 1900 as the Talented Tenth, this small but influential group of elitist black liberals has left an enormous blight on the black community.

---

[1]   http://teachingamericanhistory.org/library/document/the-talented-tenth/

Its definition and purpose has been so skewed by progressive historians that some aspiring black professionals still seek reference as members of The Talented Tenth, as a badge of honor. For those whose priorities remain the progress of the Black race, this perception could be no further from the truth. The Talented Tenth self-view of importance has always left them susceptible to the promise of prominence and power. Those who grant them prominence and power are in turn given full reign to implement their own agenda. These ideologically driven agendas, delivered through stealth and deceit have consistently been proven detrimental to the black community.

The Talented Tenth was a name ascribed by W.E.B DuBois, in 1910, to denote an educated, professional, "intelligent," traditionally mixed class of black elitists: the Black Royal Class. The term defines a view in which DuBois saw himself and others as the top of his race's evolutionary development. It was a philosophy fueled by his Eugenicists belief that the quality of his race could be improved by increasing the quality of its the gene pool. The Nazi's also embraced this belief. Increasing the quality of the Black race would require the Royalty Class Black Man to collaborate with other Eugenicists, like Margaret Sanger, to eliminate inferior and defective genes deemed a drag on the black race, through abortion and sterilization.

DuBois was the first Black American to get a PhD from Harvard. He was accepted within the northern white intellectual circles as one of the " best of his race." As an avowed Socialist, he was chosen to be the only Black Executive Board member of the newly formed NAACP by its founding Board of Directors, comprised of wealthy, white Socialist, Progressives (liberals), Marxists, Atheist and Humanists. For the next twenty-four years he would be the face and voice of the NAACP, salaried to author its outreach magazine, The Crisis. He would also serve on the board of the renowned eugenicist and KKK sympathizer Margaret Sanger, founder of Planned Parenthood. She introduced to the poor urban Black community a new birth control concept called abortion. The symbiotic relationship between DuBois and Sanger will be discussed in later chapters. In her writings she left no doubt of her contempt for the Black Race. In her own words … "human weeds," "reckless breeders," "spawning… human beings who never should have been born."[2]

The NAACP and its Black voice and face, DuBois, worked tirelessly to discredit the character, reputation and fund raising efforts of its one competing voice, capitalist, Christian and Tuskegee University founder, Booker T. Washington. Due to his message of industry, morality and self-sufficiency, the Black community had experienced tremendous success and had garnered a high degree of respect throughout the north and south. Eventually though, due to the untimely death of Washington in 1915, the seeds of socialism championed by the NAACP would overshadow his message of free enterprise and self-empowerment. The NAACP's message was a demand for "Integration at all cost" with an expectation of support from the government largess and socialist labor unions.

DuBois would later in his life join the communist party and renounce his American citizenship. Unfortunately, his "integration at all cost" message would, for the next 100 years,

---

[2]   http://www.dianedew.com/sanger.htm

deeply influence the black community's self-perception. As its entrepreneurial and academic successes were purposely downplayed, the community has seen a wholesale devaluation of everything it produces, i.e. it's goods, services, schools and businesses. Its' human resources, replete with experience, wisdom and vision were also diminished and cast aside. As NAACP driven legislation increased the demand for access to the white competitor's goods, services, schools, businesses and communities, the Free Enterprises' axiom of "supply and demand" took its natural course. There was an exponential increase in the value, both perceived and real in anything White owned, while the value of all within the Black Community decreased. As was his reflection of his goals of integration in his writing *Dusk of Dawn*.... "My own panacea of earlier day was flight of class from mass through the development of the Talented Tenth"[3]... Socialisms mantra "Class over Race."

DuBois's reward for promoting the damaging abortion agenda of Planned Parenthood and the "integration at all cost" agenda of the NAACP was national honor, prestige and a good job until his services were no longer needed. He unlike his adversary, the visionary capitalist and risk- taker Booker T. Washington, has been treated kindly in our history books as a monumental and intellectual hero.

The Talented Tenth, as described by DuBois in 1901, is alive and well today, now entitled, The Royalty Class Black Man. As it was with DuBois, they see themselves as distinct, different and above the black masses- the top tenth of their race. *They are the Elitist Class*. As they seek to "guide the

---

[3]   https://en.wikipedia.org/wiki/Dusk_of_Dawn

masses away from the contamination and death of the worst in their own... race" they act with a stunningly focused commitment to their own elevation and acceptance amongst their fellow members of the Royalty Class.

The Royalty Class Black Man is the black liberal academia. From the safety of tenured positions, they demean free enterprise while living a lifestyle afforded to them through the taxes of risk taking entrepreneurs. Empowered by their secure and protected positions they are free and unencumbered to indoctrinate their student audience to the virtue of socialism and Marxism as they bully anyone who profess views that extol the principles of capitalism. They praise their own intellectual prowess while projecting low expectations for those who do not meet their lofty post-graduate educational standards.

The Royalty Class Black Man is the black liberal politician who, at the behest of union bosses, dutifully support legislation that bars poor black children from a quality education, poor black teenagers from employment and black entrepreneurs from competing freely and unencumbered in the market place. The legislative limitations imposed on the masses are consistently hypocritical of the options they provide for their own. They ensure themselves a menu of educational choices for their own children and future entrée into white professional business networks and corporate internships, where their children can secure a good career and lifestyle.

These Talented Tenth politicians show a sociopathic empathy for the constituency that they profess to represent. They've learned well to utilize the art of "Bait and Switch," in which they bait their "low information, highly emotional and dependent" voters with visions of an effort free and happy existence. They sell themselves as saviors and the conduit through which the endlessly compassionate largess of the Federal Government can be delivered, i.e., free phones, free food, free homes, free education, and a problem-free life.

Later when their polities fail and hope of their constituents once again vanishes, they switch the Blame to sit squarely on the shoulders of others, others whom they call "uncompassionate," White and Black Americans... Conservative Christians. These Royalty Class Black Politicians instinctively know there is wisdom in Thomas Jefferson's writings when he warned of the dangers of an uneducated populace: "If a nation expects to be ignorant and free in a state of civilization, it expects what never was and never will be." [4]

The Royalty Class Black Men are the black developers and managers, the slumlords, who absconded with tens of millions in wealth from "help the poor" federal welfare funds while their poor Black tenants lived in squalor. They are the popular black entertainers who confess humbleness and connection, while selling through their degrading music and condescending message of what cannot be done. They are the community organizers whose value lies in their ability to lead yet another march. Their persuasiveness is rewarded with a position at "the front of the line" when the Federal Affirmative Action goodies arrive or a premium and coveted hosting job for MSNBC.

It has been the self-serving Royalty Class that has facilitated Socialism into its community, , the enticing

---

[4]   http://quotationsbook.com/quote/45279/#FIfbcybMAXqUUx5h.99

ideology of the original NAACP founders. They have led a proud and productive, nation leading Black middle class away from capitalism and industry, to become a community of "demanding," marching, rioting and "waiting for" the industry of others. They had overseen a once proud and independent community of hard-working farmers, risk-taking entrepreneurs, intelligent, compassionate educators and visionary builders. It has since devolved into a large percentage of men who refuse to get educated, refuse to commit to the mother of their children and who then takes offense to any suggestion of personal accountably. After six decades of this ideological reign this is the state of the Liberal Black man. It is a man who feels absolutely no shame in demanding his post-Civil War promise of 40 acres and a mule…… Neither of which he is prepared to take care of.

The resurrection of the Black community will require a painful but yet well overdue wake-up call." It will need to embrace the same enumerated solutions adhered to by every other successful American Race and community, i.e. faith in capitalism, a vision to dream, a dedication to prepare and the tenacity to win. These are the same principles that allowed the Black community to compete and obtain their American Dreams, during the early 1900s.

It will be important that the Black community recognize that the Royalty Class Black Man is not deserving of its praise and admiration. For he only prospers as the ideology of Liberalism and Socialism does, leaving in its wake divisiveness, anger and hopelessness… *Class over Race.*

THE ROYALTY CLASS BLACK POLITICIAN

"Problem profiteers... There is a class of colored people who make a business of keeping the troubles, the wrongs, and the hardships of the Negro race before the public. Having learned that they are able to make a living out of their troubles, they have grown into the settled habit of advertising their wrongs - partly because they want sympathy and partly because it pays. Some of these people do not want the Negro to lose his grievances, because they do not want to lose their jobs."

- Booker T. Washington, early 1900

"One of the advantages, and disadvantages, of representing blacks is their shameless loyalty... you can almost get away with raping babies and be forgiven. You don't have any vigilance about your performance."[5]

- Member of the Congressional Black Caucus

This segment of the Royalty Class has been particularity effective in implementing the policies of the ideology of Liberalism. As did the founders of the NAACP, they adhere to the Godless dogma of Socialism. The success of their economic philosophy can be seen in every community that they represent. Nowhere in the world has the Marxist/socialist ideology granted a different result than what is seen in the urban black communities throughout our country, i.e. hopelessness, dependency, illiteracy, anger and the lack of independent Manhood.

---

[5]   Carol M. Swain, the New White Nationalism in America: Its Challenge to Integration

This can be seen elsewhere around the world in self-declared socialist countries. These Marxist–Leninist states are inspired by the example of the Soviet Union and refer to themselves *as socialist states on the road to communism...*[6] Examples of socialist countries include China, Russia, Afghanistan, Cambodia, Cuba and North Korea. Christians should note that where Socialism reigns, God does not. The ideology of Socialism is consistent in its actions, wherever it is found. Beginning with the divisive envy of others property and wealth, it always ends with the legal confiscation and stealing of it. Disincentive follows, with the best and brightest either escaping (leaving for the suburbs) or simply ceasing to create. This predictably leaves only two economic classes of citizenry... the rich, i.e. the Royalty Black Politician and the poor, hopeless, frustrated and angry Black constituents. Though this economic Robin Hood approach always sound attractive to those trained for freeby-ism, it never has and never will succeed. Also consistent with every socialist country is that, since God is the author of Freedom, He is outlawed.

Of course there is never a lack for the latest intellectual agnostic or atheist who feels his mastery of people will force others to get it right. With the philosophy of Socialism/liberalism, *Freedom is never an option*.

Accordingly, the Socialist Royalty Class Black Politician finds the idea of free market, free enterprise and capitalism, abhorrent. Their commitment to block its presence from every aspect of their constituent's lives denies

---

6   https://en.wikipedia.org/wiki/List_of_socialist_states..

them Choice of schooling, Choice of jobs, Choice in how to protect their family, Choice in freedom to profess and follow their Christian faith and Choice of representation.

The Royalty Black Politicians are a special breed. They have mastered the skills of stealth and empathy-free betrayal. As their pro-socialist policies begin to fail they deny all accountability and pivot to blame the white Race, the racist Republicans or slavery, which ended over 150 years ago.

Prior to the Emancipation Proclamation slaves fulfilled two roles for their master, one as a field slave, the other as a house slave. Due to their proximately to white prominence and wealth, the House slaves usually lived better than field slaves, had better food and often the family's cast-off clothing. This proximity often caused the House slave to identify with his master, looking out for his well-being as he protected his owner's property, his home, and his children. House slaves benefited from their loyalty and some even came to love and care for their owners, even to the detriment of their own community. Their misguided allegiance caused them to imitate their owner's deportment and adopt his political ideology as their own.[7]

This is an appropriate description for the role of the Royalty Black Class in our society today. Their misguided allegiance caused them to imitate their owner's deportment and adopt his political ideology as their own. These are the relatively few who have shown through their policies and actions an empathy-free disconnect from the needs of black community who trust them and who they purportedly serve. W.E.B. DuBois eloquently described himself and those of

---

7   http://aalbc.com/authors/stanley_robertson.html

his stature as the "best of the race." They experienced the American Dream, the dream of prominence, power, lifestyle and education options. Yet on every significant Black proponent policy they stand in the doorway, fulfilling the power of the man behind the curtain and blocking access to opportunity and freedom for the remaining masses of their race.

> *"These people do not want the Negro to lose his grievances, because they do not want to lose their jobs"*
> *- Booker T. Washington*

For decades, regardless of the devastation experienced by their own constituents, the Royalty Class Black Politician remains loyal to the powerful liberal/socialist establishment and labor unions. They retain their power, "imitate their owners' deportment and adopt his political ideology as their own. Consistent with the more than 100-year history of the Talented Tenth (Royalty Black Class) has been its mantra "Do as I say, not as I do." As we review the policies that impact the black community, note how dependable the Royalty Black Class (The Talented Tenth) has been in standing in the doorway, obstructing entry of his race. Having passed through the doorway of the American dream they thrive and prosper, justifying the denial of access to those, who due to them, remain powerless to obtain it

> *"The Talented Tenth rises and pulls all that are worth the saving up to their vantage ground."*
> *- W.E.B DuBois*

As the Royalty Black Class continues to lift those who they believe "are worth the saving," those who are unlike themselves the poor, uneducated, unprofessional, unconnected and powerless, are due for placement on the sacrificial altar of Liberalism/Socialism/Atheism. Here is a brief review of the liberal policies they have championed and which for decades have negatively impacted millions of Black Americans.

A 1985 survey found that most blacks favored the death penalty and prayer in public schools. Most black political leaders opposed these. Most blacks opposed school busing, while most black political leaders favored it. Three times as many black opposed abortion rights, as did their black political leaders. Indeed, on many key social issues, blacks are more conservative than whites.[8] On every issue pertaining to social values of the Black community, there is a disconnect between the community at large and their Royalty Black Class elected politicians. As will be discussed in a later chapter, "Political Free Agency" will bring to an end this betrayal.

SCHOOL CHOICE

School Choice describes a wide array of programs aimed at giving families the opportunity to choose the school their children will attend. As a matter of form, school choice does not give preference to one form of schooling or another. Rather it manifests itself whenever a student attends school outside of the one they would have been assigned to by

---

[8]   Henry Louis gates jr. and Cornel West, the future of the race (vintage books, 1997)

geographic default. The most common options offered by school choice programs are open enrollment laws that allow students to attend other public schools, private schools and charter schools. It includes tax credit and deductions for expenses related to schooling, vouchers, and homeschooling.[9]

FACT: As of 2009, the Department of Education reported that literacy rates for more than 50 percent of African American children in the fourth grade nationwide was below the basic skills level and far below average. By the ninth grade nationwide, the situation was even worse, with the rate dropping below 44 percent.[10]

FACT: According to the National Association for Educational Progress 2011 Report Card, only 14 % of African American fourth graders and eighth graders performed at or above the proficient level on national reading tests. Males scored 9 points lower on average than females.[11]

FACT: Fewer than half of African American men graduate from high school. African American men make up only 5% of the college population, yet they make up 40% of the prison population [12]

In March 2013, the Black Alliance for Educational Options (BAEO) commissioned a survey of Black voters in four Southern states to gauge attitudes and opinions within the Black community on education reform, charter schools, and the need for parental choice in their community. The findings

---

9   *http://en.wikipedia.org/wiki/School_choice*

10 http://ourweekly.com/news/2013/oct/03/whats-african-american-literacy-rates/

11 http://librariesliteracyandaamaleyouth.weebly.com/module-1-literacy-and-life-outcomes.html

12 http://librariesliteracyandaamaleyouth.weebly.com/module-1-literacy-and-life-outcomes.html

indicate strong support among this significant segment of the population for greater freedom in K-12 education, widespread recognition of the need for better quality schools, and openness to charter schools and publicly funded scholarships as reform vehicles

The study found that…

- 85-89% of black voters say government should provide parents as many choices as possible to ensure their children receive a good education[13]
- Support for school choice was strongest among younger voters (ages 18-34), people with lower incomes, and those with less formal education.[14]
- BAEO's survey results showed a solid base of support for charter schools as vehicles for reform and a means of empowering families. In Alabama, Kentucky, and Mississippi, the data showed strong support for charters across all age categories, but considerably stronger among younger voters.
- In the Black community, support is highest among voters with the most limited options today, those with lower incomes and fewer years of formal education; conversely, *opposition to charter schools is strongest among Blacks with higher incomes and more years of formal education*. In general, across all demographic groups, the more familiar respondents were with charter schools, the stronger their support. Moving from initial

---

[13] http://news.heartland.org/newspaper-article/2013/08/13/southern-black-voters-over-whelmingly-favor-school-choice-poll-finds

[14] http://scoter.baeo.org/news_multi_media/20130723-Survey%20Report-NEW%5B9%5D.pdf

ballot questions about charter schools that gauged base-level reactions to informed ballot questions prefaced with facts about charters, the survey showed greater receptivity with better understanding.[15]

The Results:

Black American Voters	**85-89% Favor**
NAACP	**100% Opposed**
Congressional Black Caucus	**100% Opposed**
Education Labor Unions	**100% Opposed**

Between 85-89% of all Black Americans polled supported federally funded choice for poor black children ensuring them a quality education. Disturbing is the 10-15%, of *BLACK* Americans who stand against a parent's choice for a quality education for their child. If we seek to find the insidious faction undermining the progress of the Black community, we need look no further. These are not the voices of 1960s segregationist, but instead the betrayal of members of the elitist Royalty Black Class, whose "misguided allegiance caused them to imitate their owner's deportment and adopt his political ideology as their own." What type of responsible American blocks the opportunity for quality education for their own community's most vulnerable children? What

---

15 http://scoter.baeo.org/news_multi_media/20130723-Survey%20Report-NEW%5B9%5D.pdf

type of visionary American sacrifices the future of their race, their greatest treasure, for the sake of ideology or the welfare of socialist labor unions? "Opposition to charter schools is strongest among Blacks with higher incomes and more years of formal education." *Elitism- Class over Race.*

Look to the national leaders of the NAACP and the members of the Congressional Black Caucus. Look to the black union teachers who teach at failing schools, send their own children to successful public, private or religious schools and then vote against the poor children who they purportedly care for. As they parrot the Labor Union's mantra concerning the "welfare of the Public School System, once good students are *allowed* to leave, note that their own dear children have already exited. This poll gives a revealing glimpse of the Royalty Black Class and their lack of concern for black families, not of their class, whom they can no longer empathize with. *Elitism- Class over Race.*

A poll by the Heritage Foundation found that members of the 110th Congress send their children to private school at about *four times* the rate of the general population. Members of the Congressional Black Caucus and Congressional Hispanic Caucus, who represent populations that have performed poorly in public schools, showed particularly high rates of practicing school choice for themselves. As a backdrop to the statistics to follow, in the general populace *only 11.5 percent of American students attend private schools.*

"ROYALTY BLACK CLASS POLITICIAN" ANTI-CHOICE FOR POOR CHILDREN

Ninety-two percent of Anti-School Choice/ Pro Labor Union House Democrats, which include 100% of Congressional Black Caucus members, send their children to private schools.16 Predictably with the Royalty Class Black Politician is that the remaining 8% (the four too busy to vote) live in neighborhoods that already guarantee to their dear children the safe and quality education that all parents want for their children.[17]

Consistent with the Royalty Black Class Politician, in whatever urban community they serve, are the annual promises given to their constituents for a more hopeful pathway. They then proceed over their length of their professional politician tenure to name streets and community centers after themselves. This ironically includes the anti-Black Davis-Bacon white Labor Union set aside, urban centered office building. Salaried by their constituent's tax dollars, the Royalty Class Black Politician ensures their own children's access to the highest quality private and public schools their community has to offer. They then quietly vote (unanimously) to keep their trusting constituents' children trapped in failing and dangerous schools. The *Royalty Class Black Politician is indeed a special breed of Black folk...* ***Totally Empathy-Free.***

---

[16] http://www.heritage.org/research/reports/2003/09/how-members-of-congress-practice-school-choice

[17] http://www.heritage.org/research/reports/2003/09/how-members-of-congress-practice-school-choice

Not to be outdone, the NAACP faced demonstrations from New York City BLACK parents because of its collaboration with Education Labor union efforts in preventing their children from getting a quality education. The New York state chapter of the NAACP and local teachers' union, the United Federation of Teachers, filed a lawsuit to stop the city from closing 22 of NY's worst schools. The lawsuit also aimed to block the city from giving charter schools space to operate in buildings occupied by traditional public schools.[18]

What were these Black parents protesting? The Academy for Collaborative Education, one of the Harlem schools proposed for closing had only 3% of its students performing at grade level in English that year and only 9% in math. At Columbus High School in the Bronx, another school slated for closure, the four-year graduation rate was 40%, versus a citywide average of 63%, and less than 10% of special education students graduated on time.

Yet, despite the horrific record, the NAACP and the United Federation of Teachers has filed a suit against the Department of Education to prohibit 17 charter schools from "opening, moving, or expanding" in the Harlem area. Their suit demands that the 22 failing public schools remain open. (8) The teacher's union priorities are clear... to preserve jobs for their members and continue to collect its dues. The union and NAACP also collaborated to limit better educational options for low-income families who couldn't afford private schools and couldn't afford to move to an affluent neighborhood with decent public schools. The union knows that in a place like New York City, where space is at a premium, blocking

---

18   http://www.wsj.com/articles/SB10001424052702303745304576361630636338492

charters from operating in public buildings will hamper charter growth.[19]

Taken from a page of Socialisms' definition of supply and demand, the NAACP and Teachers Union have circumvented what is traditionally found only in the free market, capitalism's "invisible hand." Because the NAACP is a non-profit enterprise, its financial survival is predicated on contributions/donations. Due to the financial status of their urban constituents they have long ago calculated that there is a significantly more SUPPLY of funding from powerful Labor Unions than from their community. With this as their baseline, when the DEMAND comes from the unions to give them cover or to support their policies, the NAACP supplies whatever is required of them. This explains the statement by the President of the New York state NAACP chapter, Hazel Dukes, regarding the protesting black parents. Dukes, who is black, said of the parents critical of the Union's lawsuit hindering charter schools, "They can march and have rallies all day long. We will not respond."[20] Elitism- Class over Race

While 85-89% of African Americans polled favor school vouchers and a choice to allow their children to break the poverty cycle, for decades the Royalty Class has parroted the Union line, "vouchers drain away the most ambitious families and leave the public school worse off."

Liberal/Socialist/Progressives continue to show their propensity to sacrifice OPC (Other People's Children) for their cause. As they stand in the doorway barring entrance to quality education for poor Black children, the Royalty Class Black Politician divulges his true hypocrisy and betrayal.

---

[19] http://www.wsj.com/articles/SB10001424052702303745304576361630636338492
[20] http://www.wsj.com/articles/SB10001424052702303745304576361630636338492

ABORTION

Minority women constitute only about 13% of the female population (age 15-44) in the United States, but they underwent approximately 36% of the abortions.[21]

On average, 1,876 black babies are aborted every day in the United States. This incidence of abortion has resulted in a tremendous loss of life. It has been estimated that since 1973 Black women have had about 16 million abortions. Michael Novak had calculated "Since the number of current living Blacks (in the U.S.) is 36 million, the missing 16 million represents an enormous loss, for without abortion, America's Black community would now number 52 million persons. It would be 36 percent larger than it is. Abortion has swept through the Black community like a scythe, cutting down every fourth member."[22]

In the debate of who is in control of the woman's body is missing the discussion of what the physical and emotion trauma to the woman's body with an abortion. Emotional and psychological effects following abortion are more common than physical side effects and can range from mild regret to more serious complications such as depression and suicidal thoughts and actions. The emotional side effects of having an abortion are just as real as physical side effects.[23]

A highly significant 1993 Howard University study found that the increased risk of breast cancer is another side-effect of abortions. African American women over age

---

21 http://www.blackgenocide.org/black.html

22 http://www.blackgenocide.org/black.html

23 http://americanpregnancy.org/unplanned-pregnancy/abortion-emotional-effects/

50 were 4.7 times more likely to get breast cancer if they had any abortions compared to women who had not had any abortions.[24]

A 2009 poll showed that Blacks Americans opposed abortion by a 58-35% margin.[25]

Blacks Americans	**58% OPPOSED**
Congressional Black Caucus	**100% for unlimited Abortion**
Planned Parenthood	**100% for unlimited Abortion**
NAACP Leadership	**100% for unlimited Abortion**

In 2004, NAACP officially took a position favoring abortion, with then-Chairman and avowed Socialist Julian Bond saying the group was "pleased to join those insisting on a woman's right to control her own body."[26]

When Live Action uncovered Planned Parenthood clinics willingly accepting donations from donors who specifically asked that their funds go to help "lower the number of blacks in America," the NAACP remained silent.

---

[24] http://www.blackgenocide.org/black.html

[25] http://www.lifenews.com/2009/08/11/nat-5347/

[26] www.lifenews.com/2011/12/27/why-does-the-naacp-support-abortion-oppose-pro-life-bill/

That largely unreported scandal inspired Rep. Mike Pence (R-IN) to introduce legislation to deny Title X funding to Planned Parenthood. The NAACP sided with Planned Parenthood. 27 When it was uncovered, through a series of videos in the fall of 2015, that Planned Parenthood physicians were strategically aborting babies to maximize the value of their body parts for sale, the NAACP remained silent. *Elitism Class over Race.*

> *"It's a bad sign when the NAACP, America's oldest civil rights group, finds itself on the same side of the abortion debate as Margaret Sanger. The NAACP's leadership is putting political expediency and ideology before the interests of the people the organization supposedly represents. Why else would so-called advocates for the black community tacitly support the Holocaust of unborn black babies?"*
> - Jerome Hudson of the Project 21 black leadership network[28]

CONGRESSIONAL BLACK CAUCUS

Though 58% of the Black Community opposes abortion, *100% of the members of the Congressional Black Caucus,* according to the National Abortion Rights Action League (NARAL), have maintained a 100% pro-abortion voting

---

27   Ibid
28   Ibid

record. Georgia is among the states leading in abortions on black women. 100% of Georgia's abortion clinics are in urban areas where blacks reside.[29] While not in concert with the will of a majority of its voting constituents on many of the key issues, it is on this topic where the Royalty Class Black Politicians shows their degree of subservience to the ideology of liberalism. Historically over decades of conversations there is "not one" dissenting voice among them. For the Socialist, support of the abortionist and its anti-Christian message is the true Holy Grail. Members of the Congressional Black Caucus understand well that straying off the plantation on this issue would end their political career. They therefore acquiesce.

TRADITIONAL MARRIAGE
(ONE MAN AND ONE WOMAN)

The majority of African-American voters are solidly opposed to gay marriage. California's Proposition 8 ban on same-sex marriage passed in 2008, thanks to overwhelming black support. According to exit polls, 70 percent of Black Americans backed the proposition for traditional Marriage.[30] Recent gay marriage legislation in Maryland drew opposition from leading Democratic African-American legislators in the state. The same ministers organizing the get-out-the-vote

---

29   http://www.rightwingwatch.org/content/abortion-hood-campaign-revives-black-genocide-smear.

30   http://www.sfgate.com/politics/article/Black-support-for-Prop-8-called-exaggeration-3177138.php

    http://angryblackladychronicles.com/2012/03/25/splitting-the-coalition-fractured-facts-on-blacks-and-same-sex-marriage/

efforts in black churches for Obama also railed against gay marriage. Issues like these will define the priorities of the Black Christian ministers and Christian parishioners.

California's Proposition 8 ban
Ban stating marriage is exclusively one man-one woman

The Black Community	**70% For**
NAACP Leadership	**100% Against**
Congressional Black Caucus	**100% Against**
Gay, Lesbian, Bisexual and Transgender	**100% Against**

THE NAACP

NAACP Chairman and Socialist Julian Bond and NAACP President and Socialist Ben Jealous publicly took a stance against Prop. 8, that defined a marriage between a man and a woman.[31]

CONGRESSIONAL BLACK CONGRESS

Black clergy, sixty of them from 26 states, came to Washington to meet with the Congressional Black Caucus. They invited the caucus to their Monday morning news

---

31   http://prospect.org/article/naacp-takes-stance-against-prop-8

conference in the Rayburn house Office Building, where they affirmed: "Gay marriage is not a civil right" and asked for caucus support in their opposition to same-sex marriage. The members of the Black Caucus were no-shows, except one, who arrived late.[32]

LABOR UNIONS & THE BLACK COMMUNITY

"The Caucasians… are not going to let their standard of living be destroyed by negroes, Chinamen, Japs or any others."
- Samuel Gompers Federation of Labor (AFL), 1905[33]

With support from labor unions, politicians and bureaucrats often intervene in labor markets, creating laws and regulations that (they say) are needed to improve wages and working conditions for working people. The truth is that many of these efforts do harm to the economic interests of blacks, particularly black males. Most people would be surprised to learn that this harm to blacks has historically not been an unintended consequence of these pro-union policies, but the intended result.[34]

From Davis-Bacon "prevailing wage" requirements to the creation of a government agency mockingly labeled the

---

32   http://blackinformant.wordpress.com/2004/09/09/congressional-black-caucus-disses-black-clergy-rant-of-fire/

33   http://capitalresearch.org/wp-content/uploads/2014/06/LW1406-final-for-posting-140528.pdf

34   http://capitalresearch.org/wp-content/uploads/2014/06/LW1406-final-for-posting-140528.pdf

"Negro Removal Agency," the government has undermined blacks' efforts to achieve success and to make the American Dream a reality. Many federal labor laws in the United States originated in efforts to saddle black men with extra burdens and limitations, in order to (as racists often put it) "protect white jobs." Tragically, these laws, in one form or another, remain on the books today and continue to hamper the ability of blacks, especially men, to enjoy gainful employment. Yet so-called Progressives hail these laws for their supposedly humanitarian effects, and praise the sponsors of these laws for their supposedly good intentions.

The idea of restricting blacks' access to "white jobs" was planted early in the 20th Century; took root in the 1920s; and blossomed during President Roosevelt's New Deal—a "deal" created in significant part by an Alabama Klansman.[35]

Much of that "bitterness" in those communities was due to the color of the competition's skin. As legal scholar David Bernstein observes, "In particular, white union workers were angry that black workers who were barred from unions were migrating to the North in search of jobs in the building trades and undercutting 'white' wages."[36]

In 1902 W.E.B. Du Bois, the influential black spokesman and historian, found that 43 national unions had no black members, and 27 others barred black apprentices, keeping membership to a minimum. Du Bois spoke against both "the practice among employers of importing ignorant

---

35   http://capitalresearch.org/wp-content/uploads/2014/06/LW1406-final-for-posting-140528.pdf

36   http://capitalresearch.org/wp-content/uploads/2014/06/LW1406-final-for-posting-140528.pdf

Negro-American laborers in emergencies" and "the practice of labor unions of proscribing and boycotting and oppressing thousands of their fellow toilers." In a 1917 incident, employers in East St. Louis, Illinois, recruited southern blacks to take jobs for low pay to drive wages down. White workers organized a whites-only union in response. Racial tensions mounted and in July an attempt to drive blacks from their neighborhoods led to a riot in which 40 blacks and 9 whites were killed.[37]

The Law of Seed and Harvest - The fruit of a tree is inextricably tied to the seed planted. Big Labor has from its being and will always have, an alternative motive. The ultimate solutions for the Labor Union always center on what is best for the Labor Union and those few who make a great living running it. If not for the presence of Black feet in the street protesting for its cause and the transfer of corporate revenue, via black workers' dues, the Black community would hold very little value to Big Labor. Every policy that it has supported over the last 100 years shows its lack of concern for the long-term plight of the Black Race. Only the Royalty Class Black Man, continuing to prioritize his ideology over the welfare of his race, refuses to see the obvious.

A question that should be asked by all... why is there a need for Black Americans to form a separate union, the Coalition of Black Trade Unionists, within a larger Union to ensure a fair and equal treatment? Why is there a need for the little man, the black worker, to protect himself from the interest of the white controlled and dominated White Labor Union? Black members have pushed against the AFL-CIO's

---

[37] http://www.shmoop.com/history-labor-unions/race.html

effort to pull decisions and power from local communities to a centralized power at the Unions HQ's. Unfortunately this shows the failure of our progressive educational system and a lack of understanding of socialism and communism. It is the very nature of these ideologies to ALWAYS, regardless of its promises, put centralized power into the hands of a few White Union Executives. What members of the CBTU (Coalition of Black Trade Unionists) do not recognize is that the powerful Labor Union might appear to appease, but power will go where they have decided it will go. This is the mandate that defines Socialism... the centralization of power.

Members of the Coalition of Black Trade Unionists (CBTU) pushed back efforts to "streamline" and consolidate the structures of the AFL-CIO threatening to diminish the influence of Blacks in the labor force. "We are concerned about the continuing lack of diversity among various leadership bodies within the AFL-CIO, affiliated unions, state federations, central labor councils, and local unions."[38]

The facts have proven over the last 100 years that where Labor finds itself, the welfare of its predominantly white members and 100% White Executive leadership will trump the welfare of the Black community. At the very core of the Black community's problem has been the presence of the Union's influence. This exhibits itself with the now prevalent anti-capitalist attitude held by most urban Blacks Americans and the empathy-free elitist attitude of many of its wealthiest. These ideals were purposely and by subversion facilitated by an organization whose leaders were Unionist and avowed

---

[38] http://www.blackcommentator.com/124/124_cover_black_unionists.html

socialist, the NAACP. No better way to see the heart and soul of an organization than through the alliance of its founders.

Big Labor's impact can be seen today in the racist Davis Bacon Act passed in 1931 which is still law. It protects white laborer jobs at the expense of Black laborers. It supports minimum wage laws that today, price non-skilled Black teenagers out of work. Big Labor's lobbying for No Choice education continues to trap Black children in a failing school system and represents the greatest adversarial force against Black free enterprise and capitalism. Capitalism has proven to be the only system available to the masses that grants unfettered access to the American dream and middle class lifestyle.

All of the NAACP's 1910 founders were white Socialists. As we've entered a new millennium, its leadership today are Black Socialists. It is not the color of the messenger, but the ideals of the message that has left the Black community in the dismal state that it is now.... *Class over Race.* Every failed urban Black city in America testifies to the end game of this doctrine, and where the Union and NAACP leaders' home addresses are never found. Typical of the Royalty Class Black Man is NAACP's former President, Julian Bond, "When labor reaches out its hand to racial minorities, labor and minorities win. When either turns its back on the other, America loses. We all lose."[39]

The lineage of the ideology of Liberalism now boldly presents itself in the present leadership of the NAACP. In the past it was white socialist, atheists and humanist standing unseen behind the curtains. The original white founders hide

---

[39] http://www.naacp.org/pages/statements-of-support-for-the-we-are-one-days-of-action

behind its one black voice, the socialist turned Communist, atheist and former American citizen W.E.B. DuBois. The anti-American, Anti-God, Anti-Free Enterprise ideology has finally after decades, gained enough acceptance through years of progressive education that many are now proud to call it what it has always been... Socialism. A the past chairman of the NAACP, Ben Jealous, recently stepped from behind the curtain to announce his support for a self-avowed Socialist for President of the United States, Bernie Sanders. Predictably there will be the coalescing of the remaining leadership of the NAACP, Congressional Black Class and Royalty Class Black Man in their support of this doctrine of deceit and envy.[40]

---

40   nycityeye.blogspot.com/.../not-just-field-tests-across-us-parents.htm

CHAPTER 11

THE NAACP STRATEGY: THE TROJAN HORSE

The Deepest Betrayal begins with Ultimate Trust

"Hundreds of years ago Greece and Troy were at war. The Greeks came in their ships to attack Troy. For ten long years, they besieged Troy but the Trojans would not surrender. There were strong and high walls around the city of Troy. No enemy

1   http://www.bing.com/images/search?q=Trojan+War+Horse&view=detailv2&&id=58
B7E4EE1304931AE5BAC83614B8D4633CD26A62&selectedIndex=2&ccid=cy%2
bNgCdZ&simid=608047123916654218&thid=OIP.M732f8d802759a2f1fdb471be27
40ec0ao0&ajaxhist=0

could enter the city when the gates were closed. The Greeks made several attempts to break down the walls and the gates but failed each time.

The Greeks built a huge wooden horse and placed it on a large platform with wheels underneath. A few of the bravest Greek warriors including Ulysses hid themselves in the hollow stomach of the horse. When the people of Troy opened the gates and came out, they could only see the wooden horse left behind by the Greeks. They thought it was the idol of some Greek God.

They gazed at the gigantic horse in admiration and excitement and soon dragged it into the city of Troy. The capture of the wooden horse was, to them, a symbol of their victory over the Greeks. They celebrated their success with feasting and merry–making. "The danger is over, at last. We can sleep in peace now," they said to one another. Late at night, they went to sleep.

In the dead of night, when the Trojans were fast asleep, the Greek warriors inside the stomach of the horse came out quietly. They opened the gates of the city for other Greeks to enter. The Greek ships which had pretended to sail away, now turned back quickly in response to the signal from their leaders inside Troy. Soon, thousands of Greek soldiers rushed into the city. They killed thousands of Trojans--men, women and children, burnt their houses and looted the city.

Even before the Trojans were fully awake, their magnificent city was in ruins. Before they could realize what was happening, Troy was in the hands of the Greeks. Thus, the Greeks succeeded in punishing the Trojans for their refusal to hand over Helen to them. The architect of their *great victory was the brainy and wily leader, Ulysses, who brought the long-drawn war to a close by this masterstroke of cunning and foul play. "[2]*

The story of the National Association for the Advancement of Colored People (NAACP) is the tale of two visions. One is represented by a legacy of courageous Black men and women who, for decades, were willing to sacrifice all for equal opportunity for their race. Many made the ultimate sacrifice for this cause. The communities in which they were raised believed in the promise of America. They were partakers of America's free enterprise system and were steadily progressing toward self-sufficiency and independence.

The other tale of the NAACP is one of stealth and deceit. As with the Greek Trojan Horse, the attainment of trust was but the first step to a devastating betrayal. The founders of this organization understood that only through strategy and stealth could the ideology of Liberalism find a foothold within the early 1900 Black community. For close to a century the Black American intellectual, W.E.B. DuBois, has been depicted as a driving force, a co-founder and one of the original leaders of the NAACP. Though he was accepted and embraced within the integrated intellectual circles of his day, the portrayal of him as a visionary NAACP leader is a false one. It is true that he was influential in perpetuating within his race, the new strategy of integration. He was also a staunch believer in communism and admirer of Adolph

---

2   https://arunsreenivas.wordpress.com/2007/09/26/history-of-trojan-horse/

Hitler and Joseph Stalin.[3] The true visionary NAACP leaders were its twenty-one original creators… wealthy white liberal, socialists and humanist members of the Executive Board. They ran this new and influential "Black" organization from behind the curtains, where all the powers of decision for strategies, priorities and direction resided.. As has been the history of Marxist/Socialist in the countries of China, Cuba, East Germany, Soviet Union, Vietnam, etc, it is an ideology that takes advantage of desperate groups of humanity in order to further its cause. Thus, with the formation of the NAACP, white opportunists converged with black desperation in order to create a force designed to not only confront the apartheid, Jim Crow culture of the era, but to also further the notion of "an empowered working class that controlled all aspects of ownership and production."[4] In 1910, the adoption of Socialism was the endgame, as it is with today's NAACP leadership. Nowhere is this more evident than the coalescing support by the NAACP for the 2016 Socialist Presidential candidate, Bernie Sanders.

Interestingly an organization whose reputation was built on the belief of Black leadership and vision, would take 75 years to elect a Black man to the role of NAACP President. Its first three white Presidents were known for their Socialist ties: Moorfield Story (1910-1915), Joel Spingarn (1915-1940) and Arthur Spingarn (1940-1966).[5]

---

3   http://blogs.christianpost.com/thinkingoutloud/naacps-founders-were-white-socialists-10757/

4   Ibid

5   http://storyreportscomments.blogspot.com/2010/07/naacp-was-founded-by.html

In 1910, DuBois was persuaded to join the NAACP after it was already established. He was given a place on the Board, free office space, a salary and the title Director of Publicity and Research. Translated, he was the Editor and messenger for the Crisis magazine. His assignment was to deliver the Board's message to the Black community. His articles required the approval of at least two members of the otherwise All White NAACP Executive Board before its release.[6]

The concept of the NAACP began in 1909 with Mary White Ovington, a wealthy white socialist, atheist and editor. She solicited the help of Oswald Garrison Villard, editor of Nation, a newspaper self-described as the "flagship of the left" and William English Walling, also a socialist and writer. Together they conceived a strategy that would change the course of the American race relations for the next 100 years. As a means of gaining entry to the Black community, they devised a name for their all white organization that would allow them access: the National Association for the Advancement of Colored People (NAACP).

At that time the Black community was moving in a direction that was the antithesis of forced integration. Its leader and respected advocate, Booker T. Washington, was a conservative capitalist and educator. He had developed a network of wealthy white philanthropists who were funding hundreds of Black southern schools and colleges. His message was one of self-sufficiency, believing that integration between the races would be a natural consequence of increased value of skills, entrepreneurship, and moral values within the

---

[6]   Answers.com/ Q/Who was the founder of the NAACP?

Black community. The progress of this self-reliance culture had become obvious with the success of the black colleges throughout the country. It could also be seen with the success nationally of black-owned businesses. This entrepreneurial spirit was highlighted at America's first business network convention, hosted by the Negro Business League in, 1910.[7]

Booker T. Washington founded the Negro Business League in 1900 with the support of Andrew Carnegie, spotlighting many self-made millionaires and in 1913 had as their guest speaker, the President of the United States, Theodore Roosevelt.[8]

So in 1910, the NAACP (National Association for the Advancement of Colored People) was created. Instructional are the facts that there were no Colored People involved, consulted, or granted any controlling power. A small group of very wealthy white socialist liberals/progressives and atheist/humanists took it upon themselves to implement a strategy for Black race relations that had never been used in the history of mankind, called "integration."

The dichotomy between the two visions of the NAACP can be seen in the life and contribution of the NAACP's first Black President in 1975, William Montague Cobb. Born in 1904, W. Montague Cobb was a Pioneering 20th-century American scholar: a medical doctor trained in anatomy and the first black American Ph.D. in physical anthropology. As a scientist, he refuted the myths of physical and mental

---

[7] Ibid

[8] Wikipedia.org/wiki/National Negro Business League. (shuterstock.com/pic239398909/stock-photo-Theodore-Roosevelt speaking at National Negro Business League. Seated to his left is Booker T Washington

differences between the races. While chair of the anatomy department at Howard University's College of Medicine, Dr. Cobb was instrumental in the passage of the Civil Rights Act of 1964 and the establishment of Medicare in 1965. At Howard University he built one of the world's foremost collections of human skeletons for the study of comparative anatomy. He also introduced creative new teaching methods. He is recognized as the first major historian of American blacks in the medical field.

Having received his bachelor's degree from Amherst College in 1925, Dr.Cobb went on to earn his MD from Howard University. In 1932, he was awarded a PhD in anatomy and physical anthropology from Western Reserve University. He served as president of the National Medical Association (NMA) and of its Washington, DC chapter. He was editor of the Journal of the National Medical Association from 1949 to 1977. He chaired the Department of Anatomy at Howard University College of Medicine, authored 1,100 publications on diverse topics and taught over 6,000 anatomy students.[9]

Dr. Cobb was a great example of our last great generation's tenacity, grit, intelligence and ability to reach for and obtain the American Dream. His success was earned at the height of the era of legal institutional racism in our country. Unfortunately, the progress that he worked for and envisioned has been undermined by the same organization that he trusted and was committed to. The opportunities that was available to him growing up as a Black youth in the Washington DC neighborhood have long been eradicated

---

[9]   https://en.wikipedia.org/wiki/William_Montague_Cobb

by the policies of the ideology of Liberalism--with the full support and protection of his NAACP.

The irony of this great Black American's lifework begins by looking at the Washington DC community in which he was raised. His community had accepted the premise that its progress would parallel other cultures and races that had embraced what can be best described as *The American Way*. The American Way is available to all who live in this country, regardless of race, creed or color. It's a seeking spirit that asks questions, pushing boundaries in a way that is only possible in a free society where its citizens are encouraged to think. It is a spirit that disregards one's present status and instead challenges all to dream big and envision beyond all obstacles, seen and unseen. It is a spirit that yearns for education and demands more than conventional thinking. Most important it's a spirit that encourages its citizens to see each other the way that God does: from inside-out instead of outside-in. This vision will forever be embedded within our country's founding documents, highlighted by three words, "We the People."

Based on what is known of the Black community at the time of the founding of the NAACP, a question arises that needs an answer. Would the 1900 Black America community have willingly accepted an allegiance with a 100% white run and controlled organization whose fundamental beliefs were totally contradictory to its own? Within the segregated Washington DC community of Dr. Cobbs, could be found the same messaging of success principles as in my segregated Tallahassee community 50 years later. The values and vision of our community were obvious, as were the need of stealth and deceit for entry by the ideology of Liberalism.

THE 1900S BLACK COMMUNITY AND JUDEO-CHRISTIAN VALUES

Religion played a major role in the lives of black Americans. The church was often the center of their social lives, offering in many cases the only place to gather that was free of white authority, especially in the South. In churches, black Americans were able to gather and speak freely about what concerned them, including illegal and immoral practices of whites against them. Another attraction was identifying Gospels in the Bible with their own oppression and recognizing that the Bible related a personal, historical context of their lives in the South.[10] The church was usually the first community institution to be established. Starting around 1800 with the African Methodist Episcopal Church, African Methodist Episcopal Zion Church and other churches, the Black church grew to be the focal point of the Black community.[11]

Churches served as neighborhood centers where free black people could celebrate their African heritage without intrusion by white detractors. It was the center of education, where as early as 1800, they educated the freed and enslaved Blacks.[12]

As will be discussed later, a Supreme Court ruling in 1947 would forever change the obligation traditionally taken by Black Church to ensure the education of its own children. A combined effort of an atheist, the anti-Christian ACLU and

---

10   http://dmckenn2.umwblogs.org/the-color-purple/page-5

11   Albert J. Raboteau, *Canaan Land: A Religious History of African Americans* (2001)

12   Ibid

a southern Democrat Supreme Court Justice/former KKK member, would introduce to the US Constitution a new tenet. It was a concept never mentioned in our Founding documents, the separation of Church and State.

Recently, through a series of genealogy documents, I was fortunate to "meet" my oldest known ancestor who arrived to America in the belly of a slave ship. The connection to the Christian faith and commitment to the education of our race can be seen through the remarkable life of this proud and educated American citizen.

My Great, Great Grandfather Silas Burgess, was born in Africa in early 1848. He was brought to America in the belly of a slave ship with his mother and younger brother. They were sold like cattle at the infamous Potters Mart Auction House, in Charleston, SC. The plantation owner who purchased him was a Mr. Burgess. After many beatings, rapes and a child from this owner, Silas's mother informed him that she could no longer endure the torture. She told him "You are the oldest Silas. You must take care of the children. I must leave and never return." She then prepared a large meal, left all that she owned of value, prayed with her children and left never to be heard of or seen again. Whether my Great, Great, Great Grandmother's plans were to escape or to take her own life will forever be left to speculation.

Soon after she left, the plantation owner appeared looking for her. He commented, "When I find her I am going to give her a beating she will never forget." Great, Great Grandfather Silas was eight years old at the time. He later escaped with the help of some male elders and made his way to Craft's Prairie, Texas, where he got his first job building the railroad.

He was described as a very spiritual and loving human being, who was fiercely independent and highly respected by the entire community. I was fortunate to experience firsthand these exact same traits in his great grandson, my dad. Great, Great Grandpa Silas raised his large family on 101 acres of farmland, which he paid off within two years. He was politically active as a member of the Republican Party and served the spiritual needs of his community as a Primitive Baptist Minister. He founded "Zion Hill," the first church and school for Black Americans in the entire region. The church building, as a school, is where children were taught subjects from the first to seventh grades.

He prayed often to God, asking that his seed not want for bread. His last prayer was beneath a giant family oak tree. It was a prayer for health and wellbeing of the generations to come. His prayer has since come to fruition, as his progeny have been granted opportunities for higher education and being part of the American middle class. One of his great, great, great grandsons played football and graduated from Notre Dame and, like me, played a few years in the NFL. Another great, great, great grandson played football and graduated from Yale University and like his mother is entering the medical profession. Yet another very determined and tenacious great, great, great granddaughter, is a single mother who has earned her Master's, and is contracted to leave within weeks of this writing, to teach in China. This is but a small sampling of the opportunities availed to just one side of my ancestral family by an educated, grateful, proud Christian and former slave. My great, great Grandfather Silas represented the "fiercely independent" spirit and the trajectory of his race at the turn of the 1900s.

How did this post-Civil War community's commitment to education, patriotism, free enterprise and God compare with that of the 1910 white organization that would represent it throughout the 20th century? One of the NAACP's original founders was John Dewey, a humanist/atheist and founder of today's Public School system. Humanist and atheist/agnostic are synonymous. It is a theological view that holds that there either isn't a god or that there is no way of knowing.[13] Dewey was consistent in his antagonism to God, as with the 1933 signing of the Humanist Manifesto, a document that contains a complete and thorough denial of God. It sets forth man as master of his fate and declares his utopia to be achievable.[14]

His political activities included President of the Teachers' Labor Union and co-founder and advocate of the American Civil Liberties Union (ACLU). His political linkage would explain the decades of commitment of the NAACP to the Education Labor Union and his anti-God ACLU, to the detriment of millions of poor Black children. It was with the support of Dewey's ACLU, that a group of atheists successfully argued the 1947 Everson v. Board of Education case before the Supreme Court Justice, Hugo Black. Justice Black was an anti-Catholic Democrat and former member of the KKK. Legal battles concerning the separation of church and state began in laws dating to 1938 that required religious instruction in school, or provided state funding for religious schools.[15]

The Catholic Church was a leading proponent of such laws; and the primary opponent was the ACLU. The ACLU

---

[13]   http://www.andrewaasmith.com/Humanism/Humanist_vs_Atheist.html

[14]   https://upstreampolitics.wordpress.com/2013/02/05/john-dewey-the-humanist/

[15]   https://en.wikipedia.org/wiki/American_Civil_Liberties_Union

led the challenge in which Justice Hugo Black wrote "The First Amendment has erected a wall between church and state.... That wall must be kept high and impregnable."[16] It was not clear that the Bill of Rights forbad state governments from supporting religious education. Religious proponents, arguing that the Supreme Court should not act as a "national school board," and that the Constitution did not govern social issues, made strong legal arguments. However, the ACLU and other advocates of church/state separation persuaded the Court to declare such activities unconstitutional. Historian Samuel Walker wrote that the ACLU's "greatest impact on American life" was its role in persuading the Supreme Court to "constitutionalize" so many public controversies.[17]

It should be noted that the Supreme Court justice Hugo Black's Court definition of a *high and impenetrable wall between Church and State* is nowhere written or referred to in the US Constitution. It was part of a letter that Thomas Jefferson wrote to Christian parishioners.

"Believing with you that religion is a matter which lies solely between man and his God, that he owes account to none other for faith or his worship, that the legislative powers of government reach actions only, and not opinions, I contemplate with solemn reverence that act of the whole American people which declared that their legislature should 'make no law respecting an establishment of religion, or

---

[16] http://www.heritage.org/research/reports/2006/06/the-mythical-wall-of-separation-how-a-misused-metaphor-changed-church-state-law-policy-and-discourse

[17] https://en.wikipedia.org/wiki/American_Civil_Liberties_Union#Separation_of_church_and_state\

prohibiting the free exercise thereof,' thus building a wall of separation between Church and State."[18]

In this letter, Jefferson was responding to a letter he had received from the Danbury Baptists of Danbury, CT. They were a minority denomination in that area and were subjected to persecution for their beliefs. They feared that if the government were to adopt a state religion, as it had done in England, that their minority views would be trampled, and they themselves subject to further persecution. Jefferson wrote his letter to them to reassure them that they would remain free to worship as they wished, without needing to fear government interference in their religious beliefs or practices. In fact, he borrowed the term "wall of separation" from famous Baptist minister Roger Williams.[19]

"Separation of Church and State." These five little words, in their misuse, have become the rallying cry of atheists, agnostics, the ACLU and others who wish to remove God from the public forum. This anti-God segment of our nation believes that a free expression of faith in God is incompatible with any government institution, practice, program, or official.[20]

The 1947 (ACLU led) ruling has impacted the Black community in a number of ways. It ended the 150-year influence of Black churches, like the Zion Hill Church of my Great, Great Grandfather Silas. It also impacted the community's ability to use its combined religious and public resources to provide the education it deemed important for its

---

18 http://www.usconstitution.net/jeffwall.html
19 http://contenderministries.org/articles/separationmyth.php
20 http://contenderministries.org/articles/separationmyth.php

own children. The long-term impact of the 1947 ruling can be seen in the increasingly aggressive bullying and intolerance of the ideology of Liberalism that is offended by any display of the Christian religion in a public venue.

NAACP - THE ACLU INFLUENCE

* **The ACLU** court case—In June of 2002, the 9th Circuit Court of Appeals ruled in favor of California atheist Michael Newdow, saying that the United States Pledge of Allegiance is unconstitutional because it contains the words, "under God."[21]
* **The ACLU** and Americans United for Separation of Church and State have successfully sued to have displays of the Ten Commandments removed from government-owned property.[22]
* **The ACLU** has recently attacked the governor of Alabama for having voluntary Bible studies in his office. They are leading the way in removing prayer and religious symbols from public schools. They are doing all of this under the banner of their favorite catch phrase—"separation of church and state." [23]

As the NAACP dutifully sides with the ACLU and other atheist groups that continue attempts to eliminate any reference to Judeo Christian values, we're left to question:

---

21   http://www.religioustolerance.org/nat_pled3.htm

22   https://en.wikipedia.org/wiki/American_Civil_Liberties_Union

23   Ibid

Is this what the predominantly Christian Black community had envisioned in 1910? Did they sacrifice their blood, sweat and tears so that one day America would be a society that allowed the legal intimidation and bullying of their great, great, great progeny by the ACLU, socialist/liberals and atheists? Would our past great generations have tolerated organizations that supported and cheered the PC bullying of the NAACP and Democratic Party? Could those Christian, faith-based pioneers have foreseen the day when granting salutations of Merry Christmas to non-Christians, would be paramount to hate speech? Would they have ever excused, as did the NAACP and the Royalty Black Class, any political party that would vote to delete the word "God" from their National Convention Platform? Would they tolerate the boos, jeers and shaking of fists by the party's 2012 Democratic National Convention delegates, as the amendment was passed to restore a mention of God?[24]

What would our past generations say if they could observe the control that the ideology of Liberalism has over many of today's Black Christian Ministers? These ministers profess their faith in Jesus Christ and then cowardly stand in silence or boldly walk arm-in-arm with anti-God Socialists and political Atheists. The subservience of many within the ministry highlights the unequivocal demands of the ideology of Liberalism, for it is satisfied with no less than total and absolute allegiance. Do we, as did our ancestors, defend our freedom to profess our faith or do we cower to the ideology of Liberalism and put our faith in the back seat? Will our Christian ministers lead, as they have throughout the past

---

[24] http://www.wnd.com/2012/09/democrats-boo-idea-of-mentioning-god/

proud history of the Black community's fight for freedom or will they follow a new ideological Master? There is no grey line or place for ambivalence for the Black Race. The choice is simple: *"We either stand as a faith-based race or we fall as one that is not."*

As Christians, we must remain fervent in our prayers that we, as a race and as a nation, remain steadfast and valiant, trusting only in the Savior and His promises. As we do so, we will be an influence for good. We will be blessed individually, but more importantly will be a blessing to others... those of the Christian faith as well as those who are not.

Based on historical facts, we can assume some things regarding our Black ancestors of the 1800-1960s. First, they were not lukewarm, whiners, weenies and wimps regarding their faith. Second, their vision was NEVER in concert with the vision of the NAACP, whose present policies remain consistent with the ideology of those who stood behind the curtain in 1910. The NAACP was, after all, an organization of twenty-one wealthy white liberals, progressives, socialists, humanists and atheists whose core values were antithetical to values of the community they purportedly represented for the next 100 years. As an organization formed on the strategy of stealth, the NAACP is ultimately symbolic of the Greek Trojan Horse for the community of Christian, capitalist, patriotic and independent Black Americans.

THE 1900S BLACK COMMUNITY FAMILY AND THE ROLE OF THE FATHER

In 2012 the U.S Census Bureau released a report that studied the history of marriage in the United States. They discovered some startling statistics. When calculating marriage by race, from 1890 until the 1960s, the study found that African Americans age 35 and older were more likely to be married than White Americans. Not only did they swap places during the 60s but in 1980 the number of NEVER married African Americans began a staggering climb from about 10% to more than 25% By 2010. During this time, the percentage for white women remained under 10% and just over 10% for white men.[25]

These statistics show that since the 1960s there were an increasing number of Black men not committing to their family. A 1965 report by NY Democratic Senator Patrick Moynihan, "The Negro Family: The Case for National Action," supports these statistics. In the report, Moynihan attempted to sound the alarm of the detrimental impact that the ideology of Liberalism's policies of federal welfare, were having on the Black family. One of many dire conclusions was that, "The steady expansion of welfare programs could be taken as a measure of the steady disintegration of the Negro family structure over the past generation in the United States."[26]

As early as 1965, Moynihan argued "without access to jobs and the means to contribute meaningful support to a family, Black men would become systematically alienated

---

25 http://blackdemographics.com/economics/employment/
26 https://en.wikipedia.org/wiki/The_Negro_Family:_The_Case_For_National_Action

from their roles as husbands and fathers. This would cause rates of divorce, child-abandonment and out-of-wedlock births to skyrocket in the Black community—leading to vast increases in the numbers of female-headed households and the higher rates of poverty, low educational outcomes, and inflated rates of child abuse that are associated with them."

The report concluded that the structure of family life in the black community "constituted a 'tangle of pathology... capable of perpetuating itself without assistance from the white world,' and that 'at the heart of the deterioration of the fabric of Negro society is the deterioration of the Negro family. It is the fundamental source of the weakness of the Negro community at the present time..., the matriarchal structure of black culture weakened the ability of black men to function as authority figures. This particular notion of black familial life has become a widespread, if not dominant, paradigm for comprehending the social and economic disintegration of late twentieth-century black urban life."[27]

Democratic Senator Monahan's report was prophetic. How did the NAACP respond? The Senator was maligned and ignored. As predictable with the ideology of liberalism methods of silencing and intimidating opposing thought, he was accused of infusing his report with racist assumptions.[28]

The report was sharply attacked by Black civil rights leaders as examples of white patronizing, cultural bias, or racism. It was condemned or dismissed by the N.A.A.C.P. and other civil rights groups. Black leaders such as Jesse

---

27   https://en.wikipedia.org/wiki/The_Negro_Family:_The_Case_For_National_Action

28   https://www.jacobinmag.com/2015/03/moynihan-report-fiftieth-anniversary-liberalism/

Jackson and Al Sharpton accused Moynihan of relying on stereotypes of the Black family and Black men. They said the report implied that blacks had inferior academic performance, portrayed crime and pathology as endemic to the black community. They failed to recognize that both cultural bias and racism in standardized tests had contributed to apparent lower achievement by blacks in school.[9] The report was criticized for threatening to undermine the place of civil rights on the national agenda, leaving "a vacuum that could be filled with a politics that blamed Blacks for their own troubles."[29]

James Farmer, civil rights leader and honorary vice chairman of the Democratic Socialists of America, noted, "By laying the primary blame for present-day inequalities on the pathological condition of the Negro family and community, Moynihan has provided a massive academic cop-out for the white conscience and clearly implied that Negroes in this nation will never secure a substantial measure of freedom until we learn to behave ourselves and stop buying Cadillac's instead of bread."[30] In 1987, Hortense Spillers, a Black feminist academic, criticized the Moynihan Report on semantic grounds for its use of "matriarchy" and "patriarchy" when describing the African-American family. She argues that the "terminology used to define White families cannot be used to define African-American families because of the way slavery has affected the African-American family."[31]

---

29   https://www.jacobinmag.com/2015/03/moynihan-report-fiftieth-anniversary-liberalism/

30   https://www.jacobinmag.com/2015/03/moynihan-report-fiftieth-anniversary-liberalism/

31   Ibid

Psychologist William Ryan, in his 1971 book, *Blaming the Victim*, also criticized the Moynihan report. He said it was an "attempt to divert responsibility for poverty from social structural factors to the behaviors and cultural patterns of the poor."[32]

Every segment of American sociality teaches importance of individual accountability and the mastering of actions/attitudes as stepping stone for success. Honesty, hard work, preparedness and a positive attitude are imperative. Most assuredly, these were the principles that the white Liberal Ryan taught his own children, for he envisioned their future as successful and productive citizens. The ideology of Liberalism has a different standard for urban Black Americans, lowering expectations of them and considering such an act as compassionate. Acceptance of lower expectations of a race is not compassionate, but is instead debilitating, condescending and extremely racist.

When our children reach the age of maturity, capable of understanding lessons of personal accountability, responsibility and critical thinking, we teach them. For our Special Needs children, these lessons are tailored to match their capability to learn. This is an act of compassion and a wise acknowledgment of the personal limitations of the Special Needs Child. This best summarizes the perspective of the Ideology of Liberalism toward the urban Black community. Viewed as children, incapable of making necessary changes in personal conduct and choices, they suggest that personal accountability be negated from the success equation. The ideology of Liberalism then convinces its followers that

---

[32] https://en.wikipedia.org/wiki/The_Negro_Family:_The_Case_For_National_Action

their failing status has nothing to do with personal choices i.e. dropping out of school, having babies out of wedlock, the lack of personal people skills or education, dismal work habits or inappropriate appearance and dress. After imposing for decades its multiple Anti-Black policies the ideology of Liberalism then blames individual failure on racist white Conservatives and their policies.

The consequence of the condescending low expectations placed on the poor is seen in every community dominated by the ideology of Liberalism. It is also seen in every Socialist and Communist country around the world. In this environment is seen a predictable constant... *the poor remain forever and hopelessly bound/dependent in poverty.*

From its beginnings in the early 1960s until 1996, federal welfare was an open-ended entitlement that encouraged long-term dependency. There was widespread agreement that it was a terrible failure. It neither reduced poverty nor helped the poor become self-sufficient. It encouraged out-of-wedlock births and de-emphasized work ethic. The pathologies it engendered were passed from generation to generation[33] Regardless of its obvious failure, the ideology of Liberalism continued to have its way in the Democratically controlled House and Senate, as members consistently blocked any welfare reform that would stem the growing government dependency of the Black underclass. It was the Democratic Party's stand that ending dependency of recipients on the Federal Welfare Government program equated to a lack of compassion for those who were dependent on it. With the increasing statistical evidence of the detrimental impact of

---

[33] http://www.downsizinggovernment.org/hhs/welfare-spending

welfare on the Black family unit, every Socialist/Liberal organization including the NAACP demanded the status quo.... no change!

After decades of Democratically controlled House and Senate (1955-1980) and (1987-1995)[34], welfare reform was finally passed in 1996 by a Democratic President Bill Clinton, supported by a Republican controlled House and Senate. The Personal Responsibility and Work Opportunity Reconciliation Act fulfilled his 1992 campaign promise to "end welfare as we have come to know it."[35]

As a result of this reform, 31 years after the predicted devastation of Federal welfare programs, welfare and poverty rates both declined during the late 1990s. This led many commentators to declare that the legislation was a success. An editorial in the ultra-liberal magazine, *The New Republic,* was left to opine: "A broad consensus now holds that welfare reform was certainly not a disaster—and that it may, in fact, have worked much as its designers had hoped.[36]

After five decades of dominance, the ideology of Liberalism media and the Royalty Black Class, introduced a terminology that would have been considered highly offensive by early 1900 Black Americans. It was the assigning segments of Americans to a hopeless status called "the Permanent Underclass." Defined as "people who are at the bottom of a society having become victims of the poverty trap. This class is largely composed of the young unemployed,

---

[34] http://www.answers.com/Q/What_years_did_democrats_control_both_house_and_senate

[35] https://en.wikipedia.org/wiki/Personal_Responsibility_and_Work_Opportunity_Act

[36] http://www.soc.iastate.edu/sapp/PRWORA.pdf

long-term-unemployed, chronically-sick, disabled, old, or single-mothers… who are therefore, unable to rise out of it."[37]

AMERICA'S PROMISE

One of the most unique features of the Promise of America is the access it gives each its citizens to upward mobility. It provides the freest environment on the face of the earth for anyone to choose to climb if he or she wishes, with a caveat that risk and failure are intrinsic parts of the equation. There is an increasing number of Americans who demand the presence of an arbitrator who will guarantee them equal results while negating all pain. This is the false premise of Communism and Socialism, but was never the vision of Capitalism, which can be summarized *"Where there is No Pain, there is No Gain."* The American promise is one that grants multiple opportunities to try and, if necessary, to start anew. A serendipity of the American Way is access to an unseen source of strength needed to transition through growth, called Hope. The promise of the America Way is predicated on an understanding that we're only required to do our best to maximize our own full capability. This gives us faith in a fair resolution as we inch our way to the other side of defeat, disappointment and betrayal. It is a journey that every American must take, making personal chooses along the way as to whether they will remain on the thruway or take one of its many off-ramps. If the choice is to remain steady, principled and to "not grow weary in well doing" happiness

---

[37]   http://www.businessdictionary.com/definition/underclass.html

is assured through the adoption of attributes such as faith, forgiveness, diligence, patience, charity and many others.

This is the message of Conservatism. This was also the belief of the Black communities of the early to mid-1900s, summarized in three cumulatively powerful words, *"We Shall Overcome."*

How does this compare with the Way of the ideology of Liberalism?" As we reread the definition of America's "Permanent Underclass," we can see how this ideology envisions those who are convinced to depend on it most. It sees a large segment of Americans as permanently too incompetent, too lost, too poor, too Black, too uneducated, too single, too angry and hopeless, and too hapless to ever find themselves out of poverty. It is this same segment of Americans that have been left reeling from the decades of anti-black policies imposed on them, keeping them poor. These policies predictably undermined the expectations of men to fulfill their divine roles, as it simultaneously undermined women's expectation for a loyal, competent and committed partnership. As the Royalty Black Class Politicians blame others for this downward trajectory of the community that they oversaw, they confidently demand continued loyalty by promising more of the same. Only within the ideology of Liberalism/Socialism are expectations placed on individuals based on their external attributes and status. Its influence grows only as it convinces its believers to view others from outside-in verses inside-out, dividing and highlighting their differences versus celebrating their commonality.

It is the ideology of Liberalism that refuses to acknowledge the basic underpinning of the American culture, which envisions a lineage of each individual to an all-powerful and omnipotent God. This spiritual heritage, unveils an unlimited human potential, making it impossible to assign a permanent economic status to any free American.

Yes, economic limitations and misery can be mandated, as it has been in the godless regimes of Cuba, China, Russia, North Korea and Iran. Mandating constraints on rights and freedom has never been the American Way. Ours is the one country that has for two-centuries, protected the freedom choose one's own pathway. It is the country that also acknowledges that with choice comes immutable consequences based on those choices. Because personal choices within a Capitalist society define our financial status, neither wealth nor poverty is guaranteed or permanent in America. Those who choose to live with hope, a tenacious work ethic, honesty and an empathetic spirit towards others will be blessed with their personal version of the American dream.

Those who choose the route of laziness, self-centered narcissism, dishonesty, betrayal and lack of vision—the poverty of mind, body and soul awaits them. Regardless of our choice, there is a coinciding link to our personal consequences. The Law of Seed and Harvest remains in force and like the Law of Gravity and the Law of Inertia is eternally predictable.

The fickle status of wealth is reported almost daily in our reality-TV culture. Outside the arena of sports and entertainment, the stories of Black Americans obtaining long lasting, real success through the utilization of traditional success principles are very rare. Those who have done so through the free market/capitalism remain unheralded. It is not beneficial to the ideology of Liberalism to celebrate Black

Americans who have, through their own ingenuity, tenacity and willpower, proven that the American Way works. The idea that poverty is a *choice* and not a permanent condition is a contradiction to the ideology of liberalism. It is a dagger that strikes at its very core when an individual recognizes that government dependency is akin to mental, emotional and spiritual slavery. Like a malignant cancer this form of dependency eats away the essence and value of the soul. It is worse than physical slavery because it enslaves the human will, necessary to fight for and win freedom.

This is why it is imperative for the survival of the ideology of Liberalism, that the successful voices of Conservative Black Americas are ignored or silenced. If they become too vocal and too visible they are, with collaboration of the Royalty Black Class and the White Liberal Elitist's BET, demeaned, discredited and destroyed if possible. Understood by the ideology of Liberalism is the threat that these independent thinking Americans pose to their dependent base of urban Black Americans. The message that escape is possible from the sweet enticement of government dependency and its Siamese twin, poverty, could inspire others to also seek self-sufficiency.

Such is the case of Conservative Black American, Star Parker. Star was a single welfare mother in Los Angeles, California. After accepting Jesus Christ in her life, she returned to college, received a BS degree in marketing and launched an urban Christian magazine. The 1992 Los Angeles riots destroyed her business, and yet served as a springboard for her focus on faith-based and free market alternatives to empower the poor. As a social policy consultant, Star gives regular testimony before the United States Congress, and is a national expert on major television and radio shows across the country. Currently, Star is a regular commentator on CNN, MSNBC, and FOX News. She has debated Jesse Jackson on BET; fought for school choice on Larry King Live and defended welfare reform on the Oprah Winfrey Show.[38]

Star has written three books, *Pimps, Whores and Welfare Brats* (1996), *Uncle Sam's Plantation* (2003) and *White Ghetto* (2006). In 1995, she founded the Center for Urban Renewal and Education (CURE),[39] which works with black religious and community groups on social policy issues like school choice."[40] She is also a syndicated columnist for Scripps Howard News Service, offering weekly op-eds to more than 400 newspapers worldwide.[41]

Star represents the possibilities, the rags to riches & middle class American dream, for millions of near hopeless Black Americans. She is independent, smart, articulate, courageous, accomplished and proof that poverty in America is a choice. It does not have to be permanent after all. She is a great example, a role model and a voice in the wilderness for millions of young Black girls, in a community solely lacking in hopeful messaging.

What has been the response of the pro-welfare ideology of Liberalism to this successful Black American Woman who has successfully broken the chains of welfare? There is no better example of the condescending, misogynist and racist

---

38 http://www.allamericanspeakers.com/celebritytalentbios/Star-Parker#sthash. a7DfvJmP.dpuf

39 http://www.urbancure. org/

40 https://en.wikipedia.org/wiki/Star_Parker

41 http://www.allamericanspeakers.com/celebritytalentbios/Star-Parker#sthash. a7DfvJmP.dpuf

based spirit of the ideology of liberalism, than the comments of White Liberal blogger, Gaius Publius. Typical of a Liberal white racist, he accepts the premise that he is an expert on the acceptable degrees of Blackness. From his exalted perspective he sees his role as a judge capable of defining for Americans, those who are truly worthy of being called Black. Consistent with white liberal racist is the liberty and comfort that he takes in disrespecting Black Womanhood.

As America's smallest minority segment, with the audacity to step out of place, the independent Black woman is granted the highest degree of distain from white liberal racist. As Publius verbally assaults and demeans another successful Black role model, he is also confident of the praise forthcoming from his fellow backslapping Liberal PC collaborators. He will travel home to his integrated community of liberals, expecting the accepting wink and nod from the ever-predictable Royalty Black Class.

This is the gang bullying cowardice that is typical of Liberal White racism. And though it is not politically correct to call a Black American who has stepped out of their place, "a Nigger," this group of white liberal men gleefully uses such terms as Uncle Tom, Oreo, Porch Monkey, etc. to accommodate their racist distain. They will, after all, have the blessings and cover of their good Black people, the Royalty Black Class.

Imagine the racist, misogynistic and disrespectful comments made of another Black woman of our day, the First Lady Michele Obama. There are both Black and White Americans who will never see this correlation, because they have unfortunately accepted the basic premise of the ideology of Liberalism. This premise states that the sacred nature of the Liberal ideology requires loyalty that is much deeper than that required for the honor and respect of Black Womanhood. Where has this liberal premise found its most secure home? With the *Whiners, Weenies,* and *Wimps* called the Royalty Class Black Man.

Gaius Publius, representative of White Liberal Racism, defines for Americans "a good Black" verses "a self-loathing bad Black" or as he calls us… Uncle Toms. The following are his comments about national leader, a successful, vocal Christian and a Black role model, *Star Parker:*

- An African-American unemployed single mother who got abortions the way normal people use tissues and who was arrested multiple times on multiple charges.
- An African-American unemployed single mother who got abortions the way normal people use tissues and who was arrested multiple times on multiple charges.
- A right wing huckster pedaling Republican nonsense-for-pay.
- Her specialty is phony moralizing and African-American self-loathing, as in   her pathetic autobiography.
- She pimps full-time for the GOP.
- Widely considered one of the most prominent Uncle Tom's of the GOP.
- The Republican Party cleaned her up nicely before they sent her out to talk trash about poor people and tell everyone that they should read the Bible and hope for a better life in Heaven.[42]

---

42   http://downwithtyranny.blogspot.com/2010/06/palin-picks-another-loser-star-parker.html#sthash.ManNUKP7.dpuf

I believe in the resiliency of the Black Race. Though its manhood has been under attack for over sixty years, there are still millions of *Real* Black Men, alive and well, throughout our nation. These are men who are proud of their race, their heritage, our women and who are willing to defend them all. It will be these men, who will demand — not beg, plead or negotiate —for the end of the disgraceful and degrading liberal attacks on Black American women. Whether our women have reached successful pinnacles of national visibility or not, it is time for this debasement to end.

It is time we call out every *black and white elitist,* who chooses to disrespect Black Women because they believe their racist misogamy is funny and in vogue. The age of covering for obnoxious, White liberal racism is over. As the ideology of Liberalism attacks and demeans Black womanhood it shines an insightful light on its view of Black Men, who are also viewed with disrespect. From the perspective of the 1900s Black community and my proud 1960s segregated community of Tallahassee, Florida, we ask: What kind of man "remains in his place" as our women are being verbally abused and assaulted? The answer from every other proud generation of men: *Whiners, Weenies and Wimps…*

NOTICE: *For the White Liberal Racists who have taken solace in the predictable cover granted to you by the Royalty Class Black Man while you, with smug confidence and no thought of consequence, denigrate our Black Womanhood, those days are over. The resurrection of the Black community will have within, men who will insure the light of exposure and free market consequences.*

The vision of the early 1900 Black Community for the role of manhood was simple and straightforward. Considered a divine one, it was based on loyalty and faithfulness as a husband, dedication and leadership as a father and as the ultimate defender of his family, community and country. The idea of self-sacrifice was by nature intrinsic, as it came with the territory. This was NEVER the vision of the Black man by the white liberals, socialists, and humanists—the founders of the NAACP. Their ideals from the beginning were a contradiction.... an organization steeped in socialism and atheism is a dichotomy of one founded in capitalism by a community of devout Christians. From this divergence of ideals and values came the strategic need for the Greek Trojan Horse called the NAACP.

THE PRESENCE OF THE NAACP

Where was the NAACP during the last 50 years as federal welfare programs undermined the Black family, as predicted in early 1965, and saw the increase in hopelessness and the abandonment by neutered Black males? As the facts began to surface about the deepening and ever devastating urban dependency, where was the NAACP pro-growth community strategy and their MAN-UP campaign? Where was the message that is consistent within every other successful minority culture of self-sufficiency, education, work ethic and the use of "commonsense" people skills? For decades the NAACP has remained lockstep, 100% predictable and loyal to the ideology of Liberalism and the white leadership of the Democratic Party. *Not once* has it broken ranks and shown

ANY backbone to side with the millions of Black Americans who have believed in them. Instead multiple generations of trusting poor Americans have suffered through decades of NAACP supported anti-Black liberal policies imposed on them.

As recently as the mid-1960s, the Black community ranked at the top of the scale for many of America's positive success indicators, i.e. education, marriage percentage, growth of its middle class, religious commitment, percentage of entrepreneurs, etc. Fifty years later, it ranks at the top of every national negative indicator: illiteracy, crime, murder, abortion, children abandonment, child abuse, unemployment, lack of entrepreneurs, etc. What has been the cost, per the misery index, and lives lost as the ideology of Liberalism has dominated every urban city government? Each of these present war zones have been led and dominated by liberal/ socialist Black politicians, liberal/socialist Black public school administrators, liberal/socialist pro-union, anti-Black employment policies and socialist market strategies. And yet, typical of an ideology that refuses to embrace the concept of personal accountability, it lays the blame for the lack of Black progress at the feet of the white race and Conservatism.

Unfortunately, since the formation of the NAACP in 1910, Conservative values, once the bedrock of the early 1900s Black community, have had an ever-diminishing influence. Standing behind the curtain of the Crisis, were twenty-one white socialists, liberals and atheist founding Executive Board members. Their first actions where directed at attacking Capitalism by maligning the foremost capitalist and educator of that day, Booker T. Washington. They successfully set in place his reputation, within the Black community, as an Uncle Tom. They then set about, over the following decades, to undermine the loyalty that the Black community once had for the Republican Party.

Booker T. Washington, an American hero, laid the foundation for more progress by the Black race than any other man in the 20th history. It is his Tuskegee University that will be known throughout the annals of time for its contribution to WWII, the legendary Tuskegee Airman. It is also the University that given to the American market place millions and millions of talented Black graduates since 1881. It was through his collaboration with Andrew Carnegie that, in 1900, the Nations' first Business Network was established. This Black Business network served as the foundation for the exploding Black middle class throughout the 1940s, 50s and early 60s. Through his collaboration with other wealthy philanthropist, millions of dollars were sent to support black high schools and colleges throughout the south and fund secret lawsuits against racist policies. This financial support was extended for decades after his death in 1915. In 1901, he was the first Black American invited to the White House, where he dined with the Republican President Theodore Roosevelt. In his last years he was warned to slow down his work pace due to health concerns. He dismissed these warnings, and died at his beloved Tuskegee days after an arduous fund raising tour throughout the northeast. His death was due to the complications from exhaustion and high blood pressure. This is the man who the ideology of Liberalism, the NAACP and the Royalty Black Man, have successfully tainted as an Uncle Tom. His sin... as an accomplished capitalist, educator, bridge-builder and Christian, is that he delivered a message of independence, self-reliance and self-sufficiency, defining him as a Conservative. To the ideology of Liberalism this is equivalent to putting a large Silver Cross in the face of Count Dracula.

Likewise, through persistent and effective messaging the ideology of Liberalism has been successful in tainting the Republican Party as racist. This was the party whose only purpose for existence in 1860 was to present to the country its first Anti-Slavery platform. Its first Presidential candidate, Abraham Lincoln, fulfilled that promise. It has throughout the 1900s consistently advanced pro-Black policies of anti-Slavery, pro-Reconstruction, anti-KKK, anti-segregation, pro-Civil Rights, pro-God, pro-Capitalist, pro-School Choice, pro-Traditional family, pro-Job opportunity (anti-Davis Bacon), and pro-Judeo-Christian values. This is the party that the Progressive Education and the Socialist Royalty Class Black Man, has cast as racist. It has been Black Conservative Americans with these views that have been cast as Uncle Toms. Of interest is that every Pro-Black policy listed above, other than pro-Civil Rights, the Liberal/Socialist Democratic Party have stood adamantly opposed to.

The NAACP, with its effective messaging, has obscured the real roles played by the Democratic and Republican parties in regards to the progress of Black Americans. It was the Democrat President Woodrow Wilson, who ordered the segregation the United States Navy and it was the General Dwight D. Eisenhower, later Republican President, who allowed African-American soldiers to join the white military units to fight in combat for the first time—the first step toward a desegregated United States military.[43] It was the Republican President Eisenhower, in 1957, who sent the 101st Airborne to Little Rock Ark to enforce the integration mandate. Many in the Democratic establishment convulsed with rage.[44]

The support of the 1867 Post Civil War Reconstruction Act and passage of the 1965 Voting Rights Act illustrates the convoluted, yet effective messaging of the ideology of Liberalism.

The post-Civil War Reconstruction period was a defining moment that cemented the loyalty of the early Black community to the Republican Party. During the Republican legislated Reconstruction era, which began in 1867, newly enfranchised blacks gained a voice in government for the first time in American history, winning election to southern state legislatures and even to the U.S. Congress.

Within a decade, however, reactionary forces, including the Democratic Party's terrorist organization, the Ku Klux Klan, reversed the changes wrought by the Reconstruction and restored white supremacy in the South.[45] Considerable violence and fraud accompanied elections during Reconstruction, as the white Democrats used paramilitary groups (the KKK) from the 1870s to suppress Black Republican voting and to turn Republicans out of office. In North Carolina's Wilmington Insurrection of 1898 white Democrats conducted a coup d'état of city government, the

---

[43]   https://en.wikipedia.org/wiki/Desegregation#In_the_U.S._military .

[44]   http://www.politico.com/story/2007/09/eisenhower-was-key-desegregation-figure-005885#ixzz41CLzr1ZA

[45]   http://www.history.com/topics/american-civil-war/reconstruction.

only one in United States history. They overturned a duly elected biracial government and widely attacked the black community, destroying lives and property. Ultimately, white Democrats achieved widespread disenfranchisement by law: from 1890 to 1908, Southern state legislatures passed new constitutions, constitutional amendments, and laws that made voter registration and voting more difficult. They succeeded in disenfranchising most of the black citizens. The Republican Party was nearly eliminated in the region for decades. [46]

[46]   https://en.wikipedia.org/wiki/Disenfranchisement_after_the_Reconstruction_Era

[47]   http://www.bing.com/images/search?q=democratic+post+civil+war+racism&view=d
etailv2&qft=+filterui%3alicense-L2_L3_L4&id=6A527DD42FE9BAB2408CB7818
35698D979EEA756&selectedIndex=6&ccid=w%2fCHSsvL&simid=608032843156
688285&thid=OIP.Mc3f0874acbcb54733c8bac0795788224H0&ajaxhist=0

On August 6, 1965, the Civil Rights Voting Rights Act was signed into law. In the Senate, 94% of Republicans voted in favor, while just 73% of Democrats voted for it. In the U.S. House of Representatives, 82% of Republicans voted in favor compared to 78% for the Democrats. Senator Everett Dirksen (R-IL), co-author of the 1965 Voting Rights Act, helped outmaneuver Democrat opposition: "There has to be a real remedy. There has to be something durable and worthwhile. This cannot go on forever, this denial of the right to vote by ruses and devices and tests and whatever the mind can contrive to either make it very difficult or to make it impossible to vote."

The 1965 Voting Rights Act achieved for African-Americans a major goal of the GOP's Reconstruction Era-civil rights agenda, which the Democrats had blocked a century earlier.[48]

THE 1900S BLACK COMMUNITY AND CAPITALISM

Dr. Cobbs father, William Elmer Cobb, moved to Washington from Selma, Alabama, in 1899 to work for the Government Printing Office. He later established his own printing business supporting his segregated community. His entry into the Black middle class was consistent with the prevalence of the entrepreneurial mindset of that day.[49]

In that same 1900 neighborhood, where Dr. Cobb's father was able to pursue his American Dream, it is now

---

[48] http://www.freerepublic.com/focus/f-chat/2565711/posts.

[49] https://en.wikipedia.org/wiki/William_Montague_Cobb

impossible for a Black man, with the exact same skills and ambition, to do the same. It is also impossible for young black teenagers, in these urban communities, to get work experience under the tutelage of members of their own race. William Julius Wilson, a sociologist, has published numerous works about the problems of poverty caused by the loss of good-paying industrial jobs, as well as the migration of residential populations, jobs and related facilities to the suburbs.[50]

This absence of good paying jobs and entrepreneurial opportunities within the urban Black communities can be laid at the feet of Anti-Black/Pro Union policies supported by the NAACP and the Congressional Black Congress. Since 1931, the White leadership of the Labor Unions, the White leadership of the Democratic Party, and the initial White Board members of the NAACP has successfully colluded to protect an anti-Black law called the Davis Bacon Act. The Davis-Bacon Act requires that federal construction contractor's pay their workers "prevailing wages (union wages)." The law was passed during the height of the Great Depression, with the intent to protect white workers, who belonged to white-only unions, from the competing non-unionized black workers. The act continues to have discriminatory effects today by favoring disproportionately white, skilled and unionized construction workers over disproportionately black, unskilled and non-unionized construction workers. Because Davis-Bacon was passed with discriminatory intent and continues to have discriminatory effects, its enforcement violates the Constitution's guarantee of equal protection of the law.[51]

---

[50] https://en.wikipedia.org/wiki/The_Negro_Family:_The_Case_For_National_Action
[51] http://www.cato.org/pubs/briefs/bp-017.html

The passage of the Davis Bacon Act only exacerbated the financial woes of the early 1930s Black community. Its cause and effect continues today as it deprives the community of Black entrepreneurs, job opportunities for Black laborers and the tax base derived from both. While black and white unemployment rates were similar prior to passage of the Davis-Bacon Act, they began to diverge afterwards. This problem persists today. In the first quarter of 1992, the black unemployment rate was 14.2 percent, even though the overall national rate was only 7.9 percent.52

Davis-Bacon restricts the economic opportunities of low-income individuals in a number of ways. Minority contracting firms are often small and non-unionized, and cannot afford to pay the "prevailing wage." The Act requires contractors to pay unskilled laborers the prevailing wage for any job they perform, essentially forcing contractors to hire skilled tradesmen, selecting workers from a pool dominated by whites.53

Thus the Davis Bacon Act constitutes a formidable barrier to entry into the construction industry for unskilled or low-skilled workers. This is especially harmful to minorities. Work in the construction industry usually pays extraordinarily well compared to that for other entry-level positions. Such jobs could provide plentiful opportunities for low-income individuals to enter the economic mainstream. The law's impact on the ability of minorities to find work in the construction industry has been particularly devastating. The Department of Labor's initial set of regulations did not recognize categories

---

52   http://fee.org/articles/davis-bacon-jim-crows-last-stand/

53   http://fee.org/articles/davis-bacon-jim-crows-last-stand/

of unskilled workers except for union apprentices. As a result, contractors had to pay an unskilled worker who was not part of a union apprenticeship program as much as a skilled laborer, which almost completely excluded blacks from working on Davis-Bacon projects. This effectively foreclosed the only means by which unskilled blacks could learn the necessary skills to become skilled workers.[54]

As unskilled workers must be paid the same wage as a skilled worker, the contractor is forced to pay laborers considerably more than the market value of their work. For example, in Philadelphia, electricians working on projects covered by the Davis-Bacon Act must be paid $37.97 per hour in wages and fringe benefits. The average wage of electricians working for private contractors on non-Davis-Bacon projects is $15.76 per hour, with some laborers working for as little as $10.50 per hour. Thus, even minority open-shop contractors have no incentive to hire unskilled Black workers.

Ralph C. Thomas, former executive director of the National Association of Minority Contractors, stated that a minority contractor who acquires a Davis-Bacon contract has "no choice but to hire skilled tradesmen, the majority of which are of the majority." As a result, Thomas said, "Davis-Bacon closes the door in such activity in an industry most capable of employing the largest numbers of minorities.[55]

Urban community residents watch as state and federally funded projects are built all around them. Consistent is the presence of predominantly white only Union laborers, whose members take and spend their paychecks in their own

---

54   http://fee.org/articles/davis-bacon-jim-crows-last-stand/
55   Ibid

neighborhoods, supporting their own neighborhoods and schools. Also consistent is the lack of opportunity and job experience for black teenagers. This ensures that the young Black male will consistently lack responsible role models, mentors and Black entrepreneurs, most of whom would hire their own if they had the opportunity. There is also no place in this community for inquisitive Black youth to learn and experience capitalism, that is found in other minority communities, such as Asian Indian, Chinese, Japanese, Cuban, Mexican, etc.

Black American's unemployment rates are high in every urban community throughout our country. In Chicago, unemployment of Blacks has reached a high of 25%, while the rate among the white Americans is 7% and Latinos 12%.[56] Chicago is the bastion of Liberalism and the home of the prominent Royal Class Black Problem Profiteer, Jesse Jackson. The unemployment rate among teenage Black Males there is an astounding 92%.[57] This equates to 92 out of every 100 black teenage males, in one of our nation's largest cities, denied the opportunity to work and learn successful life skills. If there is any wonder why Chicago leads the nation in the murder of Black citizens, the dire hopelessness of 92% jobless, fatherless, uneducated, vision-less Black teenage males is a good place to begin seeking an answer. This is the result of pure, unadulterated, unapologetic and unaccountable Liberalism.

---

[56] http://chicagoreporter.com/chicagos-black-unemployment-rate-higher-other-large-metro-areas/

[57] http://www.iamempowered.com/article/2014/01/28/chicagos-black-male-teens-92-percent-unemployment-rate-leads-nation.

Aside from the racist Davis Bacon Act, another very popular Anti-Black/Pro-Union policy of the ideology of Liberalism is the increasing of the minimum wage. Politicians from both parties understand the devastating impact this policy has on millions of Black lives. Unskilled labor, which defines the Black male teenager, is impacted the most. With each increase of the minimum wage Black teenagers are "automatically" priced out of reach of the small business owners who would normally hire them. Between being legislated out of work by the Liberal backed Davis Bacon Act, priced out of work by the Liberal backed minimum wage, and entering a competitive market with minimum education skills (controlled by a Liberal Union Public school) the Black teenager faces the perfect storm. It keeps him unskilled, unemployed, and in time unemployable.

The Black teenager has little to look forward to but a life of crime or dependency on federal government assistance. The liberal segments of both the Democratic and Republican Parties understand the math and the common sense that drives this issue. The typical Royalty politician, Black and White, views the sacrifice of these millions of lives through multi-generations, simply as the price of doing business. It sounds compassionate enough and guarantees a pathway to re-election.

Supporters of raising the minimum wage argue it will raise the earnings of low-income workers. Labor unions are among the most prominent of these supporters, a fact that makes little intuitive sense, because very few union members work for the minimum wage. Unions, however, are not just being altruistic when they push to raise the minimum wage. A higher minimum wage increases the expense of hiring unskilled workers. This makes hiring skilled union members more attractive and could raise the earnings of union members who compete with minimum wage workers by 20-40 percent. Meanwhile, non-union, low-skilled workers (Black American youth) earnings actually fall due to reduced working hours and fewer job opportunities.[58]. This helps to explain the 92% unemployment rate among Black American boys in the Union friendly Davis Bacon, high minimum wage bastion of Liberalism, Chicago, Illinois. Nationwide unemployment for Black male teens is 83%.[59]

The facts are, according to the CBO (Congressional Budgeting Office), that the lost jobs are broadly consistent with Employment Policies Institute earlier estimates. It found that at least 360,000 jobs—and as many as 1 million—would be lost from a $10.10 minimum wage increase.[60]

High minimum wage rates lead to unemployment for teens. One of the prime reasons for this drastic employment drought is the mandated wage hikes that policymakers have forced on small businesses. Economic research has shown time and again that increasing the minimum wage destroys jobs for low-skilled workers while doing little to address poverty.[61]

High minimum wage rates price teens out of jobs. When the minimum wage gets boosted, employers frequently cut down on hiring teens who typically fill lower-priority positions. Nearly half of all minimum wage earners are

---

58 http://www.heritage.org/research/reports/2007/02/union-members-not-minimum-wage-earners-benefit-when-the-minimum-wage-rises

59 http://madamenoire.com/342987/92-young-black-males-chicago-unemployed/

60 http://www.bloomberg.com/bw/articles/2014-02-18/the-cbo-foresees-lost-jobs-from-a-higher-minimum-wage

61 www.epionline.org/minimum-wage/minimum-wage-teen-unemployment/

teenagers or young people still living with their parents. Most of the work still gets done, but customers may get stuck standing in longer lines, and teens suffer because they've been priced out of the opportunity to work.[62]

Employers are unable to afford to hire more unskilled and inexperienced workers when the minimum wage increases. Ironically, one of the stated goals of the Fair Labor Standards Act (FLSA) is to "protect the educational opportunities of minors." However, as labor becomes more expensive for small businesses, managers are forced to hire fewer workers, leaving unskilled teens and minorities out of luck.[63]

The statistical data showing the associated negative impact on millions of poor Black Americans does not faze the empathy-free Royalty Black Class leadership of the NAACP. Their jobs and lifestyles are secured as long as their loyalty remains with the ideology of Liberalism.

Dr. Cobb's father's decision to leave the security of a federal government job to pursue his own business is practically unheard of in today's Black community. There was a contiguous mindset toward independence and private ownership during the early 1900s. In 1900, Booker T. Washington founded the National Negro Business League (NNBL), committed to the economic advancement of African Americans. NNBL promoted black-owned businesses as the key to economic advancement. The League included Negro small- business owners, doctors, farmers, craftsmen and other professionals. It also maintained directories for all

---

62   Ibid
63   Ibid

major US cities and incorporated African American contacts in numerous businesses.[64]

President Theodore Roosevelt was the featured speaker at NNBL's first National Business Network convention. In 1901 Booker T. Washington was the first Black American invited to the White House, where he dined with the President.

A 1907 photograph of businessmen commemorates the 13th annual meeting of Oakland's Afro-American Council, demonstrating the ongoing presence of a black middle class. Some black entrepreneurs—including several women—managed to find financial success through hard work and good fortune. Former slave Biddy Mason used the money she earned as a nurse to invest in Los Angeles real estate, becoming a wealthy philanthropist and founding the First AME Church. Mary Ellen Pleasant, another former slave, ran several businesses and restaurants in San Francisco and used her resources to fight for African American civil rights.[65]

African Americans today are over-represented in the government sector. More than 20% of the Black working population over 16 years old are employees of federal, state, or local government, which is just over 5 percentage points higher than the national average. On the other hand a much smaller percentage of African Americans are self-employed (3.6%) than the national average of 6.2%.[66]

In the present marketplace, government employment has become synonymous with unionized, safe, secure income,

---

[64] http://www.encyclopediaofalabama .org /article/h-2131. http://www.blackpast.org/aah/national-negro-business-leaguem .

[65] http://www.calisphere.universityofcalifornia.edu/calcultures/ethnic_groups/subtopic1b.html

[66] http://blackdemographics.com/economics/employment/

and a great retirement with lifelong medical benefits. Why risk entering the free market and aspiring for greater things when Government unions give guarantees without apparent risk. All that is asked of the Federal/State employee is to show up for their 9-5 workday, take their guaranteed paid vacation and sick days, support the ideology of Liberalism through Union dues and vote for pro-Labor Union's Royalty Class Black politicians.

The downside to a lifestyle dependent on government jobs is the possibility of a reduction in forces due to bloated size and/or inefficiency. This has had a major impact on the government-dependent Black middle class in Chicago. The black middle class relies heavily on employment with the city and the school district (in Chicago). It has suffered disproportionately amid massive layoffs.[67]

Leading the Black community away from the independent seeking voice of capitalism, represented by Booker T. Washington, was the subtle and patient message of the Ideology of Liberalism. Once delivered through the NAACP's Crisis, and now through Viacom's BET, the message of socialism and atheism is finally showing a sense of brashness. Empowered by decades of dominance, the ideology of Liberalism no longer feels the need to hide in the underbelly of the NAACP Trojan Horse, as they publically fawn over every Anti-American Communist despot around the world who is willing to buy their presence.

The Royalty Black Class Entertainers, JZ and Beyoncé, derived their multi-millions in wealth through American

---

[67] http://chicagoreporter.com/chicagos-black-unemployment-rate-higher-other-large-metro-areas/

Free Enterprise. Through the free market they delivered to the trusting black urban community their Hip-Hop music promoting gangster lifestyle, sex, drugs, anti-social behavior, misogamy, anger and Black racism. Once they'd acquired their financial freedom and wealth, they were the first to stand in line to celebrate the ruthless Cuban Communist dictators, the Castro Brothers. As they flew their private jet to the communist island to be treated like Royalty, they were surely unaware of the boats below them full of desperate Cubans attempting to reach the free shores of America. An empathy-free, narcissistic soul is typical of the Royal Black Class.

And finally stepping from behind the Socialist curtain 106 years in the making is the former head of NAACP Ben Chavis. Chavis formally and proudly announced his endorsement for the agnostic, Socialist Presidential Democratic Candidate Bernie Sanders. Nowhere in the history of the world of Socialism is God allowed to reign. On the other hand, steeped in atheism, Socialism has been the source of the persecution of millions of Christians and members of other religious faiths. When Sanders was asked by talk show host Jimmy Kimmel whether he believes in God, he replied: "I am what I am. And what I believe in, and what my spirituality is about, is that we're all in this together."[68] Unfortunately, due to the influence of the ideology of Liberalism it appears this "I am what I am" and "we're all in this together" answer is good enough today for many God-fearing Christians who are willing to vote for a person who does not believe in the Judeo-Christian core values that are at the center of every

---

[68] www.christianpost.com/news/bernie-sanders-atheist-believes-god-156166/#5KjDAQxFMuxrpu5f.99

Christians life. This answer would not have sufficed for the early 1900s proud Christian Black community nor would it have held water in my 1960s proud segregated community of Tallahassee, FL.

Each of the Democratic Candidates now stumbles over themselves to fly to Harlem to kiss the ring of the master Royalty Black Class Problem Profiteer, Al Sharpton. It is through their faith in him that these candidates envision the shepherding of the urban Black vote. Ironically this predicable procession unfolds every election cycle. This is the same Problem Profiteer who has made millions by promoting, articulating and advocating for every Anti-Black policy proposed by the Man behind the Curtain. And yet he continues to have the full support of those who are purposely left ignorant by him. Thus it is those within the socialized urban community, the fatherless, jobless, illiterate, dependent and perpetually hopeless, frustrated and angry who are left to ponder this truth: "The Deepest Betrayal begins with Ultimate Trust." *Political Free Agency* will put an end to the Royalty Black Class elitist "Class over Race" representation.

THE 1900S BLACK COMMUNITY AND EDUCATION

His father's success as a capitalist, the owner of his own successful printing business, allowed Dr. Cobb to attend the all-black Dunbar High School in Washington DC. Dunbar High boasted a remarkably high number of graduates who went on to higher education and whose general student body was rated as very successful. The school was considered the nation's best high school for African Americans during the first half of the 20th century and was instrumental in making Washington DC an educational and cultural capital.

As we consider the success of Black education institutions like Duncan during this era of increasing demand of integration, we recognize the presence of a subtle message not missed by either race. Quality Black schools, communities and businesses across the nation were never targeted for integration. The demand from the NAACP, was that only white schools and businesses would forcibly share their property and resources, not Blacks. With this demand is the subtle admission of the innate inferiority of Black property/resources. As is the central theory of free-market *Supply and Demand,* the higher the demand the higher the valuation of the product being supplied. As the ideological *Demand* for the transfer of black students to white schools and tax-paying Black middle class to white communities, the result was a devaluation of Black schools, teachers, coaches, administrators and property left behind. Thousands of talented and experienced Black Americans lost their livelihoods during this initial period of integration. The Black middle class in particular took a hit, with increased closings of once successful Black businesses within their community. Apparently viewed as a necessary sacrifice for the cause, the NAACP was silent in its protest during this big economic hit on the Black Community. Following desegregation and demolition of the original facility, Dunbar High School's prestige dropped notably. Through the years the school, with an enrollment of 98% Black American, has continued to perform below standards and was among a list of failing schools identified for turnaround or closure.[69]

---

[69]   https://en.wikipedia.org/wiki/Dunbar_High_School_%28Washington,_D.C.%29

If he had known, would Dr. Cobb have supported an organization whose strategy was based on a premise that every black owned and controlled entity was innately inferior to white owned entities? Did he expect that success in this integration endeavor would mean the mass exodus of the Black middle class, as in the 1970s TV series, The Jefferson's', "moving on up and out" of their own community? Would he have agreed to give credibility to an organization whose values were the antithesis of his father's pro-capitalist generation, controlled by white liberals, socialists and atheists that would leave his once proud Alma Mata a dismal educational failure?

The educational opportunity that was once offered to Dr. Cobb's 1920 student body, is no longer available in *any* school system in the country that is now predominantly Black. Was that the vision of this extraordinary and dedicated educator? The NAACP commitment to the policies of the ideology of Liberalism and its extension, the Teacher's Labor Union, has assured that Dunbar High School, once one of our nation's best high schools, will remain a simple footnote.

The ideology of Liberalism has a strong foothold within today's public educational system. The ideals of the pro-union and pro-ACLU founders, John Dewey and Mary Ovington, can be seen in the present policies of the NAACP. Its total commitment to ideology has betrayed the community that trusted them. As it was with the lost jobs for thousands of Black educators due to its integration push, it has for decades sacrificed the education for millions of Black American children at the altar of Labor Unions.

There is no better illustration of this loyalty to class over race, than with the "very first Executive Action" by the first Black President of the United States, after taking his oath of office. Though 99.9% of the Black urban community supported his candidacy and continues to support his Presidency, President Obama's very first action in office was one of gratitude to the White-controlled Education Labor Union. He defunded a very successful school choice program that supported over 2,000 Washington DC inner city black children every year. With a graduation rate over 91% and close to this percentage electing to go on to college, Republicans, Democrats, Independents and parents praised the program.[70]

Because School Choice presents a competitive environment demanding lower cost, lower tolerance to incompetency, and measurable accountability, the Labor Union stands adamantly against it. None of these criteria is in the best interest of their members. In his first act as President, Obama stood with the 100% backing of the NAACP and Royalty Class Black Politicians to end the school choice vouchers for DC's poor Black children. They prioritized instead the protectionist policies of dues paying Labor Union adults. The results of these anti-choice policies, very popular with the Democratic Party, are drastically fewer Black children in successful "state of the art" schools. Instead, as in the private school that President Obama's daughters attend, there is a concentration of the children of the Black and White wealthy elitists. "Class over Race."

Once the Washington D.C. school choice programs ended, and the poor urban children sent back to their failing and dangerous public schools, President Obama's Department of Justice then proceed to sue Louisiana's very successful school voucher system. Consistent with the ideology of

---

[70] https://en.wikipedia.org/wiki/D.C._Opportunity_Scholarship_Program

Liberalism is its empathy–free policies, of which the Anti-School Choice targeting of the poor and the powerless, is a prime example.

THE NAACP STRATEGY

W.E.B. DuBois deserves all the credit for disseminating, thru the NAACP magazine Crisis, the new concept of integration; and creating the belief in the mind of the urban black man that he did have a right to receive—what no male group had ever received in all of human history - integration rights into another male group's established society. Prior to 1909, the idea of one race demanding a share in the proceeds, property and work of another race had never been a consideration.[71] All minorities, including Black Americans, instead addressed the barriers of exclusion, prejudice and bigotry by creating value within. They supported their own enterprises, built and expanded their own communities, and educated their own children. Prior to this new messaging, Blacks had never marched in protest against the current "separate" living arrangements.[72] By 1917, most northern urban black newspapers followed the lead of the Crisis and demanded that integration was a legitimate right for their people.

Three white members of the white society elites met in February of 1909 with representatives of the black community to get a gauge of how receptive they would be to their new

---

[71] http://www.answers.com/Q/Who_was_the_founder_of_the_NAACP
[72] Ibid

integration agenda. Overton had known DuBois from Harvard and was aware of his northern black professional group, the now defunct Niagara Movement They had organized earlier to protest Booker T. Washington's strategy and demand that white Americans commit to race-nullification, among other things.[2] Ovinton, Walling and Villard were able to persuade this group of black professionals that integration would expedite social justice. Once they knew the idea of integration would be supported, the NAACP was created in 1910. Its initial Executive Committee board was comprised of twenty-one wealthy, white socialists, liberals and at least one humanist. Most founding members were accomplished journalist, authors and editors but to DuBois would be given the role as the editor and face of the organizations magazine, THE CRISIS. The founder and "The Nations" owner, Villard funded the NAACP's budget and provided free office space in the Evening Post building for DuBois.73

The only thing required of him from the board was that he mailed copies of his CRISIS articles to each of the Executive Board Committee members for their approval before publishing. The board made every effort to control the message that was delivered to the black community.

Through The NAACP's Crisis, a campaign was launched to diminish Booker T. Washington's influence and his fund raising efforts for Tuskegee. Among the disagreements between DuBois's class of northern Royalty Class Black Professionals and Booker T Washington was their opposition to the mission of Tuskegee University and its "Industrial Education." They considered work related

---

73   http://www.loc.gov/exhibits/naacp/founding-and-early-years.html

to farming, agriculture and other businesses that required manual labor as demeaning and too closely related to slavery. They preferred programs and curriculum emphasizing Liberal Arts, as those taught at Ivy League Universities like Harvard.

As DuBois's group of northern Black professionals, the Talented Tenth, attacked the character and agenda of Washington, they also inhibited his ability to raise funds for the very successful All-Black Tuskegee University.

Although white liberals established the NAACP, it became a black parallel system to the liberal white system of power distribution. The NAACP was never a radical organization. It represented an expression of a class and regional division within the black population. Northern or northern educated blacks and the black professional class were the primary supporters of the NAACP and in this sense it was an elitist organization. The NAACP is definitely not a supporter of mass movements, such as those that would have been favored by a Vernon Johns and a Martin Luther King, Jr. Tuskegee University and the NAACP reflected the political continuum and distribution of power between conservatives and liberals. More importantly, neither the whites nor the black liberals were interested in radical change. That is still true of the situation today.[74]

Not surprisingly, when the new and revolutionary NAACP was launched, though it was created and run by White people, it wasn't in any way popular among the numerically and culturally dominant White population. In fact, white Americans steadfastly rejected the agenda. This attitude

---

[74] http://www.vernonjohns.org/vernjohns/sthprgrs.html

was likely rooted in simple and logically sound reasoning that Blacks, being a distinct people, <u>should be separate</u> and thereby achieve self-reliance, which would produce a feeling of empowerment as a people. This was Booker T. Washington's desire and pursuit. White philanthropists also believed Blacks should be separate and a self-reliant people, and therefore did not offer financial help to the NAACP in its formative years. [75]

DuBois became the favorite of another prominent atheist and liberal, Margaret Sanger. As a proponent of the KKK, pro-eugenicist, racist and founder of Planned Parenthood, she took the NAACP Strategy to new heights. A brilliant strategist, she invited DuBois and a host of other prominent middle class Royalty Class Black professionals to join her board(s) as she began her abortion foray on the black community of Harlem in 1929. The "NAACP Strategy" model, for which he served as the prototype, has served for over 100 years as an effective means of delivering to the Black community the message of Socialism by avowed Socialist. It is a message controlled by others who have remained hidden, behind the curtain. For over a century those providing the message have been the antithesis of the Black, Christian, Capitalist, Visionary and family Centered community of the early 1900s.

That model of stealth, the Trojan Horse, is still in use today by some of our nation's largest media corporations. An example is Viacom, a multibillion-dollar media corporation. Eighty per cent of the voting shares are owned by Ultra-Liberal/Progressive ideologue, Sumner Redstone.. [76] In 2001,

75   http://hubpages.com/education/NAACP-Its-Beginning

76   https://www.ft.com/content/4fa2a860-945c-11e5-bd82-c1fb87bef7af

Viacom purchased BET (Black Entertainment TV) for 3 billion dollars. The purchase of BET negated all influence of messaging to the Black community by Black Americans. No Black American serves on the controlling Viacom Executive Board of Directors, which oversees the BET programming. Though purchased in late 2000, controlled and directed since 2001 by a white corporation, Viacom, BET is still perceived by its Black audience as Black controlled. Viacom later employed a strategy that led to the bankruptcy of the last black-owned and operated, full-power TV stations in our country, Roberts Broadcasting.[77]

Roberts Broadcasting programming featured ordinary portrayals of African Americans. As mentioned previously, in 2006 there were eighteen African American-owned and operated full-power commercial TV stations, representing just 1.3 percent of all such stations. In 2013 there were none. Predictably there is silence from the Royalty Black Class and Problem Profiteers regarding concerns of lack of Black American leadership and influence in the exclusive white Executive Board Rooms of Corporate Media.[78]

James Winston, the Executive Director of Washington-based National Association of Black Owned Broadcasters expressed concern about the sale of BET. He stated, "There will not be African-American ownership at the very top, and I think that makes a difference."[79] In 2010, James spoke before a House of Representative Oversight and Government

---

[77] http://newpittsburghcourieronline.com/2013/12/30/number-of-black-owned-tv-stations-plummets-to-zero/

[78] http://newpittsburghcourieronline.com/2013/12/30/number-of-black-owned-tv-stations-plummets-to-zero/

[79] http://abcnews.go.com/Business/story?id=89100andpage=1

Reform Committee, regarding the policies being implemented that were forcing Black Entrepreneurs out of the industry. It should be noted that the liberal Democratic Party controlled the House and Senate under the leadership of the first Black President, also a Democrat. Even after hearing the concerns of the National Association of Black Owned Broadcasters, nothing was done. As is the priority of the Royalty Class Black Politician, who has never risked entry into the Free Market, there is no empathy for the Black entrepreneur. They remain unaware and unmoved that it was the Black Capitalist who was responsible for the rise of a robust 1940s, 50s and 60s middle class.

"Unfortunately, in recent years we have seen a substantial decline in the number of minority companies owning broadcast stations. This decline has been precipitated by government policies that encouraged the consolidation of the industry into the hands of a few large conglomerates, the credit crisis which has resulted in the bankruptcies of several African American owned companies, and a flawed Arbitron audience measurement service that fails to adequately estimate Black audiences." - James L. Winston[80]

Viacom paid the former BET owner Robert L. Johnson more than $2.3 billion and assumed nearly $600 million of BET's debt. At the time generating $225 million in revenue. It made him America's first Black American billionaire.[81]

The purchase granted Viacom entry into an established and trusting venue, the black urban market. This environment, already accepting of the filthy language, anti-authority and

---

[80]   http://oversight.house.gov/wp-content/uploads/2012/01/20100224winston.pdf

[81]   http://abcnews.go.com/Business/story?id=89100andpage=1

anti-women messaging of gangster rap was ripe for the ideology of Liberalism. It was also a cause of collaboration by the Royalty Black Class, once a whiff of super wealth was in the air. Johnson was quick to note that the deal had received the blessing of the **Royal Black Problem Profiteers**. He mentioned that in considering this deal he talked to several leaders in the black community, including Rev. Jesse Jackson. Together they concluded that selling to Viacom would provide a "boon to the black community."

How personally becoming a billionaire and leaving all future control of Black messaging to a powerful white Liberal controlled corporation is "a boon to the Black community" has still yet to be explained. The fact is that Johnson will not be creating new jobs for Black Americans nor will he be spending his money in Black American communities, supporting Black American business. As a wealthy member of the Royalty Black Class and a loyal Democrat, he will remain supportive of the anti-Black entrepreneur Davis Bacon Act, the anti-employment for unskilled Black teen labor, high minimum wage initiatives and the anti-school choice education for poor Black children. The statement that his wealth is a "boon to the Black community" is a stretch if looked at in the conventional way. Translated into the language of Royalty it becomes clear his real meaning. What Black billionaire, Robert L. Johnson, really meant was that his wealth was "a Boon" for the Royalty Black Class and the ideology of Liberalism. What can be counted on within the small circle of wealthy Royalty members is their support for each other. There will be a very sizable charitable "tax write-off "check clearing the bank account of our Royalty Class Billionaire written to the "non-profit" organizations of the Royalty Black Problem Profiteers', who will "pay themselves and use the remainder as a "tax write off" in their *get out the vote* effort. Their goal: to once again get the hopeless and desperate underclass Black motivated for another voting cycle to re-elect a retread of the Civil Rights "oldie but goodie" Royalty Class Black Politicians. "Let's make those old, white, racist, rich Republicans pay for what they've done to you," is the masterful message that has always worked....it has for decades. The Royalty Class Black Politician then shows their gratitude to their hopeless but trusting constituents by submissively voting for *every* anti-Black liberal policy demanded of them by powerful Liberal controlled corporations, like the all-white Corporate Board of Viacom (BET), . This is the true "boon" that Johnson envisions.... White and Black liberal elitists racing to the top for more trappings... power, wealth, lifestyle and bragging rights in their wealthy integrated neighborhoods of other Royalty.... *Class over Race.* Since none of them will be spending their money with Black owned businesses located in the Black community, it once again shows the deceit and betrayal of this empathy-free class of Americans.

"We are proud to be combining with Viacom to better serve the African-American community," Johnson said. "This provides a beacon for others. This is an opportunity for the black community to receive more information, more entertainment and more relevant news."[82] What Johnson fails to mention is that the entertainment, information and relevant news is now fed unfiltered into the young urban Black community without input from concerned, caring and

---

[82]   http://money.cnn.com/2000/11/03/deals/viacom/

visionary Black Americans. Johnson remained employed until 2006, but was not offered a seat on the Corporate Executive Board. Like his protégé, W.E.B. Dubois, he became the trusted face of a white owned corporation with its own agenda for the Black community. Like W.E.B Dubois, Johnson was simply another highly compensated employee without control. For the ideology of Liberalism, regardless of the elaborate Black facade, control will always remain in the hands of *The Man Behind The Curtain*. This defines the subtlety of the "NAACP Strategy."

This truth became apparent to the very loyal W.E.B. Dubois in 1932, when he found himself no longer in sync with the White controlled NAACP Board of Directors. After sixteen years of loyalty as editor of The Crisis delivering the Boards' message of integration and socialism to the Black community, Dubois began to see the merit in Black segregation. During the years of the Depression when the Black community was the most vulnerable, he saw segregation as an effective strategy to bind blacks together economically.[83] He recognized that integration was financially hurting the black community as Blacks continued to support white businesses, forsaking their own. His new understanding of segregation as a beneficial strategy would encourage black patrons to support their own community's black owned businesses. For this radical departure from the NAACP white Executive Board's mission, Du Bois was fired.[84] He was later re-hired but fired again for the last time, prior to the beginning of WWII.

---

[83] *http://college.cengage.com/english/lauter/heath/4e/students/author_pages/modern/dubois_we.html*

[84] Ibid

W.E.B. Dubois's legacy will rest on the divisiveness that he brought to his race as he convinced a significant number of them of the premise of the atheist-based science of Eugenics. This pseudo-science suggest that some of the Black race, based on mixed skin tone, European hair, intelligence or classical education were genetically superior than others. (The Talented Tenth). If only he could get the "ignorant" class of Black people from reproducing, the Talented Tenth would "raise up those deemed worthy."

His legacy will be his facilitation of the socialist and atheist message of the white NAACP founders that would lead his race away from the path to self-sufficiency and independence. The free enterprise message of capitalism that had been a bridge to the American Dream for every other American race, was not to be taught to his community. Instead, Black Americans have been guided to see themselves as a consumer race instead of one that manufactures and produces value of its own. It has subtly been messaged over decades that others property and presence is of more value than their own. This has facilitated the acceptance of the debilitating dependency of socialism in every US urban community.

His legacy will be his introduction into the Black community of the *Black Widow Spider* and deadly abortionist, Margaret Sanger. Abortion is now the leading killer of Black Americans and has morphed into the most hideous forms of infanticide... partial birth abortion, selective sex abortions and now "Live Birth" abortions, which was advocated in 2003 by then Senator Barack Obama[85]

---

[85] http://www.newsbusters.org/blogs/warner-todd-huston/2008/08/13/obama-lied-about-vote-against-live-birth-abortion-ban-media-mum

Perhaps after being fired twice from the NAACP and his diminishing presence in a post war of patriotic and capitalist Black Americans, DuBois felt alone with a sense of betrayal by his former circle of white liberal and intellectual socialists. He was after all, based on his own predictions as a young man, to be the Savior of his race. It's possible that it was this reflection that caused him to muse at the end of his life, "In my country for nearly a century I have been nothing but a NIGGER."[86]

Unfortunately for W.E.B. DuBois, it took his entire 90-year lifetime to recognize the empathy-free ways of his chosen ideology. At the end of his life, no longer valued by his former comrades as an All-Star player, this does confirm another age-old Eternal Truth: "You reap what you sow."

W.E.B. DuBois

---

86   http://xroads.virginia.edu/~UG03/souls/DuBoisLife.html

87   http://www.bing.com/images/search?q=W.+E.+B.+Du+Bois&view=detailv2&&id=F
F1B4FBA25843A54104D516C72E9863C67143FA0&selectedIndex=7&ccid=lFovr
hPH&simid=608038005697086219&thid=OIP.M945a2fae13c772359b91779d711d5
52aH1&ajaxhist=0

A staunch believer in communism and admirer of Adolph Hitler and Joseph Stalin.[88]

"One can hardly exaggerate the moral disaster of [religion]. We have to thank the Soviet Union for the courage to stop it."

- W.E.B DuBois

"Capitalism cannot reform itself; it is doomed to self-destruction. No universal selfishness can bring social good to all."

- W.E.B. DuBois

"Communism—the effort to give all men what they need and to ask of each the best they can contribute—this is the only way of human life. It is a difficult and hard end to reach—it has and will make mistakes, but today it marches triumphantly on in education and science, in home and food, with increased freedom of thought and deliverance from dogma. In the end communism will triumph. I want to help bring that day."[89]

- W.E.B. DuBois

The following are the original founders of the NAACP. Their occupations were diverse, including journalist,, editors, attorneys, college professors, wealthy social and political reformers, magazines owners and Labor Unionist advocates. Each was essentially socialist in philosophy and seized the

---

[88] http://blogs.christianpost.com/thinkingoutloud/naacps-founders-were-white-social-ists-10757/

[89] https://en.wikiquote.org/wiki/W._E._B._Du_Bois

opportunity to advance the socialist-progressive movement by incorporating the black struggle and anti-racism efforts during the early 1900s.[90] With another common theme of Atheism, two of the white NAACP founders also founded the nemesis of Christian organizations, the ACLU. As a Socialist opportunist, John Dewey was associated with 15 Marxist front organizations,[91] considered the Father of the Progressive, Union controlled Public School system and the pro-Labor Union advocate.

Small wonder that a bewildered Marcus Garvey stormed out of NAACP headquarters in 1917, muttering that it was a white organization.[92]

1910 WHITE FOUNDERS AND EXECUTIVE BOARD MEMBERS OF NAACP

RAY STANNARD BAKER
Socialist: **White Executive Board Member of NAACP.** Journalist, author, and biographer of Woodrow Wilson. After supporting President Theodore Roosevelt, Baker flirted briefly with socialism for several years before embracing the candidacy of Woodrow Wilson in 1912. Serving as Wilson's press secretary at Versailles, he eventually published fifteen volumes on [93]

---

[90] http://blogs.christianpost.com/thinkingoutloud/naacps-founders-were-white-socialists-10757/

[91] http://www.eagleforum.org/educate/2001/sept01/socialism.shtml

[92] http://www.kevinmacdonald.net/Jews&Blacks.pdfrters

[93] http://www.swarthmore.edu/SocSci/rbannis1/Baker/index.html

94

JOHN DEWEY– ACLU founder & Father of Modern Public School System
Atheist, Socialist and Humanist: White Executive Board Member of NAACP.

"You can't make socialists out of individualists. Children who know how to think for themselves spoil the harmony of the collective society, which is coming, where everyone is interdependent."

- John Dewey[95]

"Faith in the prayer-hearing God is an unproved and outmoded faith. There is no God and there is no soul. Hence, there are no needs for the props of traditional religion. With dogma and creed excluded, the immutable truth is also dead and buried. There is no room for fixed, natural law or moral absolutes.
-John Dewey"[96]

---

[94]   http://www.bing.com/images/search?q=John+Dewey&view=detailv2&&id=4246F71 DD481CC8FAA209D042760016F052C79E9&selectedIndex=0&ccid=jjTebp%2bX &simid=608033212515418548&thid=OIP.M8e34de6e9f97697289723d39bdca5c44 H1&ajaxhist=0

[95]   http://www.eagleforum.org/educate/2001/sept01/socialism.shtml

[96]   John Dewey, "Soul-Searching," Teacher Magazine, September 1933, p. 33

"Change must come gradually," he wrote. "To force it unduly would compromise its final success by favoring a violent reaction." In other words, implementing socialistic ideas had to be done slowly; otherwise those who truly cared about educating children would become angry and resist.[97]

John Dewey, known as "the father of progressive education," was an avowed socialist and the co-author of the "Humanist Manifesto." The U.S. House Committee on Un-American Activities discovered that he belonged to 15 Marxist front organizations. He taught the professors who trained America's teachers.[98]

JOEL E. SPINGARN – Chairman of the board of directors **Socialist: White Executive Board Member of NAACP.** Named after himself, he established the coveted Spingarn Medal, awarded yearly by the NAACP, in 1914. According to recent revelations by the *Memphis Commercial Appeal* newspaper he was also a spy for the United States Army. Spingarn was hired in May of 1918 and given the rank of major in the Military Intelligence Division (MID). Spingarn ran "a small unit of undercover agents" who were looking for "proof of subversion." The MID opened 100,000 pieces of mail a week and monitored Black publications. According to the *Appeal*: "The documents show Spingarn, who remained NAACP chairman during his tenure at MID, used his post

---

[97] http://davidfiorazo.com/2013/02/the-nea-agenda-how-john-deweysocialism-influenced-public-education/

[98] http://www.eagleforum.org/educate/2001/sept01/socialism.shtml

to obtain critical information for MID, such as a list of the organization's 32,000 members."[99]

WILLIAM ENGLISH WALLING – Chairman of the NAACP Executive Committee (1910–1911)
Socialist: White Executive Board Member and co-founder of NAACP. Author of the book *Labor-Union Socialism and Socialist Labor-Unionism* (1912). In 1908 Walling published *Russia's Message*, a book inspired by the social unrest which he and his wife had observed in Russia. He joined the Socialist Party (1910–17), His books included *Socialism as It Is: A Survey of the World-Wide Revolutionary Movement* (1912/1918). He published two other books on socialism by 1914, *The Larger Aspects of Socialism* and *Progressivism and After*.[100]

CHARLES EDWARD RUSSELL
Socialist: White Executive Board member of NAACP. Author and Pulitzer Prize winner.

Why I Am a Socialist (1910): "This is the offer of Socialism: the righting of the centuries of wrong the producers have suffered, the dawn of a genuine democracy, peace instead of war, sufficiency instead of suffering, life raised above the level of appetite, a chance at last for the good in people to attain their normal development."

---

99   http://noirg.org/articles/should-your-best-friends-spy-on-you-%E2%80%A8the-naacp-and-joel-e-spingarn/

100 https://en.wikipedia.org/wiki/William_English_Walling#/media/File:William_English_Walling.JPG

MARY WHITE OVINGTON
Socialist: White co-founder of the NAACP. A suffragist and journalist, Ovington joined the Socialist Party of America in 1905 where she met Socialist A. Philip Randolph, Floyd Dell, Max Eastman and Jack London. London argued that racial problems were as much a matter of "Class as of Race."[101]

HENRY MOSKOWITZ
Socialist: White Executive Board Member of NAACP. In 1917 Moskowitz served as the Commissioner of Public Markets in New York City. He was the founding Executive Director of the League of New York Theatres, which eventually became The Broadway League, the organization known for producing the Tony Awards.[102]

FLORENCE KELLEY
Marxist: White Executive Board Member of NAACP. Kelly was the daughter of United States congressman,

---

[101]   https://upload.wikimedia.org/wikipedia/commons/b/bc/MaryWhiteOvington.jpg

[102]   https://www.questia.com/magazine/1P3-44716911/an-naacp-crisis-time-line-1909-1954

William D. Kelley, was born on 12th September, 1859. She studied at Cornell University and the University of Zurich. While in Europe she became a follower of Karl Marx and Friedrich Engels. Over the next few years she worked on an English translation of Engels' The Conditions of the Working Class in England and this was eventually published in the United States in 1887.Kelley moved to New York City where She started the Intercollegiate Socialist Society.[103]

LINCOLN STEFFENS
Socialist: White Executive Board Member of NAACP.
Steffens was a New York reporter who published a book titled The Shame of the Cities. He is remembered for investigating corruption in municipal government in American cities and for his early support for the Soviet Union. He once famously said upon arriving back from Russia after the revolution: "I have been over into the future, and it works."[104]

[103]   http://www.socialwelfarehistory.com/people/kelley-florence/

[104]   http://spartacus-educational.com/Jsteffens.htm

105

CLARENCE DARROW

Socialist/Atheist: White Executive Board Member of NAACP. Darrow was a lawyer and unionist. In September 1905, Darrow joined with Jack London, Upton Sinclair, and Florence Kelley to form the Intercollegiate Socialist Society. Its stated purpose was to "throw light on the world-wide movement of industrial democracy known as socialism."[106]

"Socialism at least recognized that if man was to make a better world it must be through the mutual effort of human units; that it must be by some sort of co-operation that would include all the units of the state"[107]

As part of a public symposium on belief held in Columbus, Ohio, Darrow delivered a famous and powerful speech, which was later titled "Why I Am An Agnostic," on agnosticism, skepticism, belief, and religion. In the speech, Darrow thoroughly discussed the meaning of being an agnostic and questioned the doctrines of Christianity and the Bible. He concluded that "the fear of God is not the beginning of

---

[105]   2&ajaxhist=0
[106]   https://en.wikipedia.org/wiki/League_for_Industrial_Democracy
[107]   http://spartacus-educational.com/USAdarrow.htm

wisdom. The fear of God is the death of wisdom. Skepticism and doubt lead to study and investigation, and investigation is the beginning of wisdom. In the November 18, 1915 edition of the Washington Post, Darrow stated: "Chloroform unfit children. "Show them the same mercy that is shown beasts that are no longer fit to live."[108]

109

JANE ADDAMS
Socialist: White Executive Board Member of NAACP. In 1889 Addams co-founded Hull House and in 1920 she was a co-founder for the ACLU. In 1931 she became the first American woman to be awarded the Nobel Peace Prize and is recognized as the founder of the social work profession in the United States.[110] Co-founder of labor union Women's Trade Union League.[111]

---

108 https://en.wikipedia.org/wiki/Clarence_Darrow

109 http://www.bing.com/images/search?q=jane+addams&view=detailv2&qft=+filterui%3alicense-L2_L3_L4&id=85F89BFD094AEFACFA7C34D71461F81D8804D7AF&selectedIndex=1&ccid=t3omRw29&simid=608049430308063921&thid=OIP.Mb77a26470dbdfb5fd1f69d8b8b04878fo0&ajaxhist=0

110 http://www.bing.com/search?q=jane+addams+socialist&qs=AS&pq=jane+addams+socialist&sc=6-21&sp=1&cvid=48C05A726DFB459B96FF688C48636EE0&FORM=QBLH

111 https://worldhistoryproject.org/1903/jane-addams-becomes-vice-president-of-national-womens-trade-union-league

WILLIAM DEAN HOWELLS

Socialist: White Executive Board Member of NAACP. Editor of the *Atlantic Monthly*. Howells was a Christian socialist whose ideals were greatly influenced by Russian writer Leo Tolstoy.[20] He joined a Christian socialist group in Boston between 1889 and 1891.[112]

LILLIAN WALD

Socialist: White Executive Board Member of NAACP. Wald was an Employer and protégé to abortionist Margaret Sanger[113] Born in Cincinnati, Ohio, on March 10th, 1867. Wald became a nurse and Inspired by the work of Jane Addams and Ellen Starr at Hull House in Chicago, she joined Mary Brewster to establish the Henry Street Settlement in New York City in 1893. After WW1, Wald campaigned for socialist candidates and was closely associated with left-wing abortionist, trade unionist and Anarchists, Emma Goldman.[114]

---

[112] https://en.wikipedia.org/wiki/William_Dean_Howells

[113] http://www.socialwelfarehistory.com/people/wald-lillian/

[114] http://spartacus-educational.com/USAgoldman.htm

THE ORIGINAL NAACP WHITE FOUNDERS/ EXECUTIVE BOARD MEMBERS[115]

Mary White Ovington	Socialist	Journalist, *New York Evening Post*
Oswald Garrison Villard	Progressive	Owner of magazine, *The Nation*
William English Walling	Socialist	Wealthy Publisher, *Russia Message*
Dr. Henry Moscowitz	Progressive	Physician
Morefield Storey	liberal/Democrat	Lawyer and Publicist
Joel Spingarn	Progressive	Professor at Columbia
Arthur Spingarn		Lawyer and NAACP President
Inez Milholland	Socialist	World War I correspondent
Jane Addams	Socialist	Philosopher, sociologist, author
Florence Kelley	Marxist	Social and political reformer
Sophonisba Breckinridge	Progressive	University of Chicago Professor
John Haynes Holmes	Socialist and Pacifist	Unitarian minister
Charles Edward Russell	Socialist	Author and Pulizer Prize winner
John Dewey	Humanist/Atheist	The Father of Public Education
William Dean Howells	Socialist	Editor of the *Atlantic Monthly*
Lillian Wald	Socialist	Nurse, Author, Humanitarian
Clarence Darrow	Socialist/Atheist	Lawyer, ACLU Leader
Lincoln Steffens	Progressive	Reporter, *New York Evening Post*
Ray Stannard Baker	Progressive	American journalist and author
Fanny Garrison Villard	Socialist	Wealthy wife of Publisher
Walter Sachs	Socialist	

---

[115]   http://www.naacp.org/pages/naacp-history

CHAPTER 12

THE DAVIS-BACON ACT:
JOB KILLING SINCE 1931

*Reprinted by permission of Takia Hollowell and
Contagious Transformation in its entirety.
Posted on December 27, 2011*

Ever drive by a construction site and wonder, "Why aren't very many blacks visible in this industry?" During my lifetime, I've heard this question asked quite a bit. I've heard the notorious Al Sharpton recently rant against this epidemic and demand that construction sites without blacks be shut down. Even Harry Alford-I of the Black Chamber of Commerce has stated: "It is more than 44 years since the Civil Rights Act, and the construction trades are no better today than they were during the struggles of Dr. Martin Luther King Jr."

If you're wondering why jobs of this nature aren't very prevalent in urban areas, then look no further than to the monstrosity of the Davis-Bacon Act.

BRIEF HISTORY

The upheaval of the Davis-Bacon Act began in 1927 after a contractor from Alabama secured a bid to build a Veteran's hospital in Long Island, NY. As it was discovered that the contractor brought black construction workers from Alabama to conduct the work; Representative Robert Bacon was disturbed to see "coloreds" take work away from "white labor" in his district. Being that unions were created to keep blacks out of the workforce during those times, Representative Bacon developed legislation that would force contractors to pay its employees the prevailing/union wage in order to secure a federal contract. (See: US Congress House Committee of Labor, Letter of Ethelbert Stewart, pg 17, March 6, 1930) The intention was to put a stop to black labor from constantly outbidding higher paid white unions in securing federal contracts.

The racist overtone of the legislation was no hidden agenda as Congressman Upshaw openly argued on the House floor, "You will not think that a southern man is more human if he smiles over the fact of your reaction to that real problem you are confronted within any community with a superabundance or large aggression of negro labor." (Ibid, pg. 3) Fortunately during this time, their efforts failed to regulate the labor industry but the attempts did not stop there.

In Representative Bacon's relentless pursuit to legalize prevailing white union wages, he joined forces with Senator James Davis in 1931 to garner enough support for the bill to pass. During House floor debates, many other racist arguments surfaced in support of the new act. Congressman Miles Allgood stated: "See, that contractor over there has cheap colored labor that he transports, and he puts them in cabins, and it is labor of that sort that is in competition with white labor throughout the country." (See: US House of Representatives, Congressional Record, 71st Congress 3rd Session, 1931, p 6513)

The Davis Bacon Act proved to be detrimental during the Great Depression as "white salaries" were protected from cheaper black labor. Unskilled black workers were almost never admitted into unions and were not able to build a skill set or find employment. From 1931 to the 1950s, blacks were still barred from the unions of sheet metal workers, plasterers, plumbers, electrical workers, engineers, etc. (See: Herbert Hill, "Racism Within Organized Labor, Journal of Negro Education, 1961, pg. 113)

CONDITIONS OF TODAY

Despite its historical racist intentions and devastating effects on non-unionized minority workers, the Jesse Jacksons and Maxine Waters of today fight tooth and nail to prevent the Act from being repealed. You want to know what is even more disgusting? Many black Democratic leaders are aware of the Act's discriminatory history yet support it anyway. Economist Walter E. Williams points this out in his short video.

As unions support Democratic candidates with millions of campaign dollars, the elected officials in turn repay their homage by protecting the harmful legislation. Any opposition or attempt to repeal the Davis Bacon Act is demagogued as, "those evil Conservatives are just trying to hurt the middle class." Nothing can be further from the truth as its repeal would open up the floodgates for non-unionized contractors to bid on school projects, highway projects, military projects, hospital projects and more. Furthermore, its repeal would alleviate "the middle class" from footing the bill for the bloated union wages that the Act requires. Highways and schools don't pay for themselves; the taxpayer does. While the NAACP and others hold their allegiance to unions, they turn a blind eye to the higher tax burden that YOU are forced to pay as contractors can't secure bids under the local union wage (also known as "the prevailing wage). Can someone tell me how this helps the "middle class" again?

As of late, Congressman Steve King has introduced legislation (HR 745) to repeal the Act but he still needs our support to revive the issue. The Davis Bacon Act is one of many contributing factors to unemployment being almost double the national average in the black community. I would encourage everyone to write, call or e-mail their Congressman and spread the word of this egregious legislation.

CHAPTER 13

OTA BENGA:
DARWINISM'S DEMEANING OF THE
HUMAN RACE

Darwinist Proof of Evolution: 1904 New York's
Brooklyn Zoo.

The mid-19th century was both an exciting time and a critical
time for America and the world. Judeo-Christian empathy
and compassion prevailed as a majority of Americans elected

a President who stood boldly against the evils of slavery. It was an historical pinnacle time for America and resulted in a war more deadly than all other wars combined. The Civil War claimed the lives of over 750,000 soldiers and an undetermined number of civilians. Some estimated that 10 percent of all Northern males 20-45 years old, and 30 percent of all Southern white males aged 18–40 perished during this period. The blood of Americans spilled to right the wrong of generations would serve as atonement for its sociopathic acceptance of slavery.

A 14-year period following the Civil War, the Reconstruction, demonstrated further attempts by white Americans to correct past wrongs. For the first time, Black Americans, former slaves, experienced power and were elected to various positions throughout the north and south.[1] The Reconstruction period allowed the growth of prominent Black colleges, particularly throughout the Deep South, allowing access to an education that was once outlawed to Black Americans. These institutions would play a pinnacle role in establishing an upward movement of Black Americans culminating in the post WWII boom of the Black middle class.

Unfortunately, as the spirit of compassion and empathy grew throughout America, another theory that would forever reset man's view grew in popularity. In 1859, Charles Darwin introduced his new theory of evolution. This theory would change man's relationship with one another throughout the next century and give new thought to mankind's origin. Due to the theory's approach of sanitizing man from his spiritual

---

[1] https://en.wikipedia.org/wiki/American_Civil_War

origins, the godless theory spread like wildfire within the circles of academia and the intellectuals.

Darwin's hypothesis that mankind in its present state, is the descendent of the lowest state of animals, sought to undermine the foundation of Christian dogma. As soon as Darwinism made its appearance, the bourgeoisie grasped it with great zeal.[2] Taught as scientifically settled proof in these agonistic and atheist circles of the academia intellectual, Darwin's evolutionary theory spread quickly. It elevated the intrinsic value of the White Race while devaluating the value of all others, in particular the Black Race. Its foundational premise of genetic and race superiority would eventually serve as the root for a host of other atheist-based theories to come within the coming century. These theories included Malthus eugenics, Integration eugenics, and Racial Hygiene (Nazi-eugenics). Also introduced were other racist concepts and methods such as gene pool manipulation, sterilization, abortion and racial segregation.

Darwin's biological concepts of natural selection and survival of the fittest were later adapted to sociology, politics, and economics.. The evolving philosophy, Social Darwinism, has been claimed to have been the genesis for other atheist-based ideologies i.e. eugenics, racism, imperialism, fascism and Nazism, and the struggle between national or racial groups.[3] Marxism and the other anti-capitalist economic strains would follow Darwin's theory. In 1912, one Marxist theorist, Antonie Pannekoek, championed this theory: *The scientific importance of Marxism as well as of Darwinism*

---

[2]   https://www.marxists.org/archive/pannekoe/1912/marxism-darwinism.htm.

[3]   https://en.wikipedia.org/wiki/Social-Darwinism.

consists in their following out the theory of evolution, the one upon the domain of the organic world, of things animate; the other, upon the domain of society.[4]

The ideologies of Socialism, Communism, Liberalism and Progressivism blossomed from the same seed and have predictably bore the same fruit. That fruit is the negation of God as the ultimate source, as man replaces himself as the more intelligent and wiser substitute. Evidence of the new science of evolution, (an atheist-based and therefore heartless view of mankind) was on full display in 1904, at the St. Louis World Fair. and later at the New York's Brooklyn Zoo.

His name was Ota Benga. He was brought from the Belgian Congo in 1904 by noted African explorer Samuel Verner. He was touted as a representation of Darwin's missing link, man's evolutionary transition from the African ape to the evolved European White race. Ota was an African pygmy born in 1881. He was about 23 years old, four feet-eleven inches tall, and weighed a mere 103 pounds. Often referred to as a boy, he was actually a twice-married father--his first wife murdered by the white colonists, and his second spouse died from a poisonous snake bite.[5] He was first displayed in the anthropology wing at the 1904 St. Louis World's Fair with other pygmies as "emblematic savages" along with other "strange people." The exhibit was under the direction of W J. McGee of the Anthropology Department of the St. Louis World's Fair. McGee's ambitions for the exhibit were to "be exhaustively scientific in his demonstration of the stages of human evolution. Therefore, he required 'darkest Blacks' "to

---

[4]   https://www.marxists.org/archive/pannekoe/1912/marxism-darwinism.htm

[5]   http://www.rae.org/pdf/otabenga.pdf

set off against 'dominant whites' and members of the 'lowest known culture' to contrast with 'its highest culmination.'"[6] The exhibit was extremely popular and attracted considerable attention. The pygmies were selected because they had attracted much attention as an example of a primitive race.[7]

The expert scientists of the day, the anthropometricists and psychometricists, concluded that their intelligence tests proved that pygmies "behaved a good deal in the same way as the mentally deficient person, making many stupid errors and taking an enormous amount of time."[8] Nor did they do very well in the sports competition. In Bradford and Blume's words, "the disgraceful record set by the ignoble savages" was so poor that "never before in the history of sport in the world were such poor performances recorded."

It should be noted that the low state of their mental development was shown by the following facts. They have no regard for time, nor have they any records or traditions of the past; no religion is known among them, nor have they any fetish rites; they do not seek to know the future by occult means. In short, they are the closest link with the original Darwinian anthropoid ape extant."[9] The anthropologists then measured not only the live humans, but in one case a 'primitive's' head was... severed from the body and boiled down to the skull. Believing skull size to be an index of intelligence, scientists were amazed that this skull was larger than that which had belonged to the statesman Daniel Webster." When Ota was

---

6   Bradford and Blume, 1992, pp. 94-95
7   (Verner, 1906a, p. 471)
8   Bradford and Blume, 1992, p. 121
9   http://creationresearch.org/crsq/articles/30/otabenga.html

presented to Director Hornaday of the Bronx Zoological Gardens, Hornaday's intention was clearly to make a public display of Ota. Hornaday maintained the hierarchical view of races. He believed that large-brained animals were "the best evolution had to offer." His belief in the Darwinian theory also led him to conclude that there exists a close analogy of the African savage to the apes.

According to Darwin "it was more probable that our early progenitors lived on the African continent than elsewhere."[7] Ota was put on display at the Brooklyn Zoo and encouraged to spend as much time as he wanted inside the monkey house. He was even given a bow and arrow and was encouraged to shoot it as part of an exhibit. He was eventually locked in his enclosure-and when he was let out of the monkey house, "the crowd stayed glued to him."[10] The publicity began on September 9. The New York Times headline screamed, "bushman shares a cage with the Bronx Park apes." For the first time in any American zoo, a human being was displayed in a cage. Benga was given cage-mates to keep him company in his captivity-a parrot and an Orangutan named Dohong.

The display was extremely successful. Bradford and Blume claimed that on September 16, "40,000 visitors roamed the New York zoological Park... the sudden surge of interest... was entirely attributable to Ota Benga." The crowds were so enormous that a police officer was assigned full-time to guard Ota, as he was "always in danger of being grabbed, yanked, poked, and pulled to pieces by the mob.[11]

---

10 Bradford and Blume, 1992, p. 180
11 http://www.rae.org/pdf/otabenga.pdf

It was widely believed at this time, even by eminent scientists, that blacks were evolutionarily inferior to Caucasians, caging one in a zoo produced much publicity, especially by ministers and Afro-Americans. Evidently not many people were very concerned about doing anything until the Afro-American community entered the fray. Although even some Blacks at this time accepted the notion that the pygmies were "defective specimens of mankind," several Black ministers were determined to stop the exhibit. Their concern was "they had heard blacks compared with apes often enough before; now the comparison was being played flagrantly at the largest zoo on earth." In Reverend Gordon's words, "our race…is depressed enough without exhibiting one of us with the apes. We think we are worthy of being considered human beings, with souls."[11] Further, many of the ministers opposed the theory of evolution, concluding, "the exhibition evidently aims to be a demonstration of the Darwinian theory of evolution. The Darwinian Theory is absolutely opposed to Christianity, and a public demonstration in its favor should not be permitted."

Faced with continual harassment and humiliation, Ota eventually "fashioned a little bow and a set of arrows and began shooting at zoo visitors he found particularly obnoxious! After he wounded a few gawkers, (in 1910) he left the Zoological Park for good."

He eventually became a Christian, was baptized, and his English vocabulary rapidly improved. He also learned how to read and occasionally attended classes at a Lynchburg seminary. He was popular among the boys, and learned several sports such as baseball. Every effort was made to help him blend in. Even his teeth were capped to help him look more normal. Seemingly he had adjusted but inwardly he had not. Eventually he became despondent. He checked on the price of steamship tickets to Africa, and concluded that he would never have enough money to purchase one. Later employed as a laborer in a tobacco factory in Lynchburg, VA, he grew increasingly depressed, hostile, irrational, and forlorn. When people spoke to him, they noticed that he had tears in his eyes. He told them he wanted to go home. Concluding that he would never be able to return to his native land, on March 20, 1916, Benga committed suicide with a revolver (Sanborn, 1916). In Ward's words: "Ota...removed the caps from his teeth. When his small companions asked him to lead them into the woods again, he turned them away. Once they were safely out of sight, he shot himself."[12]

This story of an atheist-based science reflects the damage to real people. For generations it would spawn the spirit of racism and hatred. The tenets of evolution, rooted in a racist belief that some races are inferior and closer to the lower primates, included the polyphyletic view that Blacks had evolved from the strong but less intelligent Gorillas, the Orientals from the Orangutans, and Whites from the most intelligent of all primates, the Chimpanzees.[13]

Darwin theory was predicated on belief that when left to itself, natural selection would accomplish extinction. Without slavery to embrace and protect them, or so it was thought, blacks would have to compete with Caucasians for survival. Whites' greater fitness for this contest was [believed] beyond

---

[12] www.rae.org/pdf/otabenga.pdf
[13] http://www.rae.org/pdf/otabenga.pdf

dispute. The disappearance of blacks as a race, then, would only be a matter of time.

Each new American census showed that this prediction of Darwin was wrong. "The black population showed no signs of failing, and might even be on the rise." Not content to wait for natural selection to grind out the answer, one senator even tried to arrange a state of affairs to convince or even force blacks to return to Africa.

The failure of Darwin's theory for the extinction of the black race would lead to another evolution theory, Eugenics. In 1862, English Scientist and Darwin's cousin, Francis Galton, postulated a theory in which man could accelerate the process of evolution. It promoted the ideal of perfecting the human race by, as stated by Galton, "getting rid of its 'undesirables' while multiplying its 'desirables.'" Since charitable organizations frustrated the law of survival of the fit, those who advocated Eugenics would encourage their elimination. These organizations would also encourage proactive elimination of "inferior people and races" whose procreation, it was theorized, would lower the quality of the genetic pool.[14]

The theories presented by these two men, Charles Darwin and Francis Galton, of Evolution and Eugenics would lay a foundation over the coming century to levels of "man's inhumanity to man" never before seen in modern history. From the "scientific proof" of Ota, written of and seen by thousands, it would give intellectuals worldwide a platform for funding and implementation their social and scientific theories of Eugenics, from integration, sterilization, abortion,

---

[14]   http://www.pbs.org/wgbh/evolution/darwin/nameof/

to the ultimate Nazi-style eugenics, Racial Hygienic, later called Hitler's "Final Solution."

Eugenics was not a "white only" intellectual ideology. Black intellectual, socialist and integrationist W.E.B. DuBois subscribed to some hereditary ideas of eugenics. He wrote that the Talented Tenth of African Americans should be encouraged to have children.[15] He would serve on Margaret Sanger's abortion board (Birth Control Clinic) founded in Brownsville, NY (Harlem) and would later support Margaret Sanger's efforts to implement a Virginia statute authorizing the compulsory sterilization of a poor young white woman with an illegitimate child on grounds of feeble-mindedness, though that was never clearly established.[16]

Darwin's "big bang" theory, metaphorically, was correct. It gave rise to the foundation of every "empathy free" ideology that would plague the brand new 20th century. Its foundation of atheism would give it a presence to later metastasize within the doctrines of *communism, socialism, liberalism, Marxism, humanism, and progressivism*. It would result in the loss of millions of lives and the deaths of hopes and dreams of many more human beings, into the centuries to come.

QUOTES FROM DARWINIST THEORISTS

Samuel Verner (the explorer who brought Benga from Africa) exclaimed, "Pygmies were the most primitive race of

---

15   http://www.greatblacksinwax.org/Exhibits/W_E_B_%20DuBois.htm
16   http://www.politicsdaily.com/2009/07/28/margaret-sanger-the-other-side-of-the-story/

mankind" and were "almost as much at home in the trees as the monkeys." He also argued that the blacks in Africa should be collected into reservations and colonized by "the white race" and concerns over the social and legal relations between blacks and whites should be solved by "local segregation of the races." Verner was not a mean person, and cared deeply for other races, but this care was influenced in a major adverse way by his evolutionary beliefs[17]

Hornaday (Director of the Bronx Zoological Gardens) "maintained the hierarchical view of races... large-brained animals were to him... the best evolution had to offer." This believer in the Darwinian theory also concluded that there exists "a close analogy of the African savage to the apes."[18]

---

[17]   http://creationresearch.org/crsq/articles/30/otabenga.html
[18]   Ibid

CHAPTER 14

SECULAR SCIENCE:
THE SEED OF RACISM AND SOCIALISM

*To understand today's prominence of social and
political Elitism, it is important to understand the
secular based science that was introduced at the
turn of the 20th century. A hypothesis that was
antithetical to the dominant Christian beliefs of
that era, was immediately accepted and promoted
world-wide by fellow atheist and agnostic
intellectuals. At no other time in history, has Man's
intellectual approach to science so effectively
established itself at the very core of human
discourse.*

DARWINISM

By 1860, a year after the publishing of the *Origin of the
Species*, the theory of evolution had rapidly gained acceptance
throughout the world. An atheist, Darwin, proposed a racially-
based theory that the evolution of the white race had its
beginnings millions of years prior on the continent of Africa.
Beginning with primitive apes it would transition through

a half-man/half ape being, called the Negro, and ultimately result in the intellectually superior white race. The idea that Africa was the continent where Homosapiens would begin their journey from fish to man came from Darwin. He stated, "it was more probable that our early progenitors lived on the African continent than elsewhere."[1]

Due to academia and intellectual's natural attraction to theories devoid of spiritual linkage, Darwinism was readily accepted and taught as irrefutable science. The underpinning of the theory gave some comfort to those in the 1860s who were concerned about the ongoing Negro problem, with the end of slavery. Darwin's theory inferred that due to the inferiority of the black race, once the protective security of slavery was removed, the race would be incapable of caring for itself and would eventually become extinct. When the Black population continued to grow unabated, census after census, Darwin's theory of Evolution was forced to evolve to another spiritually voided theory. Darwin's cousin, Francis Galton, postulated that due to the altruistic attitudes of modern society, charities were not allowing natural selection "survival of the fit" to work at its normal pace. He theorized that it was possible that man could manipulate and accelerate the process of evolution. His theory, called Eugenics, found acceptance within American and European intellectual/academia circles. Eugenics is a social philosophy advocating the improvement of human genetic traits through the promotion of higher rates of sexual reproduction for people with desired traits (positive eugenics), or reduced rates of sexual reproduction and sterilization of people with less-desired or undesired

---

[1]   http://www.historyofinformation.com/expanded.php?id=2990

traits (negative eugenics).[2] Both methods were introduced and adapted at the beginning of the 1900s to promote negative eugenics, these included sterilization and abortion of the less desired. It would transition throughout the early 1900s to Racial Eugenics and then to its ultimate conclusion, the Nazi's Final Solution with concentration camps and the deaths of over 11 million people.[3]

EUGENICS

From the moment Sir Francis Galton coined the word *eugenics* in 1883, scientists were captivated by the notion of improving humanity through better breeding. Whether advocating increased procreation among the "fit" (positive eugenics), or demanding negative eugenic interventions (immigration and marriage restriction, sterilization, segregation) to reduce the propagation of the "unfit." Scientists remained convinced that eugenics promised a millennial advance in human society.4

According to Galton, a host of social problems, like alcoholism, criminality, pauperism, prostitution, tuberculosis, venereal disease, and the catch-all category of "feeblemindedness," might be eradicated by preventing the birth of those genetically destined to fill these categories. Galton believed that black people were entirely inferior to the

---

[2]   https://en.wikipedia.org/wiki/Eugenics.

[3]   https://en.wikipedia.org/wiki/The_Holocaust

[4]   http://documents.mx/documents/fighting-fire-with-fire-african-americans-and-hereditarian-thinking-1900-1942.html

white races and that Jews were capable only of "parasitism" upon the civilized nations.[5]

In the United States the eugenics movement started from a belief in the racial superiority of white Anglo-Saxons and a desire to prevent the immigration of less desirable races. In 1910, the Committee on Eugenics solicited new members with a letter that read, "The time is ripe for a strong public movement to stem the tide of threatened racial degeneracy. America needs to protect herself against indiscriminate immigration, criminal degenerates, and...race suicide." The letter also warned of the impending "complete destruction of the white race."[6] Eugenics would later be the driving force behind euthanasia, in vitro fertilization, and embryo and fetal research.[7]

It was believed that charities slowed the natural selection process and thereby slowed the cleansing pace of evolution. With her belief in eugenics, abortionist Margaret Sanger condemned charities and other forms of benevolence. She believed they only exacerbated the problems:

> *"Organized charity itself is the symptom of a malignant social disease. Those vast, complex, interrelated organizations aiming to control and to diminish the spread of misery and destitution and all the menacing evils that spring out of this sinisterly fertile soil, are the surest sign that our civilization has bred, is breeding and perpetuating*

---

5   http://www.publiceye.org/magazine/v09n1/eugenics.html
6   Ibid
7   http://www.emmerich1.com/EUGENICS.htm

constantly increasing numbers of defectives,
delinquents and dependents...to breed out of the
race the scourges of transmissible disease, mental
defect, poverty, lawlessness, crime... since these
classes would be decreasing in number instead of
breeding like weeds... such a plan would... reduce
the birthrate among the diseased, the sickly, the
poverty stricken and anti-social classes, elements
unable to provide for themselves, and the burden
of which we are all forced to carry."

– Margaret Sanger[8]

Though appearing friendly to the Black race, Sanger aligned herself with the eugenicists whose ideology prevailed in the early 20th century. They strongly espoused racial supremacy and "purity," particularly of the "Aryan" race. Eugenicists hoped to purify the bloodlines and improve the race by encouraging the "fit" to reproduce and the "unfit" to restrict their reproduction. They sought to contain the "inferior" races through segregation, sterilization, birth control and abortion.[6]

By the turn of the century, Eugenics was promoted by governments, influential individuals and by institutions. Its advocates regarded it as a social philosophy for the improvement of human hereditary traits through the promotion of higher reproduction of certain people and traits, and the reduction of reproduction of other people and traits.[9]

---

8   http://thinkexist.com/quotation/organized-charity-itself-is-the-symptom-of-a/397373.html
9   http://www.citizenreviewonline.org/special_issues/population/the_negro_project.htm

Gregory Michael Dorr, PhD, in his book, *Fighting Fire with Fire,* argues that hereditarianism and eugenics appeal to various segments of the African American community. Some African Americans, like W.E.B. DuBois and Thomas Turner, believed that relatively "fit" and "unfit" human beings existed, and that society as a whole could be improved by assuring the propagation of the fit—the best and brightest individuals, regardless of race. What emerged from this school of thought was "integrationist" or "accommodationist" eugenics, which assumed the essential biological similarity of all human races.[10]

W. E. B. DuBois shared many of the eugenic views held by white progressives. His "Talented (elitist) Tenth" was itself a eugenically weighted term. He defined members of the Talented Tenth as "exceptional men" and the "best of the race." He complained that "the negro has not been breeding for an object" and that he must begin to "train and breed for brains, for efficiency, for beauty." Over his long career DuBois time and again returned to his concern that the worst blacks were over-breeding while the best were under-breeding. Indeed, he supported Margaret Sanger's "Negro Project," which sought to sharply curtail reproduction among "inferior" stocks of the black population.[11]

DuBois subscribed to both positive and negative eugenics. He wrote that the Talented Tenth of African Americans should be encouraged to have children, (positive

---

[10] Fighting Fire with Fire: African Americans and Hereditarian Thinking, 1900-1942.. Gregory Michael Dorr, Ph.D.

[11] Liberal Fascism: The Secret History of the American Left from Mussolini to the Politics of Meaning; Johna Goldberg

eugenics) but also supported abortion and sterilization to control the quality in the gene pool (negative eugenics).[12]

STANDARD IQ TESTING—THE BEGINNING

The most enduring bequest of eugenics is the standard IQ testing. Intelligence testing began in earnest in France, when in 1904 psychologist Alfred Binet was commissioned by the French government to find a method to differentiate between children who were intellectually normal and those who were inferior. The purpose was to put the latter into special schools. There they would receive more individual attention and the disruption they caused in the education of intellectually normal children could be avoided.

However, Binet cautioned against misuse of the scale or misunderstanding of its implications. He noted that it was not intended to be used as "a general device for ranking all pupils according to mental worth." Binet also (pointed out) that "the scale, properly speaking, does not permit the measure of intelligence, because intellectual qualities are not superposable, and therefore cannot be measured as linear surfaces are measured." Since, according to Binet, intelligence could not be described as a single score, the use of his Intelligence Quotient (IQ) as a definite statement on a child's intellectual capability would be a serious mistake. In addition, Binet feared that IQ measurement would be used to

---

[12] Fighting Fire with Fire: African Americans and Hereditarian Thinking, 1900-1942. Gregory Michael Dorr, Ph.D.

condemn a child to a permanent "condition" of stupidity, thus negatively affecting his or her education and livelihood.[13]

Lewis M. Terman, best known as the developer of the Stanford-Binet IQ test, unlike Binet, believed that intelligence was hereditary and fixed, worked on revising the Simon-Binet Scale. His final product, published in 1916 as the Stanford Revision of the Binet-Simon Scale of Intelligence (also known as the Stanford-Binet), became the standard intelligence test in the United States for the next several decades. Terman was a prominent eugenicist and was a member of the Human Betterment Foundation and served as president of the American Psychological Association.[14]

Few people realize that the tests being used today represent the end result of a historical process that has its origins in racial and cultural bigotry. Both H.H Goddard and Lewis Terman, founding fathers of the modern testing industry, advocated eugenics.[15]

Due to Goddard's views on intelligence and society, he lobbied for restrictive immigration laws. Upon his "discovery" that all immigrants except those from Northern Europe were of "surprisingly low intelligence;" such tight immigration laws were enacted in the 1920s. Testing caused him to conclude that, for example, 87 percent of Russian immigrants were morons. Of course he did not take into account that they were given a test in English, with questions based on American cultural assumptions, to people who could barely, if at all, speak English. Vast numbers of immigrants were

---

13 http://iq-test.learninginfo.org/iq01.htm
14 http://en.wikipedia.org/wiki/Lewis_Terman
15 http://iq-test.learninginfo.org/iq01.htm

deported in 1913 and 1914 because of this test. According to Harvard professor Steven Jay Gould in his acclaimed book, The *Mis-measure of Man*, these tests were also influential in legitimizing forced sterilization of allegedly "defective" individuals in some states.

As with other theories proposed by the intellectuals of their day, the "settled science" of racist based evolution and eugenics, continues to unveil the legacy of man's unbridled arrogance. If not for the dire consequences of the millions of lives destroyed, their theories, with the wisdom of time, look more like Greek myths in the making.[16]

Its most damning legacy is a series of draconian state laws regarding sterilization that were upheld by the Supreme Court. The most notorious of these decisions was the 1927 *Buck v. Bell*. In that case, an 8-1 majority of the court upheld a Virginia statute, authorizing the compulsory sterilization of a poor young white woman with an illegitimate child on grounds she was feeble-minded, which was were never clearly established.

The state based its decision on the assessment of a nurse who said of the Buck family, "These people belong to the shiftless, ignorant, and worthless class of anti-social whites of the South."[17]

This decision, incidentally, was also endorsed by civil libertarians such as ACLU Co-founder/ Socialist/Atheist Roger Baldwin18 and civil rights advocates, including W.E.B.

---

16 Ibid
17 http://www.examiner.com/article/eugenic-skeletons-the-progressive-closet
18 http://www.westernjournalism.com/the-aclus-communist-atheist-roots/

Du Bois of the NAACP, both of whom Sanger counted among her supporters and friends.[19]

EARLY 20TH CENTURY "ROYALTY CLASS BLACK" EUGENICS

W.E.B. DuBois, in his article "Black Folk and Birth Control," criticized the "mass of ignorant Negroes" who bred "carelessly and disastrously." He said that the increase among [them] ... "is from that part of the population least intelligent and fit, and least able to rear their children properly."[20] In 1932 DuBois also contributed an essay on birth control to *Margaret Sanger's Birth Control Review.* He accepted the conventional eugenic wisdom that "the more intelligent class" exercised birth control, which meant that "the increase among Negroes, even more than the increase among whites, is from that part of the population least intelligent and fit, and least able to rear their children properly." He chided that African Americans "must learn that among human races and groups, as among vegetables, quality and not mere quantity really counts." DuBois adhered so strongly to this notion that he allowed this article to be reprinted, unchanged, again in 1938. DuBois felt that these distinctions were scientific and unbiased. Apparently, many others shared his view.[21] *Elitism Class over Race.*

---

[19]   http://www.politicsdaily.com/2009/07/28/margaret-sanger-the-other-side-of-the-story/

[20]   http://www.citizenreviewonline.org/special_issues/population/the_negro_project.htm

[21]   W. E. B. Du Bois: The Souls of Black Folk, The Negro

DuBois believed in the hereditary superiority of the Talented Tenth, whether the top ten percent of the white population, or the top ten percent of the black population. This opinion appears throughout his writing. In "Souls of Black Folk," DuBois confirmed his belief in "the rule of inequality." Simply stated, he believed that "of the million black youth, some were *fitted to know and some to dig.*" He made this inborn fitness the basis of his call for education according to ability.[22]

Charles S. Johnson was Fisk University's first black president. He later served on the National Advisory Council to the Birth Control Federation of America (BCFA) becoming an integral part of the Negro Project. He wrote that "eugenic discrimination" was necessary for blacks. It was his belief that high maternal and infant mortality rates, along with diseases like tuberculosis, typhoid, malaria and venereal infection, made it difficult for large families to adequately sustain themselves. Further, "the status of Negroes as marginal workers, their confinement to the lowest paid branches of industry, the necessity for the labors of mothers, as well as children, to balance meager budgets, are factors [that] emphasize the need for lessening the burden not only for themselves, but of society, which must provide the supplementary support in the form of relief."[23]

Another black writer, Walter A. Terpenning, considered birth control for blacks as "the more humane provision" and "more eugenic" than among whites. He felt birth control information should have first been disseminated among

---

[22] Ibid

[23] The Negro Project: Margaret Sanger's Eugenic Plan for Black Americans

blacks rather than the white upper crust. He failed to look at the problematic attitudes and behavior of society and how they suppressed blacks. He offered no solutions to the injustice and vile racism that blacks endured.[24]

It is interesting to note that Supreme Court Justice Oliver Wendell Holmes, a liberal member of the court, wrote to his friend, British eugenicist Harold Laski, about his decision in the case, "I... delivered an opinion upholding the constitutionality of a state law for sterilizing imbeciles the other day and I felt that I was getting near the first principle of real reform." In his zeal to codify eugenics in American jurisprudence Holmes wrote, "three generations of imbeciles are enough."[25]

A Cornell-trained biologist, Dr. Thomas Wyatt Turner, taught eugenics at Tuskegee, Howard, and Hampton Universities. Like W.E.B. Dubois and other black intellectuals, Turner identified with the Talented Tenth. He felt that people like himself and his students, as the eugenically fit, whose intellectual achievements and social status certified their genetic worth, should marry and procreate to increase the proportion of "fit" individuals in the black population. Turner explicitly argued that if African Americans used biology and eugenics to "uplift" the race to meet white norms, then whites could no longer use biology to deny black equality.[26]

The subtle message of the Elitist Talented Tenth, is that, through positive or negative Eugenics, it can pull itself up and away from the lesser *Untalented* 90%. It is a message

---

[24] http://www.citizenreviewonline.org/special_issues/population/the_negro_project.htm

[25] http://www.examiner.com/article/eugenic-skeletons-the-progressive-closet

[26] www.wfu.edu/~caron/ssrs/Dorr.rtf

that denotes a race dominated by its inferior class. There is no question but that the abortionist, Margaret Sanger, found an advocate in W.E.B. DuBois.

Within this setting of "accepted" genetic science in academia and intellectual circles, Sanger was able to charm the black community's most distinguished Black professional, W.E.B DuBois. DuBois, one of the community's more prominent and respected leaders, championed the ideology of Liberalism. As such, DuBois can be credited with helping to establish one of society's more devious political precedents. It is a precedent that is unique to the Black Race and has left an indelible imprint on its progress of those attempting to experience the American Dream. It has manifested itself in the compliance of an entire race of more than 40 million Black American allowing another race to dictate who speaks as "leaders" on its collective behalf. That group of handpicked, well paid spokesmen, the Royalty Class Black Man, has not deviated from its given script for more than 100 years.

THE SCIENCE OF RACISM

Scientific racism is the use of scientific techniques and hypotheses to sanction the belief in racial superiority, inferiority or racism.[27] Racial hygiene was a set of early twentieth century state sanctioned policies by which certain groups of individuals were allowed to procreate and others not, with the expressed purpose of promoting certain characteristics deemed to be particularly desirable. The most

---

[27]   http://en.wikipedia.org/wiki/Scientific_racism

noteworthy example is the extensive implementation of racial hygiene policies by Nazi Germany. It should be noted that similar policies were implemented throughout Europe and North America.[28]

Adolf Hitler read racial hygiene tracts during his imprisonment in Landsberg Prison. He thought that Germany could only become strong again if the state applied to German society the principles of racial hygiene and eugenics. Hitler was a firm believer and preacher of evolution. His book, *Mein Kampf,* clearly set forth a number of evolutionary ideas, particularly those emphasizing struggle, survival of the fittest, and the extermination of the weak to produce a better society.[29]

In organizing their eugenics program the Nazis were inspired by the United States' programs of forced sterilization, especially the eugenics laws that had been enacted in California.[30]

Darwinism did not produce the Holocaust, but without Darwinism, especially in its social Darwinist and eugenics permutations, neither Hitler nor his Nazi followers would have had the necessary scientific underpinnings to convince themselves and their collaborators that one of the world's greatest atrocities was really morally praiseworthy. Darwinism—or at least some naturalistic interpretation of Darwinism—succeeded in turning morality on its head.[31]

---

[28] http://en.wikipedia.org/wiki/Racial_hygiene

[29] http://www.islamdenouncesantisemitism.com/thesocial.htm

[30] http://en.wikipedia.org/wiki/Nazi_eugenics#Hitler.27s_views_on_eugenics

[31] Richard Weikart http://en.wikipedia.org/wiki/From_Darwin_to_Hitle

CHAPTER 15

PLANNED PARENTHOOD:
THE SOPHISTRY OF MARGARET SANGER

The masthead motto of her newsletter,
The Woman Rebel, read: "No Gods, No Masters"

"Consistent with her deep belief of racial supremacy and purity of the Aryan race Margaret Sanger is responsible, more than anyone else, for keeping alive international racism. Sanger played the attractive hostess for racist thinkers all over the world. Organizing the First World Population Conference in Geneva in 1926, she invited Clarence C. Little, Edward A. East, Henry Pratt Fairchild, and Raymond Pearl—all infamous racists."[1] In 1931 Sanger founded the Population Association of America with Fairchild as its head. Fairchild, formerly the secretary-treasurer of the American Eugenics Society and the leading academic racist of the decade, wrote *The Melting Pot Mistake*, which denigrated the Jews, referring to them as the inferior new immigrants who would threaten the native Nordic stock.[2]

---

[1] Birth Control Review, November, 1926
[2] Allan Chase, The Legacy of Malthus, p. 656.

Today, on an average, 1,876 black babies are aborted every day in the United States. Though minority women constitute only about 13% of the US female population (age 15-44), they underwent approximately 36% of the abortions. According to the Alan Guttmacher Institute, black women are more than 5 times as likely as white women to have an abortion [3]

As the results of one hundred years of steady, progressive and effective messaging, Planned Parenthood has gained support from segments of Americans that just decades ago would have been deemed impossible. The ideology of liberalism has convinced close to 50% of Americas of all religious faiths, colors, and backgrounds of the merits of embracing the beliefs of Planned Parenthood's founder Margaret Sanger. Her views of Black Americans and other minorities once deemed unacceptable, like "human weeds," "reckless breeders," "spawning... human beings who never should have been born"[4] have been safely tucked away categorized under the PC term of "Choice." Over the course of several decades our nation has had its once intrinsic ideals that values each soul as one of promise, slowly eroded away. We've watched an organization, through shrewd patience and sophistry, gain credibility and admiration doing singularly what all former racist groups... the KKK, the Confederate Army, thousands of heinous slave owners and Jim Crow era lynch mobs, could not do combined. On a scale matched only by the Nazi Government's genocide machine, Black

---

3   http://www.blackgenocide.org/black.html
4   Margaret Sanger, Pivot of Civilization

Americans represent 12.3 percent of the U.S. population.[5] Since 1973, abortionists have killed over 16 million black babies, representing over 40 percent of todays population of 40 million Black Americans. Sadly, even with the knowledge of its racist beginning and the disproportionate impact on one race, Planned Parenthood's abortion clinics remain well entrenched. Even with mounting scientific evidence of the negative long-term emotional and physical toll on Black mothers or the spiritual searing our race's soul, this tenet of Liberalism has effectively imbedded itself into the core of our community. We, unlike all the generations before us, have accepted an empathy-free disconnection that allows us to *simply not care.*

As a sociopathic chameleon, Sanger was able to simultaneously and effectively ingratiate herself into two separate and opposing groups, the White Racist KKK organization and the Black Racist Royalty Class Professionals. Her talent for sophistry can be attested by her ability to fulfill the needs of her diverse audience. The science of eugenics allowed Royalty Class Black elitists to accept their superior status to others of their race, the darker and less educated ones. This perception was based on their perceived superior gene value of their mixed ancestry. White racists accepted their superiority based on their hatred of anyone that is different from themselves..

Scientific Racism—This form of racism is based on genes, rather than skin color or language. The issue is not color of skin or dialect of tongue, *but 'quality of genes.*

---

5   http://www.bing.com/search?q=how+many+black+americans+are+there+in+the+usa&andqs=SC&andpq=how+many+bloack+americans+&andsk=SC4&andsc=8-26&andsp=5&andcvid=F19D656538AC4B9888C9AA7EEBC030DD&andFORM=QBLH

Therefore, as long as blacks, Jews and Hispanics demonstrate a *good quality gene pool*–as long as they act white and think white–they are esteemed equally with Aryans. As long as they are, as Margaret Sanger said, 'the best of their race,' then they can be [counted] as valuable citizens." By the same token, individual whites who showed dysgenic traits must also have their fertility curbed right along with the other inferiors and undesirables. Scientific racism is an equal opportunity. Anyone with a *defective gene pool* is suspect. And anyone who shows promise may be admitted to the ranks of the elite.[6]

Racial Supremacy—Consistent with her deep belief of racial supremacy and "purity" of the "Aryan" race "Margaret Sanger is responsible, more than anyone else, for keeping alive international racism. She played the attractive hostess for racist thinkers all over the world. Organizing the First World Population Conference in Geneva in 1926, she invited Clarence C. Little, Edward A. East, Henry Pratt Fairchild, and Raymond Pearl--all infamous racists." In September 1930 she invited Nazi anthropologist Eugene Fischer, whose ideas were cited by the Nazis to legitimize the extermination of Jews, to meet with her at her home.[7]

HISTORY OF PLANNED PARENTHOOD

Planned Parenthood itself reports that of the 132,314 abortions it did in 1991, 23.2% were on African Americans,

---

[6] http://www.cwfa.org/the-negro-project-margaret-sangers-eugenic-plan-for-black-americans/

[7] http://www.ewtn.com/library/PROLIFE/PPRACISM.TXT

12.5% were on Hispanics, and 7% were on other minorities. Thus, the total abortions on minorities are 42.7%. But minorities comprise only 19.7% of the U.S. population. Therefore, relative to population percentage, Planned Parenthood strategically aborts minorities three times a higher rate than whites.

"When an organization has a history of racism, when its literature is openly racist, when its goals are self-consciously racial, and when its programs invariably revolve around race, it doesn't take an expert to realize that the organization

- **1916**—Margaret Sanger, a member of the Socialist Party of America,[8] opened the first birth control clinic in Harlem. The clinic serviced the poor immigrants who heavily populated the area — those deemed "unfit" to reproduce.[9]

- **May 1926**—*The KKK.* "I accepted an invitation to talk to the women's branch of the Ku Klux Klan... I saw through the door dim figures parading with banners and illuminated crosses...I was escorted to the platform, was introduced, and began to speak.... In the end, through simple illustrations I believed I had accomplished my purpose. A dozen invitations to speak to similar groups were proffered."[10]

- **1939**—*The Negro Project*: "We should hire three or four colored ministers, preferably with social-service

---

8   http://spartacus-educational.com/USAsocialismP.htm

9   http://www.lifecoalition.com/?p=101

10   Ibid

backgrounds, and with engaging personalities. The most successful educational approach to the Negro is through a religious appeal. We don't want the word to go out that we want to exterminate the Negro population and the minister is the man who can straighten out that idea if it ever occurs to any of their more rebellious members."
– Margaret Sanger[11]

- **2002**—*The Born-Alive Infants Protection Act* (BAIPA). Illinois and Federal legislature that eventually passed, BAIPA was meant to make illegal death "by neglect" of babies born alive but unwanted by their mother.[12] Three attempts were made in the Illinois legislation 2001, 2002 and 2003 to provide legal protection for "babies born alive." All three attempts were opposed by then Illinois Senator Obama.[13]

- **2012**—*"After-Birth Abortion."* (Live Birth Abortion/ Infanticide). Alberto Giubilin, a philosopher from the University of Milan, and Francesca Minerva, an ethicist from the University of Melbourne, have made the case that since both the unborn baby and the newborn do not have the moral status of actual persons and are consequently morally irrelevant, what they call "after-birth abortion" should be permissible in all the cases

---

[11]   939 Margaret Sanger- regarding her "Negro Project"_

[12]   http://www.redstate.com/diary/warner_todd_huston/2008/08/14/obama-lied-about-vote-against-live-birth-abor/

[13]   http://www.factcheck.org/2008/08/obama-and-infanticide/

where abortion is, including cases where the newborn is perfectly healthy.[14]

- **2015—***Selling of Baby Body Parts.* In the fourth undercover investigative video of Planned Parenthood officials discussed the harvesting and selling of aborted baby parts—internal organs and tissue—a medical assistant, with the doctor, is shown in a Planned Parenthood office picking organs from a dead baby out of a glass pie dish and at points saying, *"here's the heart ... this is part of the head ... here's some intestines."*[15]

Who would have guessed in 1916 that a decision by the black community in Harlem, New York to open its doors to the first abortion center would progress within 100 years to the election of a Black President who would defend the practice of "Live Birth Abortion," a United States Justice Dept who would not investigate the selling of body parts of babies statistically killed to maximize their market value and Democrat and Pro-Abortionist Republicans who refuse to do anything about this abortion cartel....

THE NATURE OF ETERNAL LAWS

There are eternal laws of nature that serve as touchstones by which all human progress is measured, i.e. math, science,

---

14   http://www.lifesitenews.com/news/shock-ethicists-justify-infanticide-in-major-medical-journal

15   http://www.cnsnews.com/news/article/michael-w-chapman/planned-parenthood-baby-body-parts-video-was-crack-little-bits-skull

chemistry, etc. Each law is predictable, irrefutable, and cannot be altered by man's wishes or wisdom. Regarding our relationship to these laws, as individual or collectively as a nation, it is simple. We can choose the blessing that comes from understanding and respecting them or we can chose to work through the consequences of our ignorance. As per the law of gravity, the effects of eternal laws are both reliable and predictable. Always present, the Law of Gravity cannot be changed or altered by the laws of man. It can be suspended temporality, by other eternal laws that are counteractive to it, like The Law of Lift or Momentum., In time, regardless of race, creed, or color, the Law of Gravity will once again claim its own, *what goes up must come down.*

So it is with the Eternal Law of Seed and Harvest. The blossoming of an apple tree is tied inexplicably to the planting of an apple seed, the fruition of a tomato plant originates with the sowing of a tomatoes seed... it is immutable. In keeping with this law, the planting of the seed of bigotry, deception and evil begets the fruit of bigotry, deception and evil. The seed and fruit thus described is called Planned Parenthood, the sower of the seed, its founder, Margaret Sanger.

As we consider the documented goals of this organization and its founder's it will be helpful to understand the soil in which the seed of Planned Parenthood was planted. During the late 1800s, Americans' hearts, minds and souls were receptive to a new scientific theory whose influence would be felt throughout the world. The world was in the process

of embracing Darwin's theory on the origin of man, and Galton's theory that artificial means could improve the human species. The consequence of Darwinism and Eugenics would over the following century result in the suffering and loss of millions upon millions of lives. The country's acceptance of their racist-based science would stunt American's heart and prolong the acceptance of minority groups as equals for decades. The seed of Darwinism, sowed by a white intellectual atheist was founded on a premise that man began as a primitive ape, progressed in time to a primitive, sub-human black race and ultimately to its greatest creation, the white race. A naturalist, Charles Darwin's thinking and writing on the subject of evolution and natural selection would cause him to reject the evidence for God in nature and ultimately to renounce the Bible, God, and the Christian faith. [16]

The seed of Eugenics, again sowed by the white intellectual atheist Darwin, was predicated on an idea that later in the 1800s there would be a need to control inferior populations through population control. Defined in this manner, "The essence of evolution is natural selection; the essence of eugenics is the replacement of 'natural' selection by conscious, premeditated, or artificial selection in the hope of speeding up the evolution of 'desirable' characteristics and the elimination of undesirable ones."[17]

This philosophy of "survival of the fit" would lead Eugenicist believers to adamantly oppose charities that saved or improved the lives of the downtrodden. Francis Galton, a cousin of Charles Darwin who coined the word eugenics believed that "the proper evolution of the human race was thwarted by philanthropic outreach to the poor: misguided

---

[16] http://creation.com/charles-darwins-slippery-slide-into-unbelief
[17] http://www.emmerich1.com/EUGENICS.htm

charity encouraged the "unfit" to bear more children."[18] This spiritually devoid science, over the next 100 years, would lead to the demeaning of life and the subsequent mistreatment and extermination of minorities around the world. As governments worldwide declared classified groups as "inferior class" and sub-human, these groups would be treated with untold cruelty, actions justified by the science of Darwinism and Eugenics. It is in this environment in which millions within "civilized" societies would tolerate in full sight, man's inhumanity to man, tolerance that would eventually empower the century's greatest tyrants and mass murderers Hitler, Stalin, and Mussolini.

The acceptance of these theories led to a hardening of America's heart and spirit. What followed was a callous consciousness that would evolve to self-centered elitism. It is this spirit of elitism that today defines the ideology of liberalism, socialism, communism and the progressive movement.

Margaret Sanger's embrace of the race-based science of Darwinism and Eugenics combined with a mix of atheism and Marxism proved to be a potent concoction resulting in what could be best described today as a sociopath, an individual "devoid of conscience." She spent her entire adult life gaining the trust of the black race, as she would simultaneously spend her life's resources attempting to eliminate them. Her view of the Australian Aborigine people is instructive of her racist and evil personality. Like many eugenicists of her era, Sanger saw Australian aborigines as under-evolved and of little value except where they could be studied to gain better knowledge

---

[18] http://www.emmerich1.com/EUGENICS.htm

of evolution. She certainly believed that they, and other black people, should not be allowed to enter the white gene pool. She had a strong drive to promote contraception and negative eugenics (to prevent the birth of 'weaker' human elements.)"

"It is said that a fish as large as a man has a brain no larger than the kernel of an almond. In all fish and reptiles where there is no great brain development, there is also no conscious sexual control. The lower down in the scale of human development we go the less sexual control we find. It is said that the aboriginal Australian, the lowest known species of the human family, just a step higher than the chimpanzee in brain development, has so little sexual control that police authority alone prevents him from obtaining sexual satisfaction on the streets."[19]

SANGER—THE SIREN

In Greek mythology, Sirens were dangerous creatures, portrayed as seductresses who lured nearby sailors with their enchanting music and voices to shipwreck on the rocky coast of their island. There is no better example of the bewitching and destructive nature of ideology of liberalism than Planned Parenthood. It has been for the black community, it's most seductive siren.

No organization in our history has torn at the fiber of the family as has Planned Parenthood. Its founder, Margaret Sanger was both genius and beguiling in her strategy, both heartless and ruthless in her betrayal. An Atheist, Socialist

---

[19]   Margaret Sanger- Sanger, *"What Every Girl Should Know"* 1920, p. 47

and racist, she has over the course of her life, able to seduce the support of some of the most educated and successful Black Americans of her day. She was able to accomplish what the KKK found impossible to do over decades of intimidation, for as evil as were the KKK's many atrocities, they could not defeat the determined, courageous and united black community. Sanger on the other hand relied on stealth networking to disarm the community she had targeted. Some of those she used were enthralled as she fed their egos with platitudes and prominence as others were attracted by her feigned concern for their race. Her international, multi-billion–dollar organization today continues to reward prominent members of black community. Those who give their allegiance to her program are granted political power, wealth, acceptance and face time on BET, MSNBC and other liberal media outlets.

Peddling her wares wrapped in pretty packages labeled "women's health" and "family planning," her program has been a plague on the black community for over 100 years. It has hardened the very soul of a race that continues to kill hundreds of thousands of its own babies each year.

SANGER–IN HER OWN WORDS

To understand Sanger's program and strategy it will be instructive to hear directly from her own words:

KU KLUX KLAN

"I accepted an invitation to talk to the women's branch of the Ku Klux Klan... I saw through the door dim figures parading with banners and illuminated crosses... I was escorted to the platform, was introduced, and began to speak.... In the end, through simple illustrations I believed I had accomplished my purpose. A dozen invitations to speak to similar groups were proffered."[20]

HUMAN WASTE

"[Slavs, Latin, and Hebrew immigrants are] human weeds... deadweight of human waste... [Blacks, soldiers, and Jews are a] menace to the race... Eugenic sterilization is an urgent need... We must prevent multiplication of this bad stock."[21]

LARGE FAMILIES

"The most merciful thing that a large family does to one of its infant members is to kill it." [22]

---

[20] *Margaret Sanger: An Autobiography*, P.366) (25)

[21] Margaret Sanger, 1933 Birth Control Review

[22] Margaret Sanger, *Women and the New Race* (Eugenics Publ. Co., 1920, 1923)

HUMAN WEEDS

On blacks, immigrants and indigents: "human weeds," "reckless breeders," "spawning... human beings who never should have been born."[23]

CHARITIES

"Organized charity itself is the symptom of a malignant social disease. Those vast, complex, interrelated organizations aiming to control and to diminish the spread of misery and destitution and all the menacing evils that spring out of this sinisterly fertile soil, are the surest sign that our civilization has bred, is breeding and perpetuating constantly increasing numbers of defectives, delinquents and dependents."[24]

ON THE EXTERMINATION OF BLACKS

"We do not want word to go out that we want to exterminate the Negro population," she said, "if it ever occurs to any of their more rebellious members."[25]

"The mass of significant Negroes still breed carelessly and disastrously, with the result that the increase among Negroes... is in that portion of the population least intelligent and fit."[26]

---

23   Margaret Sanger, *Pivot of Civilization*, referring to immigrants and poor people

24   http://thinkexist.com/quotation/organized-charity-itself-is-the-symptom-of-a/397373.html

25   http://www.dianedew.com/sanger.htm

26   Margaret Sanger, *Pivot of Civilization*

CATHOLICS

The "salvation of American civilization"—the sterilization of those "unfit" to procreate. She condemned the "irresponsible and reckless" rates of procreation among those "whose religious scruples prevent their exercising control over their numbers." "There is no doubt in the minds of all thinking people that the procreation of this group should be stopped."[27]

BOARD OF DIRECTORS

Sanger was relentless and productive in networking her way into the black community with the help of respected black intellectual professions. She and other eugenicist of her day believed that lighter-skinned races were superior to darker-skinned races. [28] There were other Royalty Class Black professionals like W.E.B DuBois who held the same eugenicist philosophy, as Sanger. It was this Eugenic and evolutionary foundation that would initiate DuBois' proposed Talented Tenth beliefs in which intellectuals, European-looking blacks, like himself, would be looked upon as the Saviors of their race. It was this philosophy that justified his advocacy for abortion within his community and integration (race normalization) outside of it. These beliefs were predicated on the idea of evolutionary group of "betters" (Royalty Black

---

[27] March 1925 international birth-control event in New York City

[28] McCann (1994), pp 150–4. Bigotry: p 153. See also p 45, *The selected papers of Margaret Sanger*, Volume 1.

Class) within the black race, which would eventually "Raise Up" and (integrate or race neutralize themselves) themselves away from the remainder of their race.... Away from those who have been deemed not worthy of acceptance by the Royalty Class.

"...developing the 'Best of this Race' that they may guide the Mass away from the contamination and death of the Worst, in their own and other races."

- W.E.B DuBois

W.E.B. DUBOIS
Sanger's Harlem Birth Control Center: Board Member

DuBois, in his article "Black Folk and Birth Control," said, "inevitable clash of ideals between those Negroes who were striving to improve their economic position and those whose religious faith made the limitation of children a sin." He criticized the mass of ignorant Negroes who bred "carelessly and disastrously so that the increase among [them]... *is from that part of the population least intelligent and fit, and least able to rear their children properly.*" He called for a more liberal attitude among black churches. He said they were open to "intelligent propaganda of any sort, and the American Birth Control League and other agencies ought to get their speakers before church congregations and their arguments in the Negro newspapers."[29]

---

[29]   http://blackgenocide.org/archived_articles/negro03.html

CHARLES S. JOHNSON (EUGENIST)
Fisk University's First Black President: Board Member

Johnson served on the National Advisory Council to the BCFA, becoming integral to the Negro Project. He wrote eugenic discrimination was necessary for blacks. He said the high maternal and infant mortality rates, along with diseases like tuberculosis, typhoid, malaria and venereal infection, made it difficult for large families to adequately sustain themselves.

Further, "...the status of Negroes as marginal workers, their confinement to the lowest paid branches of industry, the necessity for the labors of mothers, as well as children, to balance meager budgets, are factors [that] emphasize the need for lessening the burden not only for themselves, but of society, which must provide the supplementary support in the form of relief."[30]

DR. DOROTHY FEREBEE (EUGENIST)
Black Physician and Sanger's Board Member

"For a eugenic .... it was integral to the implementation of eugenics to eliminate the 'unfit'. Eugenics is "a science that deals with the improvement (as by control of human mating) of hereditary qualities of a race or breed." Negative eugenics focused on preventing the birth of those it considered inferior or unfit. The pseudo-science (racial hygiene theory) of negative eugenics influenced social policy and eugenics-

---

[30]   Ibid

based legislation (Immigration Act of 19243, segregation laws, sterilization laws) and led to the racial hygiene theory adopted by the Nazis."[31]

"The future program [of Planned Parenthood] should center around more education in the field through the work of a professional Negro worker, because those of us who believe that the benefits of Planned Parenthood as a vital key to the elimination of human waste must reach the entire population, also believe that a double effort must be made to extend this program as a public health measure to Negroes who need is proportionately greater."[32]

- Dr. Dorothy Ferebee Chairman of the Family Planning Committee of the National Council of Negro Women

"Negro professionals fully integrated into the staff... who could interpret the program and objectives to [other blacks] in the normal course of day-to-day contacts; could break down fallacious attitudes and beliefs and elements of distrust; could inspire the confidence of the group; and would not be suspect of the intent to eliminate the race."

- "Planned Parenthood as a Public Health Measure for the Negro Race," January 29th, 1942, Dr. Dorothy Ferebee

There are many unsung heroes throughout this era as the black community progressed from its former state of slavery. Nothing is more indicative of the courage of this generation

---

[31]   http://www.toomanyaborted.com/thenegroproject/
[32]   Ibid

than what can be seen through the efforts of the black fraternities and sororities during that time. A prime example of this was the AKA Sorority, one of the many prominent national black women service organizations. Initiated by its International President, Ida Jackson, The AKA's from 1933 to 1940, became America's first mobile medical clinic servicing poor Blacks throughout the south.

The program, called The Mississippi Health Project, with the above quoted Dr. Ferebee of the Howard University Medical School appointed as Director, would facilitate over 46 Black female doctors' participating over the summer months.[33]

Over a seven-year period this program stands as one of the most impressive examples of voluntary work ever conducted by black physicians in the Jim Crow south. Throughout the era of segregation, black physicians in the south contributed their time, money and expertise to improve the health of their communities. Their stated goals for the Mississippi Health Project reflected a commonalty with others, like Booker T. Washington, to uplift and offer a hand-up to self-sufficiency: (1) To improve the health of negroes in a section of the country where medical services were limited; (2) To create and encourage Negro efforts for self-improvement; and (3) To stimulate a sense of pride and appreciation for the AKA service programs. 34 It ended due to the fuel shortage at the beginning of WWII. These female doctors drove their own

---

[33] "Changing the Face of Medicine: Dr. Dorothy Celeste Boulding Ferebee." National Institutes of Health. 2007-02-19. Retrieved 2007-09-28.

[34] AKA sorority, The 1936 Mississippi Health Project in Bolivar County,(Detroit and London:Gale Research Inc., 1992

vehicles from the Northeast over southern backwoods and rural roads delivering medical support, supplies and hygiene education to over 15,000 uneducated, indentured rural families throughout Mississippi.[35] It was initiatives by selfless Black leaders, like Ida Jackson, that would provide a window for southern rural Black Americans to see for themselves the possibility of the American Dream. In the summer of 1934, Ida Jackson initiated the Summer School for Rural Teachers to train future teachers. She worked with a total of 22 student teachers and 243 school children. In addition, she held night classes for 48 adults. By obtaining 2600 books for the school's library, Jackson made it "the largest library owned by white or colored in all Holmes County." [36]

Sanger's ability to network and befriend those within the leadership of the black community can be seen in the contradiction of Dr. Dorothy Boulding Freebee. Dorothy Freebee would oversee a program that required a courageous commitment and charity to the most vulnerable of her race.. "It is curious that she would simultaneously sit on the advisory board of Planned Parenthood, whose founder was committed to the "weeding out" of her race's "unfit." As a Eugenics proponent, Sanger's view on charity was very clear *"[Charity] conceals a stupid cruelty, because it is not courageous enough to face unpleasant facts."* [37]

The composition of Sanger's Planned Parenthood board could very well highlight the sociopathic effectiveness of Sanger to befriend and persuade her victims of her "good

---

35 McNealey, E., Pearls of Service, p. 181

36 McNealey, E., Pearls of Service, p. 181

37 The Pivot of Civilization 1922- Chapter 5, "The Cruelty of Charity"

intentions." It should be noted in Ferebee's talk, "Changing the face of Medicine," it seemed to reflect Sanger's influence as she discusses "the elimination of human waste" when speaking of others of her race. Though there where professional blacks who shared the preeminent philosophy of a genetically superior Talented Tenth, many of the well-meaning black middle/upper class were simply seduced into the web of the deceitful black widow spider, whose motives were ultimately 180 decrees different from theirs.

Sanger was able to move her agenda though the community by understanding the different visionary camps within and being able to morph the message of her cause to be attractive to her victims. By giving the appearance of making their cause her cause, she increased her influence and the effectiveness in spreading her message. She would use as her messengers black professionals who deeply cared for their own community, as indicated in the Mississippi Health Project. These visionary professionals would use their own financial resources to travel down southern hot and dusty rural roads to serve and uplift the poorest and most downtrodden among their race.

Sanger would simultaneously tailor another message for the middleclass elitists represented by W.E.B. DuBois. These professionals perceived themselves superior to other members of their race based on education, professional occupation, being "light-skinned" and by their acceptance into white society's inner circles. By introducing Sanger as a friend, they proved to be the perfect Trojan Horse for Sanger's goal to ingratiate herself within the black community.

SANGER'S STRATEGY

Prior to 1939, Sanger's abortion outreach was limited to the black community, her Harlem clinic and speaking at black churches. Her vision for the reproductive practices of Black Americans expanded after the January 1939 merger of the Clinical Research Bureau and the American Birth Control League to form the Birth Control Federation of America. Dr. Clarence J. Gamble, of Procter and Gamble fame, was chosen to be the Birth Control Federation of America, Southern Regional Director.[38] Best articulated by the racist abortionist, Dr. Gamble, is the strategy of Planned Parenthood, its perception and deception. In a November 1939 memorandum, entitled *Suggestions for the Negro Project*, he recognized that black leaders might regard birth control as an extermination plot, so suggested (to Sanger) black leaders be placed in positions where "it would appear" they were in charge.

Another project Director lamented to Sanger: "I wonder if Southern Darkies can ever be entrusted with... a clinic. Our experience causes us to doubt their ability to work except under white supervision"[39]

Margaret Sanger might well have been one of the 20th century's greatest strategists. She was among the America's first influential contributors to the concept of 'personal relationship networking.' Today social liberals consider her as one of the primary leaders and inspirations of the liberal

---

[38] http://www.cwfa.org/the-negro-project-margaret-sangers-eugenic-plan-for-black-americans/#sthash.fBtDxRY1.dpuf

[39]

social and sexual revolution of the 1960s.[40] US Secretary of State Hillary Clinton said that she admires "Margaret Sanger enormously, her courage, her tenacity, her vision" and that she was "really in awe of" Sanger's early work in Brooklyn, New York.[41]

Though Sanger's strategy of sophistry has not changed over the last 100 years, the size and scope have changed with its adoption by other like-minded individuals.. The success of the early White-managed Planned Parenthood and NAACP was predicated on their strategic use of Black Americans as facades, "giving the appearance" that they were in charge. This new century's version can now be seen in large and powerful corporations like Viacom (BET), Comcast/NBC (MSNBC) and the white controlled Labor Unions (AFL/CIO) that strategically deliver their message to the masses through their employed Black spokesmen. Black ownership, Black control and legitimate Black leadership have never been congruent with the ideology of Liberalism.

Sanger continues to cast a dark shadow over the Black community decades after her death as her legacy continues to "weed out the unfit" among Black Americans. As with her pre- 1939 efforts had focused on the community of the Harlem clinic and black churches,[42] her present organization has retained that legacy. New research released by Protecting Black Life (an outreach of Life Issues Institute) reveals that 79% of Planned Parenthood's surgical abortion facilities

---

40 http://www.ukapologetics.net/10/sanger.htm

41 http://www.lifesitenews.com/news/archive/ldn/2009/apr/09040306

42 http://www.cwfa.org/the-negro-project-margaret-sangers-eugenic-plan-for-black-americans/#sthash.fBtDxRY1.dpuf

are located within walking distance of African American and/or Hispanic/Latino communities. The group has a new map (*http://www.protectingblacklife.org/pp_targets/*) which serves as a powerful visual — illustrating in full color on a website portal integrated with Google Maps functionality just how Planned Parenthood targets minorities. This interactive site gives viewers an up close and personal look at just how close these facilities are to their neighborhoods.[43]

As mentioned earlier in this chapter, Sanger's organization has since 1973 been responsible for the deaths of over 16 million black babies, equating to 40% of the total number of blacks living in America today. Some would consider the targeted elimination of that number of lives within one race... genocide. Not the Royalty Class Black Man.

Added to the NAACP /Sanger strategy is one Liberalisms' most effective plays... requiring an agreeable black spokesman who is willing to do what is politically incorrect for White Americans to do. This involves the silencing of all competing and independent Black voices via personal attack, vilification and destruction of reputations if necessary. Considered racist if Liberal White men took these same actions, the Royalty Class Black Man is given carte blanche to turn his vitriol onto successful members of his own race. Because his ultimate goal is not to find solutions for his own race through intellectual debates, the Royalty Class Black Man plays his appointed role as the ideology of Liberalisms' Attack Dog.. He displays his anger at new

---

43   http://www.lifenews.com/2012/10/16/79-of-planned-parenthood-abortion-clinics-target-blacks-hispanics/

thought even though old thought has proven a dismal failure for the Black community (A boon for the Royalty Class). He then dutifully and predictable returns to his traditional and limited vocabulary of past intimidation terms like Uncle Tom, Oreo, Porch monkey, etc. (Again see Kevin Jacksons' book *Race Pimping* for a one-page list.) Their prototype was an accomplished intellectual and... the "Best of his race," W.E.B DuBois. Today's ideology of Liberalism no longer requires a person of accomplishment or intelligence. It only needs a "willing opportunist," someone who can, on cue, rally the emotions of the hopeless and angry urban Black community when called upon. The same community is kept angry, through its anti-White messaging, by the "Black in Name Only, BET (Black Entertainment News Channel). The contracted Royalty Black Class Problem Profiteers, Jesse Jackson and Al Sharpton fill this role once required of the Socialist turned anti-American Communist W.E.B DuBois.

Sanger would continue throughout the decades to hone her message and deepen her influence into black professional network, as she prepared to implement the 1936 Negro Project. Ironically, if she were alive today she would silently detest most of the liberals who today defend and honor her... Blacks, Jews, Christians, immigrants, and soldiers. She has left us with 50 years of documented writings, actions and words that conclusively define her. She was an avowed atheist, eugenicist, Socialist, pro-Nazi supporter, pro-KKK supporter, anti-Catholic and racist and yet today's Liberal ideologues view her as a Saint and will twist the truth like a pretzel to defend her.

CONCLUSION:
Robin A. Brace, January 2010, UK Apologetics

"Margaret Sanger's ethics and moral evaluation were very deeply flawed and her seeming liking for vulgarity, bad taste and for provoking anger when it might have been avoided, often brought her into needless conflicts. Meanwhile her atheism, and her easy acceptance of racism and eugenics and her approval of the principle of euthanasia (if not the actual practice of gassing the physically and mentally unfit) mean that - overall - we must consider Sanger as an evil little lady who will not escape the judgment of God for her part in being one of the architects of the hideous moral revolution of the 1960s/1970s, a sexual revolution which, it is now clear, has caused enormous damage, including the utterly disgraceful fact of millions of aborted babies. This, we believe, will finally stand as one of the most hideous stains on 20th/21st century western society. Most 'enlightened' westerners don't even think of this as important, but there is a God in Heaven who is keeping an account."[44]

---

[44]   Robin A. Brace, January 2010, UK Apologetics

CHAPTER 16

COMMITMENTS AND CONCLUSION

GOD

"Where the Spirit of the Lord is, there is liberty"- 2 Corinthians 3:17

The Resurrection of our present Black Community to the proud, independent and self-sufficient community of the 1950s and 60s may seem a daunting task to some. There are unfortunately millions of Americans who have never seen firsthand the visionary, courageous, loyal, entrepreneurial, selfless and spiritual leading Black man. Due to the agnostic nature of Liberalism and its abhorrence to Manhood, Americans from all backgrounds, cultures and colors are now experiencing the same void.

The damage to our country over the last few decades can only be addressed with a recommitment to proven and indispensable pillars present in days of old. Change must first occur from within beginning with desire, open minds and a willingness to accept basic truths.

Among the first of these truths is that as Americans we live in an Exceptional country. It is a nation that grants each citizen, regardless of color, age, gender or starting point, an "opportunity" for an exceptional life. Though all will not choose to take advantage of the opportunities available, all Americans benefit from those who do. *The poorest among us rank among the world's richest.*

What is the source of America's Exceptionalism? It is during a search of the world's most obvious wealth supplies, where the hidden secret of the American difference is found. American Exceptionalism, for instance, is not found in the abundance of natural resources. If so, Russia or Saudi Arabia, instead of America, would have been the world's destination for millions of emigrants over the last two centuries. Russia is the world-leader in gas and timber reserves while Saudi Arabia holds over 20% of the world's oil reserve.[1]

If Exceptionalism was measured in land mass or in the diversity of forests, streams, lakes, mountains and deserts, America would rank fourth behind Russia, Canada and China. New Zealand would lead the world due to its #1 ranking with its perfect climate.[2] China and India would lead the world as number one and two, if Exceptionalism were based on populace ranking.[3] Russia, Botswana and the Democratic Republic of Congo would rank first through third, if diamond reserves were the standard.

American Exceptionalism is therefore not due to material or natural wealth, climate, or population size. It stems instead from a source that is not obvious to the naked eye. From its very beginning America's blessing and protection has rested

---

[1] http://www.thecountriesof.com/top-10-countries-with-most-natural-resources-in-the-world/

[2] http://science.howstuffworks.com/nature/climate-weather/atmospheric/10-countries-with-perfect-climates10.htm with

[3] http://www.infoplease.com/ipa/A0004391.html

on the faithfulness of its people to a God who is the author of all blessings.

With the signing of the Mayflower Compact, Americans established themselves uniquely among all of the world's nations, as a covenant making and covenant-keeping people. After a perilous 66-day journey from Holland, a small group of Christian Pilgrims built a settlement based on Judeo- Christian beliefs. What followed has been a two-century journey by generations of Americans attempting to understand and adhere to those beliefs. The Mayflower Compacts' baseline for individual rights, freedom and a law-abiding society, were later enumerated in the Declaration of Independence and the Constitution. No other country has duplicated the culture of America in its devotion to God and allowing the freedom, in a multitude of ways, to worship him. We have thus, for the rest of the world, best represented the "the light of the world... A city set on a hill."

The promised umbrella of protection and prosperity continues to be available to all American cultures and communities, including the Black Community. The evidence of which can be seen over the last century of success and contributions when, as a community, it had adhered closest to its Judeo-Christian roots.

A second Truth lies in the foundation of the freedoms enumerated in the US Constitution. It is a recognition that an individual's right to Life, Liberty and the Pursuit of Happiness relies on the only financial model that grants this opportunity: Free Enterprise. It is inherent within a free society that the individual is allowed to use his/her dream power, creativity, faith and tenacity to compete for and acquire capital. This is where access to our nations' promises is secured. It is Free

Enterprise that permanently lowers the economic drawbridge and provides an onramp for anyone who dares to dream. It is paved, well-lit and has for 200 years proven stable enough to carry the weight of untold millions of Americans, regardless of the baggage that they bring with them.

It was the American Free Enterprise system that allowed for the successful settling of my African ancestors in America. It is a story that began with the arrival of an eight-year-old African boy, in the belly of a slave ship. It is a story that continues decades later of a politically engaged, proud American citizen known for his "fierce independence," a spirit that I define as the American Way. He was a successful entrepreneur, property owner, proud patriarch and a pillar of his community. His legacy can now be found within the lives of hundreds, if not thousands, of his progeny. As noted earlier, one of his Great, Great, Great Granddaughters has, through her fiercely independent spirit and tenacity, earned an opportunity to fulfill her life's dream of teaching in China. As she does so, she grants her young son exposure to a new culture and language allowing him to expand his scope of unlimited possibilities of American Exceptionalism. His "opportunities" will be exponentially greater than that of my restrictive 1960s segregated south upbringing, my dad's 1930s KKK plagued era or that of his Great, Great, Great, Great, grandfather Silas's 1842 arrival in the belly of a Slave Ship. It is within the eternal perspective of time, and through the eyes of history where the improving heart of the America can be clearly seen. For it is a culture that has proven with the passing of time, as a predictable society that ALWAYS looks to find its better self. This is an innate quality deep within the DNA of diverse and covenant-keeping American People.

PRINCIPLES: POLITICAL FREE AGENCY

"I guess you'd call me an independent, since I've never identified myself with one party or another in politics. I always decide my vote by taking as careful a look as I can at the actual candidates and issues themselves, no matter what the party label." - Jackie Robinson[4]

There is no better way to learn the meaning of "Principled" than to witness it firsthand. In an earlier chapter I spoke of an experience, in the early 1960s, of witnessing my father's response as two young white boys attempted to remove my mother from a "White Women Only Restroom." My Dad did not hesitate to rush to my mother's aid, the odds against him not being a factor. This example of Manhood was one of countless ones that I was fortunate to witness throughout my life. It was during a reflection of this experience over 50 years later that my dad shared one of his final lessons with me... the longevity of Principles. It was from a generation who did their best to live by them.

Neither Mom or Dad ever brought up the "rest room" incident again with us as children, nor did they complain of victimization at the hands of horrible white racists. They had the uncanny ability to deal with issues in front of them, fight for what was right and then move on. Their attitude could be best summarized by something my mom told me as a teenager, while standing in our kitchen. "Burgie... remember to never let someone else's problems become yours." From a very wise mother, it was a message for the ages.

---

[4]   http://www.brainyquote.com/quotes/authors/j/jackie_robinson.html

Shortly after arriving home I fortunately walked past my parents' room as they were discussing how my Dad was going to respond to the "rest room" affront. He told Mom of his plans to cut up and return his gas card to the headquarters of this particular gas station chain. When dad was 85, a year prior to his passing, we were reflecting on memories of earlier years and I shared with him my experience, as a 10–11-year-old, of witnessing that incident from the backseat of our car. His response confirmed the true meaning and timeless value of being Principled. With a smile and sense of pride, he confirmed my recollection and added that he has never since bought a "drop of gas" from that gas chain. I was left to ponder my Dad's decision over five decades prior and his commitment to it. Did his personal boycott make a difference to this multi-billion–dollar gas supplier? No. Did it make a difference to the principled self-esteem of my Dad and to his oldest son? *Absolutely.*

To achieve its Resurrection, the Black community will need to commit, once again, to build a community of Principled Men. It must set aside the valueless facade of color, personality, popularity and promises and stand once again, for principled representation. Principled representatives will innately adhere to an eternal truth… "if you teach the people true knowledge, they will govern themselves."[5] They will view the empowerment of self-sufficiency that stems from education and engagement as a birthright of their constituents.

The qualities of a Principle populace… *honesty, charity, empathy and loyalty* are revealed from inside-out and not outside-in. It is the heart to heart connection found at the core

---

[5]   Pioneer-Tribute to Brigham Young-pg7

of the Judea-Christian doctrine and those who profess a love and devotion to Jesus Christ. To have its day of Resurrection, the Black community must cease to vote for its representation solely based on race and color. This is and has always been the ways of the racist. Those who encourage the external judgment of others, whether they are Black or White, are simply racist. Racism never was and will never be the pathway to happiness. The Black community must remember "to never let someone else's problems become yours." When Americans allow the hatred of the racist to turn us into hateful racists, they've won. What resides within the soul of a racist, Black or White, is perpetual and passionate anger, instantaneous and unreasonable judgment and negative spirit that guarantees an unhappy existence. Simply put, they've won. There are some Black Americans who actually believe that the Black race is exempt from racism, because of their victim status. This thinking is not only absurdly self-condescending but also convoluted. This nonsensical justification of acceptance of Black racism highlights the lack of critical thinking skills that has become evident within today's progressive public school system. It is why, if we hope to resurrect the Black Community, it is imperative that parents have the Freedom of Choice to send their dear children elsewhere. *Common Sense* is not a welcomed attribute of the ideology of Liberalism.

A Principled community must vehemently reject the concept of party loyalty. The political careers of men and women in either Democratic or Republican Parties should not be the priority of the voter. Instead opportunity, accountability and a well thought out /articulated plan, based on the community's best interest. As *Political Free Agents*, a principled community will demand competition and will value the best-qualified agent for change… regardless of color, race or gender. As it is in every other arena of competition, talent is colorblind. A *Political Free Agent* embraces this truth.

For three decades, until 1993, NFL players had fought for free agency. Being on the frontline for some of the early NFL pioneers resulted in careers that were prematurely ended or altered with trades that were meant to send a message to other players. If players became too outspoken on this issue, they were simply blackballed, as was the infamous case of former Minnesota Vikings Super Bowl QB, Joe Kapp in 1970.[6] It was understood on both sides of the negotiating table that Free Agency would result in paradigm shift within the NFL. Once secured with the 1993 collective bargaining agreement, teams were forced to compete for player services and the environment in which he worked and played improved dramatically. Locker rooms, weight rooms and stadiums transitioned from being fit for Spartan warriors to spacious accommodations with a touch of luxury. Billion-dollar football stadiums now litter the country, not only for a better fan/customer experience, but to attract the best NFL talent. As players freely choose their teams, based on self-interest, they are able to demand tens of millions of dollars more for performing the same functions prior to free agency. The agreement had an immediate impact on salaries, increasing wages for the 1993 season by 38 percent.[7]

Now would be a good time to highlight in real dollars, in a real world example, the empowerment of Free Agency.

---

[6] https://en.wikipedia.org/wiki/Joe_KappThere

[7] Quinn, Kevin G. (2010). "Getting to the 2011-2020 National Football League Collective Bargaining Agreement." *International Journal of Sport Finance*.

In 1973 as a 1st round choice of the NY Jets, I was drafted as the NFL's 13th pick and first Defensive Back. Once drafted, I had two options. One was to sign with the Jets, and hopefully negotiate as close as possible to the predetermined contractual cap set by them. The second choice was to search for an interested Canadian football team to play with. In a closed monopoly and with no other bidders, my capital potential was predetermined and capped regardless of my potential value to the team. I'll never know how close I came to my ceiling, but I felt accomplished with the addition of an addendum that the Jets would pay for the remainder of my college education at the University of Miami. Including my $50,000 signing bonus, my three-year contract totaled $128,000, with only the signing bonus guaranteed. The remaining $78,000 was to be earned year-to-year. This equated to a sweet, low-risk deal for my employer and a very happy employee, clueless of his true market value. In today's inflationary dollars my bonus would have equated to approximately $800,000. As we fast forward to the free agent environment of the 2015 NFL. The 13th pick in that year's draft was by New Orleans for OL Andrus Peat. Peat's four-year contract was fully guaranteed for $11.39 million with a $6.55 million signing bonus.[8] Free Agency empowers the valued individual or group in any Free Market endeavor where it is introduced. It will likewise be so as a principled Black community chooses to become independent *"Political Free Agents."*

---

8   http://www.nfl.com/news/story/0ap3000000493786/article/new-orleans-saints-sign-andrus-peat-to-4year-deal

A principled Black community will be comprised of *Political Free Agents*, who vote across party lines based on its own values and best self-interest. It should demand thoughtful debate and competitive ideas on specific policies and issues. It should demand education and the respect of "intelligent" engagement from its representatives. Once policies and issues are understood, the populace can determine what is in its best interest. When a community is respected for its *Political Free Agency*, competition guarantees that it will never again be taken for granted or neglected. Engagement, knowledge, accountability and independence are the keys to an empowered community. This will insure that our Constitution will work as it was intended... on the behalf of "We the People."

WOMANHOOD

"When our young women refuse to lower their standards, it forces our young men to raise theirs. It is the power of motherhood that defines the character and heart of our nation. The environment they design for our children today will define the souls and vision of our leaders tomorrow, both inside and outside of the home."
- Burgess Owens

One of the most admirable traits of our past great generations of Americans, Black and White, was the honor, respect and the protection that was given to the sanctity of

Womanhood. It was once taught in homes and communities through the use of the simple salutations of Yes Ma'am and No Ma'am. Young men understood from their earliest training that the disrespect of their mother and other woman was simply not tolerated. Not only were excuses not considered, dire consequences from his father was guaranteed. Young men were trained to beware of the enhanced self-esteem that is innate to Manhood with opportunities to work, provide, to lead and to be a willing buffer for others. His willingness to intercede and sacrifice self, brought with it the compensation of worth. In every home and community where edification and the honor of Womanhood is found, is also found Manhood.

The Sacred nature of Womanhood is taught universally, but nowhere has it been held with such high esteem as within the Judeo-Christian ideals of the American culture. It is through dedicated Mothers, that mankind witnesses its closest experience of the pure unconditional love of Christ. It is Motherhood that gives birth, shape souls, and forms the character of our nation. It is through her teachings, example and spiritual intuitiveness that our daughters are taught to fight the worldly message that encourages the lowering of their moral standards. Simultaneously through a connection that is divinely unique, Motherhood encourages her sons to raise their standards. It is by its very nature, a sacred trust of the highest order.

Men can only stand aside in wonderment and admiration viewing the sacrifice, dedication, courage and patience that accompanies the Mother phase of Womanhood. It is the nature of Mothers and Wives that encourages a self-sufficient and self-confident man to search even further within, to find his better self. It is for approval and respect of Womanhood that men find a deeper commitment for courage, a stronger clarity of vision, a deeper willingness to risk and the desire to begin again, if he fails.

Centered on his respect for Womanhood, Manhood discovers his divine nature and is therefore willing to seek for more wisdom, vision, leadership, courage, and a heart for self-sacrifice. It demands respect for himself, his family, race, country, God and seeks for the survival and progress of all for whom he is responsible. The desire to acquire these attributes will lead him to embrace the politics and ideology that correctly mirrors his mission. The principled Black Man will no longer leave this responsibility to someone else. The Black community and our nation will be blessed with the return of Black Manhood.

Black Manhood will not leave his family defenseless, for it is within his divine nature to be the ultimate source as PROTECTOR. As a Husband and Father he identifies abandonment as cowardly, selfish, irresponsible, empathy-free and godless narcissism. Within a community of real men, these male facades are called out for what they are... Failures... Whiners, Weenies, and Wimps.

Black Manhood will not allow the continued perception of his race as beggars and victims, for it is within his divine nature as a LEADER to command respect. He sets the standards for his race and is determined to be victorious against all with whom he competes.

Black Manhood will not tolerate failure and incompetence in the teaching his children, for it is within his divine nature as a VISIONARY to insure the success of his entire race though the raising of an intelligent, thinking, confident and self-sufficient posterity.

Black Manhood will not allow another Man to demean Black Womanhood, for it is within his divine nature as a DEFENDER to act and to demand its respect. He understands that the future of his race, the successful raising of his children, depends upon the edification of Womanhood. He also inherently knows that inaction or cowardice on his part negates respect from others and his right to be called a Man.

Black Manhood will not allow the wanton killing of his posterity for it is within his divine nature as PROCREATOR. He inherently recognizes the God-given potential in his seed and is drawn to his responsibility as a Father. Because he accepts his own value, he will not allow the demeaning of his family or race as less than human or insignificant. He will not allow his children to be destroyed for convenience or for profit. He believes in the innate majesty of his spiritual lineage and refuses to accept the doctrine of those who attempt to tie him to the lowest denominator of the animal kingdom. He is aware of his value in the eyes of God and as a Father, recognizes that same spiritual royalty within his children.

Black Manhood will not leave the spiritual growth of his family to someone else, for it is within his divine nature as its GUIDE to humbly seek for protection, guidance and blessing for his family. He learns to put aside his pride, ego, and the worlds enticing distractions to become his family's ultimate SERVER. He understands that to best insure his success, he must depend on daily inspirational guidance and that his personal example is the best means of teaching his family to rely on those same powers.

One of America's more poignant love stories comes from the Civil War. It is one that illustrates the strength and commitment of true Manhood and Womanhood to each other. Viewed through the temporal eyes of a brief lifetime it is a story of tragedy. But through the eyes of eternity it is an example of a loving bond that has found eternal happiness.

Sullivan Ballou (March 28, 1829 – July 29, 1861) was a lawyer and successful 31-year-old politician from Rhode Island. As a volunteer for the Union Army he is best remembered for the eloquent letter he wrote to his wife one week before he fought in the First Battle of Bull Run. It was a battle that took his life.

July the 14th, 1861
Washington D.C.

My very dear Sarah:

> *The indications are very strong that we shall move in a few days—perhaps tomorrow. Lest I should not be able to write you again, I feel impelled to write lines that may fall under your eye when I shall be no more.*
>
> *Our movement may be one of a few days' duration and full of pleasure—and it may be one of severe conflict and death to me. Not my will, but thine O God, be done. If it is necessary that I should fall on the battlefield for my country, I am ready. I have no misgivings about, or lack of confidence in, the cause in which I am engaged, and my courage does not halt or falter. I know how strongly American Civilization now leans upon the triumph of the Government, and*

how great a debt we owe to those who went before us through the blood and suffering of the Revolution. And I am willing—perfectly willing—to lay down all my joys in this life, to help maintain this Government, and to pay that debt.

But, my dear wife, when I know that with my own joys I lay down nearly all of yours, and replace them in this life with cares and sorrows—when, after having eaten for long years the bitter fruit of orphanage myself, I must offer it as their only sustenance to my dear little children—is it weak or dishonorable, while the banner of my purpose floats calmly and proudly in the breeze, that my unbounded love for you, my darling wife and children, should struggle in fierce, though useless, contest with my love of country.

Sarah, my love for you is deathless, it seems to bind me to you with mighty cables that nothing but Omnipotence could break; and yet my love of Country comes over me like a strong wind and bears me irresistibly on with all these chains to the battlefield.

The memories of the blissful moments I have spent with you come creeping over me, and I feel most gratified to God and to you that I have enjoyed them so long. And hard it is for me to give them up and burn to ashes the hopes of future years, when God willing, we might still have lived and loved together and seen our sons grow up to honorable manhood around us. I have, I know, but few and small claims upon Divine Providence, but something whispers to me—perhaps it is the wafted prayer of my little Edgar—that I shall return to my loved ones unharmed. If I do not, my dear Sarah, never forget how much I love you, and when my last breath escapes me on the battlefield, it will whisper your name.

Forgive my many faults, and the many pains I have caused you. How thoughtless and foolish I have often been! How gladly would I wash out with my tears every little spot upon your happiness, and struggle with all the misfortune of this world, to shield you and my children from harm. But I cannot. I must watch you from the spirit land and hover near you, while you buffet the storms with your precious little freight, and wait with sad patience till we meet to part no more.

But, O Sarah! If the dead can come back to this earth and flit unseen around those they loved, I shall always be near you; in the brightest day and in the darkest night—amidst your happiest scenes and gloomiest hours—always, always; and if there be a soft breeze upon your cheek, it shall be my breath; or the cool air fans your throbbing temple, it shall be my spirit passing by.

Sarah, do not mourn me dead; think I am gone and wait for me, for we shall meet again.

As for my little boys, they will grow as I have done, and never know a father's love and care. Little Willie is too young to remember me long, and my blue-eyed Edgar will keep my frolics with him among the dimmest memories of his childhood. Sarah, I have unlimited confidence in your maternal care and your development of their characters. Tell my two mothers his and hers I call God's blessing upon them. O Sarah,

I wait for you there! Come to me, and lead thither my children.

— Sullivan[9]

The letter was never mailed. It was found in Ballou's trunk after he died and was reclaimed and delivered to Ballou's widow by Governor William Sprague. Sprague had traveled to Virginia to reclaim the effects of dead Rhode Island soldiers.

Sarah Ballou, who was only 24 years old when her husband was killed, never remarried. She raised her two sons alone, supporting her family with a government pension of $29 per month and the money she earned by giving piano lessons. In 1875, she became the secretary of the Providence public school system, where she served until 1899. She then moved to East Orange, New Jersey to be near her son William. She died at East Orange, New Jersey on April 19, 1917 at age 80, and was laid to rest beside her husband in Swan Point Cemetery in Providence. The original copy of the letter Sullivan Ballou wrote to Sarah a week before the First Battle of Bull Run has never been found and, according to one story, was buried with her.[10]

This story has touched the hearts of millions of Americans. Within it resonates the love, loyalty and sense of completeness that every couple wishes for but unfortunately too few experience. What Sullivan and Sarah shared in their short life was a commitment that best illustrates the engine

---

[9] https://en.wikipedia.org/wiki/Sullivan_Ballou
[10] http://civilwarwomenblog.com/sarah-ballou/

that has driven the American Way… an *Eternal Faith* in the spiritual connection to God, Family and Country.

Within his wife Sarah, Sullivan Ballou had identified the totality of Womanhood. His commitment to her was total, as was his belief that the cause for which he would die was for her benefit and to his Gods honor. He loved, honored and saw within her the builder of his young son's character to be men. Within Sullivan, Sarah found the full complement of Manhood. One of which she knew could not be replaced by another. She spent the remaining 56 years of her life committed only to him.

No more loving tribute of an eternal nature could have been given by a man to his wife, than in Sullivan's' last paragraph written to Sarah during the last days of his earthly sojourn.

"As for my little boys, they will grow as I have done, and never know a father's love and care. Little Willie is too young to remember me long, and my blue-eyed Edgar will keep my frolics with him among the dimmest memories of his childhood. Sarah, I have unlimited confidence in your maternal care and your development of their characters. Tell my two mothers his and hers I call God's blessing upon them. O Sarah, I wait for you there! Come to me, and lead thither my children."

COUNTRY: THE 54TH

11

The 54th Regiment Massachusetts Volunteer Infantry

The 54th Regiment Massachusetts Volunteer Infantry was an infantry regiment that saw extensive service in the Union Army during the American Civil War. The regiment was one of the first official African-American units in the United States during the Civil War.[12]

By most accounts the 54th Regiment left Boston with very high morale. This was despite the fact that Jefferson Davis' proclamation of December 23, 1862, effectively put both African-American enlisted men and white officers under a death sentence if captured. The proclamation was affirmed

---

11   https://commons.wikimedia.org/wiki/File:Memorial_to_Robert_Gould_Shaw_
and_the_54th_Massachusetts_Volunteer_Infantry_Regiment,_Boston.JPG#/media/
File:Memorial_to_Robert_Gould_Shaw_and_the_54th_Massachusetts_Volunteer_
Infantry_Regiment,_Boston.JPG

12   "54th Regiment!". Massachusetts historical Society. Retrieved December 6, 2014

COMMITMENTS AND CONCLUSION

by the Confederate Congress in January 1863 and turned both enlisted soldiers and their white officers over to the states from which the enlisted soldiers had been slaves. As most Southern states had enacted draconian measures for "servile insurrection" after Nat Turner's Rebellion, the likely sentence was a capital one.[13]

The regiment gained recognition on July 18, 1863, when it spearheaded an assault on Fort Wagner near Charleston, South Carolina. Two hundred and seventy-two of the 600 men who charged Fort Wagner were "killed, wounded or captured." At this battle Colonel Shaw was killed, along with 29 of his men; 24 more later died of wounds, 15 were captured, 52 were missing in action and never accounted for, and 149 were wounded. The total regimental casualties of 272 would be the highest total for the 54th in a single engagement during the war. Although Union forces were not able to take and hold the fort (despite taking a portion of the walls in the initial assault), the 54th was widely acclaimed for its valor during the battle, and the event helped encourage the further enlistment and mobilization of African-American troops, a key development that President Abraham Lincoln once noted as helping to secure the final victory. Decades later, Sergeant William Harvey Carney was awarded the Medal of Honor for grabbing the U.S. flag as the flag bearer fell, carrying the flag to the enemy ramparts and back, and singing "Boys, the old flag never touched the ground!" While other African Americans had since been granted the award by the time it was presented to Carney, Carney's is the earliest action

---

[13] https://en.wikipedia.org/wiki/54th_Massachusetts_Infantry_Regiment

for which the Medal of Honor was awarded to an African American.[14]

Commitment, Courage, Patriotism, Valor, Leadership: these attributes denote the character of the 54th Regiment. It is in this same light that I perceive today's Black Conservative. Though they are not required to spearhead assaults on southern fortress walls, they voluntarily attack the spiritual, physical and emotions walls of enslavement built over decades by Liberalism and Socialism. As was the punishment proclaimed by the 1862 Confederates for servile insurrection, the adversary today is as merciless in their response to Black Americans who declare independence. They seek to demean, silence and destroy their character and livelihoods using, as their first line of offensive, the Royalty Class Black Man.

As did the 54th Regiment, today's Black Conservatives fight their battles deep within enemy territory leaving behind the safety and comforts of home. They are willing to sacrifice acceptance, financial perks and power, and in some case their chosen livelihood for the sake of their cause. Their cause is a worthy one, for it is a fight for future generations of millions of Americans. It is a cause that is determined to recapture the courage of its Manhood and the respect of its Womanhood. It is one that seeks to keep bright the light of opportunity for all in a country defined by its "American Way."

Pioneers Thomas Sowell and Walters Williams have for decades been voices in the wilderness, representing Black Conservative thoughts and reason. There are many others who now join them on the battlefield of debate, often against seemingly insurmountable odds. They are willing to walk

---

[14]   https://en.wikipedia.org/wiki/54th_Massachusetts_Infantry_Regiment

into the Lion's Den of Liberalism... often solo, without back up, ostracized, and demeaned. With the use of White Liberal organizations like BET, that are "Black in Name Only," they are portrayed as caricatures. These are Americans who are determined to keep the bridge of opportunity permanently accessible to all others. They are committed to pulling our country back from the dark abyss of Socialism and ensuring the light of liberty shines brighter than ever before. Like Harriett Tubman... *"they love freedom more."*

For these modern day members of the 54th Regiment, the path to victory within our free society will be through our American Free Market system. It will be imperative to amplify these voices through the grassroots support of like-minded Conservative Americans...with their hearts, minds and free market support. It is the American Way to reward that which it deems of value, through our system of Capitalism. There has never been, in the history of our nation, a message of more value than that of today's Black Conservative. The century long sacrifice of success and innocent lives within the Black community is a foreshadow of things to come for our nation, if corrective actions are not taken. Our nation today stands at the precipice of Socialisms' hopeless abyss. As we view the historical stealth of this ideology and its dismal failure within the Black community, Americans now have an opportunity to make a clear stand for Liberty and agency. As it has for over 200 years, the American people predictably choose to fight for Freedom once they realize they're in a fight and aware of the stakes. At stake for our nation is a future of mental, spiritual and physical dependency/slavery wrought by Socialism and its kissing cousins, Liberalism and

Communism. We see the evidence of this in every community nationwide and every country worldwide, where it resides.

According to a Pew Research Center Research 28% of Black Americans espouse Conservative values regarding God, Country and Family. Nineteen percent of Black Americans identify as Religious Right even though only seven percent (support) the Republican Party.[15] It is from this segment of the Black Community where our nation will find its initial source and example of *"Political Free Agents."* As our young nation fought for Freedom from the oppressive rule of England, only one-third joined the fought as Patriots. Another one-third chose to fight against freedom, as Tories, while the remaining segment chose apathy or ignorance, as by-standers. So it will be the task of the one-third Conservative- leaning Black Americans, to make the sacrifice of their ancestors over the last century, worthwhile. It will be these principled, conservative and issue-based Americans who will play a part in pulling our nation back from the abyss.

How can the American hearts, minds and free market best support these Black Conservative efforts? The 1800 post Civil War message by Fredrick Douglas still remains true today:

" 'What shall we do with the Negro?' I have had but one answer from the beginning. Do nothing with us! Your doing with us has already played the mischief with us. Do nothing with us! If the apples will not remain on the tree of their own strength, if they are worm-eaten at the core, if they are early ripe and disposed to fall, let them fall! I am not for tying or fastening them on the tree in any way, except by nature's plan,

---

[15]   https://en.wikipedia.org/wiki/Black_conservatism_in_the_United_States

and if they will not stay there, let them fall. And if the Negro cannot stand on his own legs, let him fall also. All I ask is, give him a chance to stand on his own legs! Let him alone!" [16]

It is the American Way that allows citizens to show their preference of values, principles and policies, through the power of their vote. So it is with our free market system, that through the voluntary flow of capital, we vote the value of products and services. The power of our capital facilitates increased availability with the increase of demand. It will be the free market, through the voice of the Black Conservatives, that the message of Political Free Agency will have its day in the market place. And it will be this message, *Political Free Agency* that will ensure the Black community is never again taken for granted or ignored by either political party. The education and engagement required to be a principled *Political Free Agent* will also ensure our protection from the seductive power of Socialism.

By embracing Political Free Agency and demanding options, the ideals of Conservatism can once again be debated and judged on its merit vs. being silenced and hidden via Political Correctness. Parents will have the choice to educate their children in an environment that best reflects their ideals and priorities. The ideals of Capitalism, God-centered values, respect for self and others, education, Life, Liberty and the pursue happiness will be taught as American Values instead of White Values. They will be embraced, once again, as the core stepping-stones to true, long lasting success.

One of the primary premises of this book is to highlight the influential nature of Womanhood. To insure that this

---

[16]   http://www.lexrex.com/enlightened/writings/douglas.htm

influence is appreciated we should encourage our young women, of all colors, backgrounds and cultures to read and hear the thoughts and reasoning of Conservative Black women. Their stories of overcoming, boldness and courage to stand against "group think," for their strongly held principles are *instructional*. With knowledge of their struggles and victories they are also *inspirational*. These are times when our young women sorely need instruction, inspiration and strength, as they fight the downstream pull of Liberalism's immorality cesspool. Today's Black Conservative Women are a great resource for all, but in particular for our young women.

The pioneer Black Conservatives listed below, and many others throughout our country, deserves our thanks and our free market vote. We do so as we read and promote their books, listen to their shows, buy from their businesses/ advertisers and support their efforts to spread the message of conservatism. They are Political Free Agents who are issue driven, diverse and fiercely independent in their views, solutions and political preferences. Though as individuals driven by "diverse and independent thought there is a guaranteed area of consensus among all of them... their love and appreciation for America and the Liberty that it embodies. *"It is the American Way that maintains that freedom is a birthright and represents a perpetual source of hope for every seeking soul around the world."*

Deneen Borelli

Website: http://deneenborelli.com/
Book: *Blacklash: How Obama and the Left Are Driving Americans to the Government Plantation*

Herman Cain

Website: http://www.caintv.com/
Book: *The Right Problems: What the President, Congress, and Every Candidate Should Be Working On*

Stacey Dash

Facebook: https://www.facebook.com/OfficiallyStaceyDash
Book: *There Goes My Social Life: From Clueless to Conservative*

Larry Elder

Website: http://www.larryelder.com/
Book: *Dear Father, Dear Son: Two Lives... Eight Hours*

Harrison Faulkner

Website: http://harrisfaulkner.com/publicity.html
Book: *Breaking News: God Has a Plan: An Anchorwoman's Journey Through Faith*

Brenda Flank

The Conservative Alliance for Community Growth
Website: https://www.conservativeallianceforcommunitygrowth.org/

Alveda King

Website: http://www.
alvedakingministries.com/
Book: *King Rules: Ten Truths for
You, Your Family, and Our Nation
to Prosper*

Bishop E.W. Jackson

YouTube: https://www.youtube.com/
watch?v=Oi_KaZ53eDg
Book: *Ten Commandments to an
Extraordinary Life: Making Your
Dreams Come True*

C.L Bryant

Website: http://theclbryantshow.com/
Documentary: *Runaway Slave*
http://www.runawayslavemovie.
com/

Kevin Jackson

Website: http://theblacksphere.net/
radio/
Facebook: https://www.facebook.
com/TheBlackSphereRadioShow
Book: *Race Pimping: The Multi-
Trillion Dollar Business of
Liberalism*

Angela McGlowan

Facebook: https://www.facebook.
com/amcglowan
Book: *Bamboozled: How
Americans Are Being Exploited by
the Lies of the Liberal Agenda*

Rev. Jesse Lee Peterson　Website: http://
rebuildingtheman.com/home/
Book: *The Antidote: Healing
America from the Poison of Hate,
Blame and Victimhood*

Star Parker　Website: http://www.urbancure.org/
Book: *White Ghetto: How Middle
Class America Reflects Inner City
Decay*

David Webb　Website: http://davidwebbshow.com/

Allen West　Website: http://www.allenbwest.com/
Book: *Guardian of the Republic:
An American Ronin's Journey to
Faith, Family and Freedom*

Armstrong Williams　Website: http://www.
armstrongwilliams.com/
Book: *Reawakening Virtues:
Restoring What Makes America
Great*

CONCLUSION

As a member of a proud 1960s segregated Black community in Tallahassee, FL, I'm grateful to be able to reflect on the many changes seen and experienced over my lifetime. The NFL, a game that I watched in the 60s and participated in during the 70s and 80s has produced thousands of millionaires. Unlike in a past era, the color of the athlete has no bearing on his opportunity to participate, but instead is predicated on his character, content and contribution potential. We have a society in which Black Americans have earned, been elected and have built businesses to the highest levels available within our society. Our nation has elected for two terms, a Black President. There are no schools, jobs, positions or business opportunities that are off-limits based on skin color. With opportunities in more abundance and availability than at any time in American history, the Black community is also angrier and more frustrated than at any time in American history. As Asians, Hispanics, Eastern Indians, Filipinos and a multitude of other minorities successfully assimilate, they are admired for their business acumen, academic skills and work ethic. They compete and win on the world stage and, though a smaller minority, are not typically viewed needy of affirmative action status. Though their success is rare in the ranks of professional athletes or star roles on weekly TV series, these Americans are prominent players in their communities, involved in their children's school PTAs, are hiring and training the youth of their race and are present at their family's dinner table. They are unfamiliar with the mindset of victimization and are therefore very rarely seen marching behind professional protestors. Is this because they're too busy working, studying, improving, risking, overcoming and committing? Or is it possible that within their homes, parents have taught them that the attainment of the American Dream is still available through hard work, study and risk taking? Maybe it was due to a father and mother who showed their belief everyday by getting up, going to work and not whining to their children when challenges and setbacks come their way. For sure these minorities, of all races, color and languages, have been taught to disregard the Progressive Public School system's message of entitlement. They were granted within their homes, the best head start that parents can give their children as they leave to compete in the free market ... *an attitude of gratitude for being an American.*

Though I still wear the faint scars of racial intimidation attempts during my 10th grade year at Rickards High school, the greatest blessing is the recognition that the internal scars of anger and the temptation to become a racist, disappeared decades ago. Many of my former white high school teammates are now Facebook friends, as we occasionally discuss the good ole days, the life lessons learned since and politics. My greatest nemesis that first year of integration, Larry, has since passed on. I regret not having the opportunity to spend time with him reflecting on those days, as 16 and 17 year olds, as we were doing our best to overcome the prejudices of our fathers. Instructional were four years after High School, when Larry and I had the opportunity to play on the same College

All-American Team. My former nemesis/potential friend for that week spent much of his time with Black players. I have a memory of him walking into a room of players, relaxing after practice and being the only white player present. He had changed. I hope that he continued to do so…attempting to find his better self.

Over the years, I've reflected on those years of change for Larry and me and have discovered some great life lessons. During those times when we experience the anger and the negative actions of a few, remember the kindness and charity of the many, many more. It is within this vast majority of good where we find the true heart of America. For those who believe that others are incapable of change, ask yourself… are you? If the answer is yes, than it is also possible for all those around you to do the same, regardless of race, creed or color.

"The key to your universe is that you can choose"- Carl Frederick

This represents the American Way, a society of individuals continually falling short of our personal potential and our Nations' stated promise. As we mature, learning to reflect and repent, we do so with the purpose of finding happiness within the best of ourselves. This approach of self-inspection and active engagement is defined within the Judeo Christian tenets that teach that change and second chances are possible. It teaches that serving our fellow man brings with it the serendipity of loving our fellow man… the perfect antidote for hate and distrust.

For us to see the best that America has to offer, our nation must reject the anti-god ideology of Socialism that divides instead of unifies. We must reject the ideology that gains its power by encouraging Americans to judge each other based on our exterior criteria, be that Black or White, rich or poor, old or young, white collar or blue collar, male or female, religious or not, ect. We must reject the ideology that was able to gain its foothold into the American culture only through stealth and strategically fake facades. We must again demand of ourselves actions that helped our earlier generations make it through. We must once again serve, educate, sacrifice, worship, protect and defend, Man-up and Woman-up. In doing so the promise of our Nation will be reflected in the lives of an increasing number of other Americans who find themselves grateful for the opportunity to take part in our American Way.

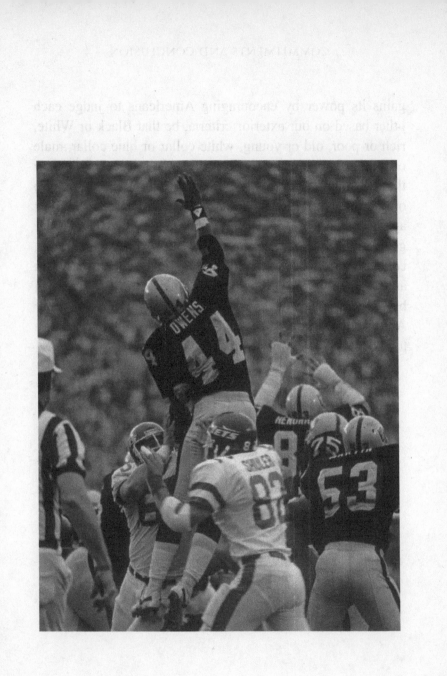